D0875464

Nationalism
in the
Twentieth Century

Nationalism
in the
Twentieth Century

Anthony D. S. Smith

Martin Robertson

First published in 1979 by Martin Robertson & Co. Ltd., 108 Cowley Road, Oxford OX4 1JF

ISBN 0 85520 275 0

Phototypeset by Santype Ltd. Salisbury
Printed and bound by Richard Clay at The Chaucer Press, Bungay

Contents

Preface

The breakdown of tradition and religious authority in many parts of the world has encouraged a search for new kinds of salvation and progress. Some of these salvation routes are personal and individual, others are social and communal. Of the communal ideologies, some are limited and localised in their objectives, while others make more universal and global claims.

Perhaps the most important and enduring of the more limited modern ideologies is nationalism. Nationalism combines a programme on behalf of a specific community with a more universal vision of culture-groups. It therefore stands midway between purely local movements like populism and nativism, and the great 'world salvation' ideologies of racial fascism and socialism or communism. It also differs from these more universal ideologies in basing itself on a pre-existing mass sentiment, and in emphasising practical construction at the expense of utopian or chiliastic visions.

My aim in this book is to chart the relationships, conceptual and historical, between nationalism and other ideologies, notably fascism and communism, and to explain some of the reasons why nationalism continues to appeal to so many people in different parts of the world today. Nationalism in the twentieth century has survived the challenges posed by fascism, racism and communism, and is now experiencing something of a resurgence. The movement and ideology has also undergone an unusual expansion and diversification, both in content and organisation. Today we can find every type of nationalism, from ethnic separatism and conservative bureaucratic nationalisms in the West to the populist and communist nationalisms of some developing countries. Yet the 'nationalist' colour of these varied movements is readily discernible, and the nationalist component nearly always predominates over others.

Both analytically and chronologically, the book continues my earlier discussion of approaches and typologies of nationalism in *Theories of Nationalism*. It elaborates the basic definitions of nationalism arrived at in the earlier work, and seeks to demonstrate the varied guises under which nationalism has appeared in our century. It does so by contrasting nationalist ideas and activities with those of other, related, movements, as well as by relating those ideas and activities to their specific social and cultural contexts. The aim throughout remains analytic and comparative, in the belief that these tasks are prerequisites to evolving any more general theories of the whole phenomenon of nationalism. The task of a general theory must await further studies of the origins of nationalism. Instead, my aim here is to chart the later developments of the nationalist movement as a whole by examining crucial 'moments' in its career during our century, and in the final chapters to offer some hypotheses about the general conditions of the *persistence* of nationalism today, conditions that, I would argue, are no longer identical with those that fostered the initial *emergence* of nationalism whether in eighteenth-century Europe or in nineteenth-century Asia, or even in early twentieth-century Africa. For, although certain elements of those initial conditions have persisted in a general manner, their forms have changed; and other elements, indeed new conditions, have made themselves felt, influencing the course of nationalism and hastening its resurgence. For this reason it becomes necessary to develop models and theories of the persistence and revival of nationalism, both at a general and at a regional level.

These general considerations of method have accordingly determined the structure of the book. In the first two chapters I aim to set out the main strands in contemporary nationalist ideologies. The first chapter recapitulates the main assumptions inherent in all nationalist thought, and analyses how national ideals were interpreted and expanded by varying groups in different situations during the late eighteenth and nineteenth centuries. The second chapter elucidates further some of the chief motifs of nationalism by juxtaposing its ideals to the chiliastic visions of older religious millennialisms. Contrary to some opinions, nationalism is revealed as an optimistic, secular and practical ideology, far removed in spirit from the supernaturalist pessimism of millennial movements.

The next three chapters examine the main challenges to nationalism in our century. The first of these, fascism, is one of the great 'world salvation' movements, especially in its racial Nazi form; and it is sharply distinguished from nationalism at the conceptual level. The many historical links between the two movements, especially in interWar Europe, are then examined, and the transition from nationalism to fascism, especially in Germany, and its general causes are then traced. Fascism's ability to subvert nationalism, albeit temporarily, was powerfully aided by racist ideas, and the next chapter is devoted to an analysis of the relations between racism and nationalism. Again, racism needs to be distinguished from nationalism in order to grasp their common roots, and to understand why racism can both challenge and accentuate national feeling. In certain circumstances, racial and colour feeling can even revive a lost national identity, as it has done among African and black peoples in the pan-African movement. Third, there is the more recent challenge of that other great 'world salvation' movement, communism. There are sufficient parallels between Marxism and nationalism to permit some symbiosis, and social and political conditions in many developing countries may well favour the rise of a 'communist nationalism'. But even here, the alliance is often uneasy, and the kind of communism adopted tends to become too denatured to resist the appeals of a populistic nationalism.

The last three chapters consider the main reasons for the persistence and resurgence of nationalism today. First, there is the problem of current Western 'neo-nationalisms': why should they emerge now in well established, industrialised, usually democratic states with well educated citizens? The answers are sought in the social composition of the movements' leaderships, and in the general geopolitical situation of decline in which these states now find themselves, and which makes them unable to cope with minority demands. Second, and at a broader level, nationalism's appeals today are based upon 'internal' as well as 'external' factors. Internally, nationalism feeds upon very ancient sentiments of ethnic association, and on the cyclic operation of impersonal modern bureaucracies. The latter uphold the authority of the State, so engendering a bureaucratic nationalism. But, by contrast, they also create the conditions for a revolt against reason and a flight into romantic protest, which can again be converted into an ethnic nationalism. Externally, the growth of a world state system reinforces balance of power considerations, and sets national élites against each other in a competition for world status. Even supranationalism turns out to parallel traditional nationalisms on a continental scale. We are therefore unlikely to witness the early demise of nationalism, despite massive industrialisation and high levels of education.

The fact is, that we have arrived at the point where nationalism appears to be a self-reproducing phenomenon, given the persistence of the world state system in any form. Hence, cosmopolitan hopes for an early withering-away of nationalism are doomed to disappointment, for they are based on a failure to grasp the importance today of the conjunction of ethnic sentiments, secular ideals and changing elements of modernisation and its social concomitants. It is at these levels that we may begin to discern a common thread in all the manifestations of nationalism.

ANTHONY D. SMITH
London, February 1978

CHAPTER I

The Development of the National Ideal

Of all the visions and faiths that compete for men's loyalties in the modern world, the most widespread and persistent is the national ideal. Other faiths have achieved more spectacular temporary success or a more permanent footing in one country. Other visions have roused men to more terrible and heroic acts. But none has been so successful in penetrating to every part of the globe, and in its ability to attract to its ideals men and women of every sort, in all walks of life and in every country. No other ideal has been able to reappear in so many different guises, or to suffer temporary eclipse only to re-emerge stronger and more permanently. No other vision has set its stamp so thoroughly on the map of the world, and on our sense of identity. We are identified first and foremost with our 'nation'. Our lives are regulated, for the most part, by the national state in which we are born. War and peace, trade and travel, education and welfare, are determined for each one of us by the nation-state in which we reside. From childhood, we are inculcated with a love of country and taught the peculiar virtues of our nation. And though in later life some may dissent from the patriotic ideal, and a few turn 'traitor', the vast majority of citizens will retain a quiet loyalty to their nation, which in a moment of crisis can swell into a fervent devotion and passionate obedience to the call of duty.

What is this national ideal that can command such loyalty in so many countries, and how has it developed? For it was not something original or natural to man, like his physique or family. The first clear statement of this ideal occurs during the French Revolution. Here we read that the only sovereign is the nation, that man's first loyalty is to the nation, and that the nation alone can make laws for its citizens.[1] There too we hear for the first time the call to arms for the defence of the fatherland (*patrie*), and the idea that a 'citizen' of France has certain rights and duties towards his nation.[2] Although the French Revolution was not the first to unfurl a flag or compose an anthem, it was the first moment that self-governing citizens did both for the 'national' cause, and not to celebrate a dynasty. And it was the first time that citizens sought to impose a single culture and language on all the regions of their country, to break down all the barriers between those regions, to become one nation devoted to a single ideal.[3]

But what was this national ideal? Fundamentally, it was a belief that all those who shared a common history and culture should be autonomous, united and distinct in their recognised homelands. But, whereas the French, like the English, could assume, to a large extent, a common history and culture, other subject populations could not. The French did not have to emphasise their distinctiveness or identity. They could concentrate on achieving self-government and unity, on overthrowing the absolutist *ancien régime* and on breaking down feudal barriers between the regions. But Germans and Italians and Greeks, who soon took up this national ideal in the wake of Napoleon's conquests, could not assume such a deep sense of common history and culture, or even that minimum of territorial unity that the French, with their almost 'natural' boundaries, possessed.[4] They therefore had to devote much more attention to arousing their compatriots to a sense of their new 'national' identity and distinctiveness. From the very first, therefore, the 'national ideal' began to expand its content to suit new interests and other needs.

The history of the development of the national ideal is a tale of its continual expansion and transformation to accommodate the different interests and needs of successive waves of adherents and devotees. But it is also the story of a protean ability to remain constant through all its transformations, in the teeth of the various challenges it has had to meet from other faiths and ideals.

At the root of the 'national ideal' is a certain vision of the world and a certain type of culture. According to this vision, mankind is 'really' and 'naturally' divided into distinct communities of history and culture, called nations. Each nation is distinct and unique. Each has its peculiar contribution to make to the whole, the family of nations. Each nation defines the identity of its members, because its specific culture moulds the individual. The key to that culture is history, the sense of special patterns of events peculiar to successive generations of a particular group. An historical culture is one that binds present and future generations, like links in a chain, to all those who preceded them, and one that therefore has shaped the character and habits of the nation at all times. A man identifies himself, according to the national ideal, through his relationship to his ancestors and forebears, and to the events that shaped their character. The national ideal therefore embodies both a vision of a world divided into parallel and distinctive nations, and also a culture of the role of the unique event that shapes the national character.

But the national ideal involves something more even than a special vision of the world, or a particular culture of the historical event. It also entails a certain kind of solidarity and political programme. The national ideal leads inevitably to 'nationalism', a programme of action to achieve and sustain the national ideal. The solidarity that a nationalist desires is based on the possession of the land: not any land, but the historic land; the land of past generations, the land that saw the flowering of the nation's genius. The nationalist therefore wants to repossess the land, to make it into a secure 'homeland' for the nation, and to 'build' the nation on it. The solidarity he desires is therefore based on territory. Without territory, you cannot build the fraternity and solidarity that the national ideal requires. You cannot instil in people a sense of kinship and brotherhood without attaching them to a place that they feel is theirs, a homeland that is theirs by right of history. Nor can they realise their peculiar identity and culture in the future, unless they possess a recognised homeland.

But for this to be realised, the homeland must be free. It cannot be ruled by others of a different historical culture. The nationalist therefore is drawn into politics, into the struggle for self-government and sovereignty in his homeland. Not all nationalists want complete sovereignty. Some may prefer the autonomy of 'home rule', or federation with another state. But all want recognition of their right to the homeland, and freedom from interference in their internal, especially cultural, affairs. And since such recognition and freedom are often difficult to secure in a federation with a stronger state, nationalists usually prefer outright secession in order to set up a sovereign state of their own, for whose defence and administration they will be wholly responsible. In that state, they will be free to create those institutions and arrangements that will best answer to the peculiar needs of their nation and its historical culture.

Nationalism, therefore, involves four elements: a vision, a culture, a solidarity and a policy. It answers to ideological, cultural, social and political aspirations and needs. Its success over two centuries is partly attributable to the range of needs that it satisfies. But equally important is the manner in which nationalists can adapt the vision, the culture, the solidarity and the programme to diverse situations and interests. It is this flexibility that has allowed nationalism continually to re-emerge and spread, at the cost of its ideological rivals, from 1789 until today.

The central theme of this book is the revival and re-emergence of nationalism in the twentieth century, despite the serious challenges from other faiths. In the succeeding chapters I shall examine in more detail the nature and roots of the national ideal, and the chief challenges to its primacy in our century. Nationalism undoubtedly suffered temporary eclipses in Europe after both World Wars, and even today it faces severe tests in several Asian, African and Latin American countries. Yet it has throughout always managed to hold its own against other ideologies, and to reappear in new guises and with a different emphasis. By way of conclusion, I shall try to offer some suggestions for the resurgence of nationalism and its continuing appeal today. It is impossible, however, to grasp the role of nationalism in the contemporary clash of ideologies without setting it in its historical context and recalling the main lines of nationalism's origins and development in the late eighteenth and nineteenth centuries. In the following brief survey, therefore, I shall merely isolate some of the main phases and strands in this historical development.

ENLIGHTENERS AND ROMANTICS

When Rousseau and the French revolutionaries began to grope their way towards a national ideal, they were not working in an intellectual vacuum. Luther's translation of the Bible into German had initiated an interest in vernacular languages in place of Latin, and Renaissance humanism had spread an enthusiasm for ancient literature and art. With the decline of religious intolerance in the late seventeenth century, the interest of the early Enlightenment in pagan antiquity had sparked off a number of important cultural debates. The first of these, the Quarrel of the Ancients and Moderns, turned on a comparison between the several virtues of antiquity and the eighteenth century, and tended towards the optimistic conclusion that it was possible to surpass the ancients in the arts and sciences. The second debate concerned the relative merits of Greeks and Romans, especially after explorers and artists like Stuart and Revett had opened European eyes to the purity and nobility of Greek art.[5] Third, and cutting across the other debates, was the divide separating those who favoured a more imperial or 'Augustan' ideal of antiquity, as exemplified in the Roman Empire, and those who preferred the 'doric' simplicity and plain dignity of the 'republican' ideal, with Sparta, early Republican Rome and sometimes Athens as their models.

The last of these debates carried, of course, contemporary political allusions, and one can trace a definite progression from a cultural and social republican nationalism in Rousseau or Diderot to a more definite political nationalism in artists like David, and writers like Sieyès.[6] The vision of a world of culturally distinct nations, each of which required social unity, formed the embryo of a 'national' ideal, and it was left to Girondins and Jacobins to implement the ideal in political organisation. For confirmation and justification of their actions, they had only to turn back to their specific reading of those ancient models that appeared to embody their ideals. What they all admired in Sparta or early Rome was the simple life-style of a Cincinnatus, the martial valour of a Leonidas, and the self-sacrifice of a Brutus or Cato. What impressed them so much was the spirit of civic participation they discerned in those societies, and the primacy of the community over its individual members, who voluntarily accepted their subordination to the community. Within its fixed and recognised territorial limits, the *polis* of antiquity seemed to furnish an ideal of voluntary community and to embody a truly 'national' spirit of solidarity.[7]

The return to antiquity in the eighteenth century was by no means confined to any one stratum. Kings, bureaucrats, nobles and merchants shared the general European enthusiasm for the classical world, for the Grand Tour and the discoveries at Herculaneum, Pompeii, Palmyra and Athens. But after 1760 a more serious view of the antique ideal began to catch the imagination of some of the intellectuals and middle classes. The resulting 'republican' ideals of neoclassicism were directed in particular against the hedonism, cynicism and artifice of corrupt oligarchies and regimented absolutisms throughout western Europe. On the Continent, especially, neoclassicist republicans were in revolt against the arbitrariness of despotic rule, the artificiality of hierarchy and the fragmentation of society, and on all these counts they struck a responsive chord with the rising middle classes.[8]

In France, the main ally of the radical intelligentsia was the manufacturer and entrepreneur, who desired a unified republic free of internal barriers and aristocratic privilege. In Germany, at first the intelligentsia was more isolated and fragmented; but here too a middle class was emerging, and together with some of the lower clergy was voicing cautious support for constitutional reform and a more Germanised culture.[9] To the east, in Poland and Hungary, dispossessed and impoverished aristocrats after 1800 began to rally to the national cause.[10] In the Balkans, too, the intelligentsia in exile were soon joined by wealthy merchants and dealers, and by many of the lower clergy, in their struggle for independence from Ottoman rule.[11] The national ideal was even transported to Latin America, where Spain's own war of independence against Napoleon from 1808 allowed Bolivar and San Martin to lead the wealthier urban creoles against Spanish imperial rule.[12]

The accession of such different strata to the national ideal tended to expand and transform its content, with the result that after 1800 the neoclassical French radical example ceased to be the sole model. Less democratic and more mystical versions of the national ideal became prominent, particularly in central and eastern Europe; and it is often thought that this more 'romantic' kind of nationalism was caused by the lack of a strong bourgeoisie in these countries, who could support the intelligentsia.[13] But factors other than class structure were as influential in the rise of a romantic and 'organic' nationalism. After all, England, the country with the most advanced bourgeoisie in the late eighteenth century, was also the first to develop a powerful Romantic movement.[14] The other factors included political resistance, not only to Napoleonic rule but to all the revolutionary and rationalist innovations which that rule inaugurated. Besides, many of the populations he conquered were divided and partitioned, yet their intelligentsias could point to a history as long as the French, and to languages beginning to emerge from literary obscurity. In Germany, Poland, Italy and the Balkans, therefore, a more romantic emphasis upon the historic culture began to develop–an interest in ethnic customs, an attachment to vernaculars, nostalgia for tribal and medieval pageantry and society, religious yearnings–much of which had been foreshadowed in the pages of Rousseau and Herder, those twin links between enlightened neoclassicists and romantic medievalists.[15] Indeed, this first phase, which saw the birth of the national ideal and lasted from the 1750s until its diffusion under Napoleon, is at once neoclassical and 'pre-Romantic'; the neoclassical yearning for an austere antiquity goes hand in hand with the early Gothic revival, and together they become synthesised into a powerful political ideal.[16]

RADICALS AND TRADITIONALISTS

The second phase opens with the wars of resistance against Napoleon and lasts till 1848. The emphasis now falls upon the demand for unification and political independence, as Hungarians, Germans, Poles, Italians, Greeks, Serbs, Argentinians and Chileans demand an end to alien control and territorial unification as a democratic right and historic need. In most cases, nationalists base their claims on both radical and conservative principles, though in Latin America, at first, the radical-democratic rationale of the Enlightenment and French Revolution prevailed in the struggle against a traditionalist Catholic Spain.[17] In eastern Europe, radical intellectuals tended to be swamped by more traditionally minded strata, aristocrats and lower clergy. In their battle against 'enlightened despots' in Austro-Hungary, Russia and Prussia, their national radicalism soon acquired a mystical, even messianic, quality. Thus the dream of a resurrected Poland, likened to a suffering and crucified Christ-redeemer, inspired Mickiewicz and his circle in exile after the abortive revolt of 1830.[18] In the Balkans, the earlier classical romanticism of a Korais or Rhigas was soon challenged by more traditionalist 'Byzantine' dreams, as priests and peasant leaders in Greece and local chieftains in Serbia assumed the leadership of a struggle that was as much religious as national, with the Orthodox pitted against an infidel Islam.[19] In Germany, too, there was a religious revival after 1810. German nationalists like Jahn, Arndt and Müller took up the romantic medievalism of Tieck, Schlegel and Novalis, and dreamed of the restoration of the medieval German Reich. The same romantic vision of organic unity and Christian Germanism inspired Wagner and the *völkisch* propagandists after 1848.[20] In Italy, there arose a similar desire to accommodate Catholicism and the papal heritage in the writings of conservatives like Gioberti; and even radicals such as Mazzini gave their yearnings for national independence a religious hue. All over Europe, from Ireland to Karamzin's Russia, the national ideal was being expanded to encompass a cult of traditionalism.[21]

Yet this was also the era of liberal and radical nationalisms. Despite their vagueness and inconsistency, Mazzini and his followers in the Carbonari stood for a united, democratic Italy, with a republican constitution based on French models. Mazzini's organisation, Young Europe, gave political form to Herder's belief in the special quality of each nation and to Rousseau's admiration for the peculiar institutions and customs of peoples like the Jews, Corsicans and Poles.[22] In France itself, the liberal nationalist tradition was carried on by the historian Michelet, against the theocratic and counter-revolutionary visions of conservatives like de Maistre and Bonald.[23] Germany too found spokesmen for the national aspirations of the Rhineland middle classes, in such liberal constitutionalists as Rotteck and Welcker. But after 1830 French liberal influence was supplanted by more conservative Anglo-Saxon models, and historians like Dahlmann began to advance a more hierarchical and monarchist national ideal.[24] Until 1848, however, the rising national ideal was largely tied to liberalism in most European countries.

IMPERIALISM AND SECESSION

The reaction after the 1848 revolutions, the split between liberalism and nationalism that appeared during that year, and above all the drive towards consolidation at home and annexation overseas soon undermined the liberal–nationalist ideal. As might be expected, these developments strengthened traditionalist versions of nationalism; but they also created a new kind of imperialist nationalism, and saw the zenith of the national secession movements in eastern Europe.

From 1848 to the 1890s, traditionalist nationalisms constituted a powerful force in European politics, and could even be found as far away as Japan. The ruling class and the monarch were glorified as the embodiment of the nation, its hierarchy and traditions expressing the essence of the nation's historic culture and social unity. At the same time, these nationalisms possessed an aggressive modernising drive, with strong militarist overtones. Some of these themes appear in the writings of the Slavophiles in Russia, but their classical home is Bismarck's Germany where Lagarde and above all Treitschke offered a forceful defence of the German state and national unity which had none of the liberal constitutionalism of Burke's earlier organic nationalism.[25]

In opposition to this dynastic and military nationalism, the various subject peoples evolved their own national ideals. Essentially, they were concerned with the right of populations with distinct historic cultures to secede from an empire and set up their own nation-states. The ethnic content of this secession nationalism went far beyond anything conveyed by the Kantian principle of 'self-determination', even after it had been emended by Fichte and his followers. Nor was it limited by the Romantic German criterion of language. Among Serbs and Croats, Poles and Czechs, Hungarians, Rumanians, Bulgars, Ukrainians and Jews, religion, customs and above all historic antagonisms helped to define the content of the national ideal for ethnic minorities locked into vast empires.[26] Ethnic secessionists were simultaneously democrats and conservatives. They fought oppressive and arbitrary tyrants in the name of all the people in an historic nation; yet the very need to assert their separate origins and historical identities against rulers and detractors inevitably lent a mystical and backward-looking hue to their rebellion. The rescue of history, customs and language encouraged the past to shape their futures as much as to serve them.[27]

Since these ethnic secessionisms have often been regarded as the embodiment and touchstone of all nationalisms and their classic expression, we should remind ourselves that in fact they constitute only one version of the national ideal as it expanded in the nineteenth century. Europe itself was evolving other versions. One of these, a new imperialist nationalism, had global consequences. Particularly after 1870, this idea of an imperial duty to annex, educate and westernise overseas alien peoples to become acceptable citizens of the metropolitan country gained a fervent following in several western European states. France furnishes the classic example. In Africa, French colonial policy aimed to 'assimilate' the African élite in countries like Senegal and the Ivory Coast and turn them into black Frenchmen, with the same political rights as metropolitan Frenchmen. To this end, African *evolués* were taught French history and inculcated with a love of French literature and language.[28] More crudely, Russian administrators sought to Russify, and often Christianise, non-Russian ethnic groups that the tsarist drive in the Caucasus and central Asia was annexing during the mid nineteenth century. But here the means were more drastic. They involved a massive influx of Russian colonists and an insistence on the use of Russian as the *lingua franca*, methods that soon stirred considerable resentment among the Islamic and Turkic peoples.[29]

In a sense, imperialist nationalisms were self-contradictory. They envisaged a world of parallel nations, each possessing its own historical culture, yet were bent on wiping out that culture in order to ensure imperial assimilation and homogeneity. The British, indeed, seemed to sense the problem. At any rate, they tried, unsuccessfully, to avoid the contradiction by their policy of indirect rule through local chiefs, particularly in Africa. Even so, the national ideal was inevitably distorted, and in the era of racial Darwinism it soon bred racist ideals which threatened to undermine the whole concept of nationalism.[30]

POPULISM AND ANTI-COLONIALISM

After the economic crisis of the 1870s, and the scramble for empire, two new versions of nationalism appeared which were to prove very influential in the next century: populism and anti-colonialism.

Populism was largely a reaction of members of lower strata and some deracinated intellectuals to the reality of the threat of massive industrialisation. The growth of large cities and slums, the swollen tide of urban unemployed, the expansion of an academic proletariat, all linked to the spread of industrial capitalism, posed a major threat to the livelihood and status of these uprooted strata. Populism idealised the small businessman and extolled the beauties of agrarian life and the small town, in opposition to the bigness of industry, cities and unions. So when some intellectuals began to identify the small man with the 'people' and the people with the 'nation', urging a return to rural and small-town simplicities, the ensuing populist nationalism found a mass following.

There are, of course, several varieties of populism. The version that flourished among American small farmers expressed their fundamental hostility to capitalism and city life in the form of a democratic xenophobia. A second variety, the populism of an intelligentsia that appeals to the peasantry and extols peasant communal institutions, emerged in Russia during the 1870s, and has provided an inspiration for several communist nationalisms in underdeveloped countries in this century.[31] Finally, there was the populist nationalism of recently urbanised lower middle classes, especially in ethnically mixed areas like central and eastern Europe. In this case, racist demagogues soon inflamed the fears of unemployed and uprooted immigrants, and identified the 'real' nation with folkish and racial elements rooted in the soil of the motherland at exactly the moment when the migrants felt most uprooted. Here is one link between nationalism and racial fascism, and one route towards the ultimate subversion of the national ideal.[32]

The 1870s also witnessed the first stirrings of reaction to European imperial nationalisms among Asians and Africans. After the initial resistance to colonial intrusion had petered out, a new kind of liberal nationalism arose among the westernised élites. In India, for example, an Anglicised intelligentsia joined forces with a rising merchant class to form the Congress Party in 1885. At first their demands were mainly liberal and constitutional, an attempt to achieve greater representation and more equal rights within the Empire. Only later, and under the influence of a more traditionalist nationalism led by Tilak, did the liberals raise the anti-colonial banner and demand sovereignty.[33] British West Africa witnessed similar developments. At first, the new urban élites were more interested in securing adequate representation in legislative bodies or the colonial administration in Sierra Leone, the Gold Coast and Nigeria. Under the influence of Horton and Blyden, they wanted to demonstrate the parity of an African nation with the

Christian West; and only later, after the Great War, did they begin to demand self-government and independence for the colonies.[34]

With the partial exception of India, the countries of Asia and Africa were barely touched by industrialism or commodity capitalism in the nineteenth century, and what native bourgeoisies there were, were largely subservient to foreign interests.[35] The result was that the national ideal was confined to small circles of intellectuals, students and professionals, whose political education tended to be based upon the liberal–democratic and Christian principles professed in theory by their imperial masters. Their nationalism, therefore, while generally liberal and democratic in orientation, lacked a deep cultural content and popular appeal. It was only through an alliance with traditionalist religious or racial sentiments that the national ideal could gain a mass audience and acquire a historical content.

Outside Europe, then, three types of nationalism emerged in the later nineteenth century. The first resembled the European version of traditionalism, and took root in Japan, where the emperors and their advisers used modern methods and concepts to uphold the traditional content of Japanese national culture–in contrast to China, where the older concept of a dynastic 'civilisation' had not yet been superseded by the new ideal of the 'nation'.[36] A second type of nationalism was found mainly in the Middle East, where east European-style ethnic secessionism was taken up by Armenians, Georgians and, later, Arabs.[37] Finally, westernised intelligentsias in India, Egypt and West Africa were beginning to introduce the first liberal-constitutional phase of an anti-colonial nationalism, which was well suited to their pre-eminent position as pace-setters of modernisation prior to the era of independence.[38]

THE UNITY OF NATIONALISM

From even this brief survey, it can be seen how easily the national ideal has been expanded and diversified to fit a variety of geopolitical situations and social needs. There has, in fact, never been a single version of nationalism, and it is vain to search for some 'genuine' doctrine or 'true' movement to act as a criterion for all subsequent cases.[39] From its eighteenth-century origins, we meet different concepts of the ideal in the writings of Bolingbroke and Burke, Montesquieu, Rousseau and Sieyès, Jefferson, Herder and Fichte, Alfieri and Mazzini. As far back as the early 1930s, Carlton Hayes demonstrated this ideological richness and variety.[40] And it is therefore hardly surprising if an ideal that lacks a central tradition, single prophet or biblical text or canon, should have undergone so many transformations.[41]

Despite this protean variety, these versions of nationalism are closely interrelated. They form different members of a single ideological family with its special vision, culture, solidarity and programme. Though each nationalism adds its own motifs and theories, it always remains a doctrine of the history and destiny of the 'nation', an entity opposed to other important modern collectivities like the 'sect', 'state', 'race' or 'class'.

In fact, the following chapters aim to unfold this national ideal and doctrine in relation to the ideological challenges it has had to meet during the course of this century, by those who espouse the claims of rival collectivities. Despite its many guises, nationalism emerges as a unity with clear contours as it meets the successive challenges of millennial, fascist, racist and communist movements. Already in the nineteenth century, nationalism had to meet the criticisms of orthodox religious leaders and of some liberal democrats. Later it began to face the challenge of Marxist socialism. But only in this century did the challenge become a total one. Nationalism was called upon to withstand the onslaught of first a racial fascism, and then a developmental communism. In both cases, it has met and outlived the crisis posed by these two opposed 'world salvation' movements, by contracting, expanding and transforming itself as the situation appeared to demand. In doing so, it has been quite ready to borrow the myths and slogans of its rivals, and it has often been exploited by them. Yet it has always outlasted them, showing itself to be more attractive, more flexible and more tenacious than its competitors.

CHAPTER 2

Nationalism and the Millennium

The desire for a kingdom of perfect freedom and justice in the here and now has a long and distinguished history. We find it in the Sumerian epic of Gilgamesh, in the ancient Israelite prophecies, and in the example and teaching of Jesus and his followers. During the Middle Ages, chiliastic and revolutionary movements spread across Europe denouncing papal corruption and preaching the imminent demise of this world and its divine replacement by another, which would embody a state of absolute purity and justice. Only believers who had repented their misdeeds in time could share in the thousand-year rule of Christ and his saints, shortly to be inaugurated; for the rest there was damnation or purgatory, till the second and final resurrection. In the divine millennium there could be no place for disbelievers, corruptors or materialists, for only the elect would taste the joys of salvation.[1]

Both these medieval millennialisms and those later ones that flourished in Africa and Asia under colonial rule have attracted much scholarly attention, as much for their basic similarities as for their many differences, which include the cultural context and period, the degree of activism evinced, and the presence or absence of a messiah figure. For all these obvious differences, it still remains reasonable to identify some common characteristics which justify us in labelling such movements as 'millennial'; and it may be helpful to define these movements very generally as salvation movements, which announce the imminent end of this corrupt world and the advent, through divine agency, of a new golden age of terrestrial perfection for God's elect. In this definition, neither the thousand-year kingdom nor the messiah are mentioned, since the medieval movements did not emphasise the role of the messiah while the colonial movements did not refer to the rule of the saints for whom they often substituted the return of the ancestors.

All these movements, however, were inspired by a belief in the apocalypse, in which this wicked world would be swept away at one stroke and God would institute, either directly or through His representative, the golden age of perfection and justice on earth.[2]

Apart from this general similarity, certain features recur in most millennial movements, and these have been excellently summarised by Yonina Talmon.[3] To begin with, millennialism has a linear conception of time. It envisages a revolutionary leap into the perfect future from a past that is both corrupt and ambivalent. Second, salvation must be terrestrial. The elect can only be saved on this earth, and the kingdom of God likewise must be instituted here and now, through the fruits of the earth, as 'Cargo cult' symbolism expressed it so vividly. Third, salvation was held to be collective but limited. It was not the individual who was to be saved, nor the whole world, but a special group, the 'chosen people', bearers of good tidings who waited and watched and prayed for the hour of judgement. Fourth, millennialism is always and everywhere supernaturalist. Only God can actually save; only He can institute the kingdom. Man cannot bring salvation; he can only be ready for it. Prayer, vigilance and repentance may help; but the act of judgement, and with it damnation or election, belongs solely to God. Fifth, and slightly modifying the last feature, was a common belief in a mediator, who might be the messiah, or a prophetic announcer like Joachim of Fiore or Ndungumoi in Fiji, or a redeemer—leader like Simon Kimbangu or André Matswa in the Congo. There was also a tendency for millennial movements to throw up a political organiser and fundraiser, who might be a different figure from the charismatic leader. And finally, though the movement could range from a stable, exclusive sect to an amorphous, ephemeral and inchoate string of networks, there was always a hard core of dedicated believers, fanatical followers of the charismatic mediator. Such then were some of the main features of these irrational, antinomian mass movements that have sprung up in most periods and in most religious traditions.

As interest grew in these movements, there arose the conviction among some students that we would do well to view them as precursors, and even progenitors, of secular mass movements like nationalism and communism. Secular ideological movements were increasingly regarded as heirs and surrogates of the earlier millennialisms, and an attempt was made to trace out the European lineage of nationalism and communism back to medieval chiliasms. An extension of this view implied the idea of a triple progression: from millennialism to nationalism, and then to communism, each stage according with the state of social consciousness of the masses during that historical period.[4] The link might be temporal, or simply evolutionary: nevertheless, the idea of a link that also represented a progression of consciousness proved highly attractive.

It goes without saying that these arguments are put forward by conservatives as well as radicals, and while for the conservative the alleged millennial element within nationalism damns it out of hand, for the radical the same feature helps to redeem what would otherwise be a dangerous deviation from the real task. For a conservative like Kedourie, nationalism is the secular heir and successor of a Christian millennialism, which is thus responsible for all its absurdities;[5] for socialists like Hobsbawm and Worsley, 'pre-political' millennialisms foreshadow and herald truly political movements like nationalism, which in turn announce the coming, in the appropriate social conditions, of the universal movement of socialism and communism.[6] Nevertheless, both the 'secular heir' and the 'triple progression' theses agree in assigning a central role to the millennial element in defining and energising the nationalist movement. Millennialism, in short, is the most potent source of nationalism.

It is just this fashionable view that I wish to dispute. Far from 'millennialism' constituting a central motif and primary source of nationalism, it has in fact played a minor role in the genesis and diffusion of nationalist ideas and movements – and that however broadly millennialism is defined. Nationalism does not announce the imminent end of this world and the advent of another; it does not reserve salvation for believers; it has no place for the supernatural; and despite Fichtean or Mazzinian rhetoric, it does not see itself as building the 'kingdom of God' on earth, only attempting to make the earth a more tolerable habitat for a certain category of person. What is true is that certain, usually atheist but 'messianic', believers in a single cosmopolitan world, having found that the world was not yet ready for their high ideals, transferred their fervent expectations on to their 'nation', lending its nationalism a touch of romantic and ardent exuberance. In that attenuated sense and in that sense alone can a messianic 'millennialism' be said to have crept into nationalism. But it bears no relationship to a truly religious millennialism, and it is therefore misleading to regard nationalism as a secular heir or progression from a millennialism with which it has such tenuous links. We shall not gain in an understanding of nationalism by viewing it through the lens of millennialism; rather, we need to examine more traditional religious sources of nationalism, as well as some of the new non-religious ideas that collided with traditional beliefs. For nationalism can only be understood as a fusion of strands from several sources, religious and non-religious, as they came into conflict at the dawn of the modern era; and it is just this confluence of different sources that allows nationalism to combine, transform, yet always remain a recognisable ideology.

MILLENNIAL ROOTS

The view that I wish to dispute – the 'millennialist' theory of nationalism of both the conservative and radical varieties – is supported by two kinds of argument: those based on affinity and those showing a covariance between the two movements. The first attempt to demonstrate a close proximity between the ideas and consequences of the two kinds of movements; the second aim to show a high correlation, with chiliastic millennialism always preceding the birth of nationalism. I start with the arguments from affinity.

First, nationalism and millennialism are held to exhibit and generate a similar fervent new morality. Both espouse an ideal of terrestrial social justice with puritanical zeal, and preach a universal ethic of acosmic love and revolutionary fraternity. For millennialists, this is an imitation of Christ's all-embracing love; for nationalists, it is a form of social cohesion and fraternity, third of the ideals inscribed by the French revolutionaries. In both movements, the virtuous elect are separated by their morality from an individualistic and materialist world. The new ethic commands its devotees to sever all ties with family, class, church and state, in order to unfetter the soul from a corrupt and degrading past. The elect can only partake in the radiant future salvation by a thorough inner purging of the spirit and through arduous struggle and zeal. Only by sternly renouncing the joys of this life, and by completely devoting oneself, body and soul, to the new life of virtue and brotherhood, can the believer hope for any redemption. And only through collective virtue can the kingdom of justice be established on earth.[7]

Ideologically, therefore, millennialism and nationalism speak the same language and exude an identical spirit. The Franciscan Spirituals devoted themselves to prayer, poverty and chastity; their nationalist heirs in Jacobin France and Arndt's Germany trod the same path of self-denying virtue and organised brotherhood. Similarly, there is a strong parallel between the two kinds of movements in their social consequences. Both mobilise and unify large numbers of people who were previously scattered in self-sufficient villages and small market towns, and were altogether outside the political arena in the main cities. Millennial Bible-singing evangelical groups gathered villagers together, inspired them with a common ideal and common grievances, and thereby broke down their narrow localism and fragmented lives. True, millennialism is a largely 'pre-political' movement. It does not have a theory of worldly power as such. Yet it has managed to weld the politically inexperienced and inarticulate villagers and the poor together, whether they be landless proletarians, recent immigrants, serfs and semi-feudal peasants in depressed areas, or ethnic minorities. A case of the latter kind occurred in the Congo, where Balandier studied the 'sacred nationalism', as he called it, of the BaKongo who dreamed of the restoration of their ancient kingdom.[8] Here too Kimbanguism helped to mobilise and politicise the rural population, and was closely linked to their ethnic nationalism. Indeed, part of nationalism's appeal lies in its ability to coalesce and unify around a common goal otherwise divergent interests, thereby undercutting and suppressing all forms of sectionalism and regionalism. In other words, nationalists simply carry on the work begun by the chiliasts: they create large units and erase old local ties and sympathies.[9]

Closely linked to its mobilising role is the propensity for both types of movement to draw élites and masses together. So all-encompassing and urgent is the new morality that it sweeps away all social barriers, including those of property and status. Besides, the leaders of millennial movements are not drawn from the upper class; more often, they are aspirant but rejected lower middle-class men, or alienated, marginal misfits. They form an ideal focus for every kind of local grievance and discontent, especially in a society that has no legal channels for the expression of such grievances. Their nonpartisan position as outsiders allows them to mould together all the separate interests and grievances into a single, powerful movement. A Sabbatai Zvi could attract Jews from Turkey as well as Poland; his Zionist successors can unite in one fold Jews from Russia, Germany, Morocco and Yemen, each group having its own specific memories and life-styles. In this way, the nonpartisan élite becomes identified, and identifies, with their followers, while former distinctions of wealth and status lose their edge in the new moral community forged by the struggle.[10]

Ideologically, too, nationalism is as revolutionary as millennialism. It aims to reverse the status of the disprivileged, to make the last first. It announces the advent of a new era when the community will be reborn, and the ethnic fraternity, the true believers, will find salvation and peace. Reform is insufficient; the revolution is at hand. Only the total overthrow of the old order can ensure man's perfectibility and the arrival of God's kingdom, and only man's zeal and activism can prepare the revolution of the heart, for which both movements strive.[11]

The arguments from covariance point in the same direction. They show that, in many cases, nationalism and millennialism coincide. Perhaps the best-known examples come from the Congo. Kimbanguism flourished in the 1920s, soon to be followed by Simon Mpadi's Kakists and then Matswaism. Simon Kimbangu himself was born in 1889, failed his English mission exams, and in 1921 was 'touched by the grace of God'. He thereupon became a catechist, healer and prophet, forming xenophobic, Bible-singing congregations which practised adult baptism and confession. Proclaiming himself the messiah of the Ki-Kongo, he condemned magic, revived the ancestor cult and announced the imminent end of this corrupt world. Soon his followers came into conflict with the Belgian authorities, particularly when they began to proclaim that loyalty to God precluded any allegiance to the colonial administration, whose demise was daily awaited. The Belgians arrested, tried, condemned and deported Kimbangu, and he died in prison in 1950. His successors met a similar fate, Matswa being deported to Chad in 1930, and Mpadi being imprisoned four times. For Balandier, it has proved impossible to avoid linking these millennial movements with BaKongo or neighbouring nationalisms, manifesting themselves in periods of severe economic dislocation and colonial exploitation.[12]

Similar connections between millennial movements and an incipient nationalism can be found in Nyasaland and the Sudan. According to Shepperson and Price, John Chilembwe's nativist revolt against white authority in Nyasaland in 1915 owed a great debt to the activities of the wandering evangelist missionary, Joseph Booth, who seems to have introduced the ideas of the Watchtower movement into southern Africa in the first decade of this century.[13] Undoubtedly, their beliefs in the imminent advent of the Kingdom played an important part in Chilembwe's religious nativism.[14] Similarly, Islamic beliefs in the advent of the Mahdi's chiliastic kingdom affected nationalism's early phases, not merely in the Sudan itself but as far afield as Senegal and the Cameroons. Here too we find millennial prophets breaking down existing kinship ties and preparing the minds of men and women for radical political change.[15]

In Asia, too, millennialism has frequently anticipated, we are told, an incipient nationalism. Thus in Burma, the revolt of Saya San in 1930 in the Burmese countryside immediately preceded the formation of the Thakin movement of nationalism, drawn from the intellectuals. Saya San meanwhile had proclaimed himself the restored Buddha–king and appealed to the peasant masses to evict the British, but his rebellion was soon crushed.[16] In China, the Tai-ping rebellion in the 1850s combined Christian and Chinese ideas, and antedated Chinese nationalism.[17] And in the remote steppes of central Asia, among the high Altai Mountains, Oirot Khan, the last great Oirot ruler, 'appeared' on a white steed in 1904 to an Oirot shepherd, Chot Chelpanov, to announce the end of tsarist rule. Burkhanism, the 'White Faith' of the small, impotent and impoverished tribe of the Oirots, attacked Russian Orthodoxy and Russian rule, looked to the victorious Japanese, and sought a messianic return to ancient native legends and traditions stemming from the descendants of Genghis Khan.[18]

Traces of an anti-colonial nationalism may also be discerned among the millennial 'Cargo-cults' of Melanesia.[19] Thus in 1885 a well travelled Fijian, Ndungumoi, claimed bodily invulnerability, set himself up as a prophet and preached the future submission of European traders and missionaries to their Fijian subjects, once the material supplies or 'cargo' reached them. Ndungumoi's followers came to believe that the Bible was their creation, which the Whites had stolen along with their wealth and goods. Soon Ndungumoi was able to raise funds for the traditional prestige feasts, and for a paramilitary force; however, when he told his followers to burn their crops in readiness for the advent of the millennium, he was summarily deported and gaoled.[20]

In Europe, too, some millennial movements carried political overtones. Thus, after the terrible Chmielnicki massacres of 1648–50, thousands of Polish Jews flocked to the message of the false messiah, Sabbatai Zvi of Smyrna, who claimed he was an emanation of the divine, basing himself on the Cabbalistic text of the Zohar. Though the rabbis condemned him, and the Sultan forced him to convert to Islam, the masses who had suffered physical and economic ruin continued to believe in him, as they were later to believe in Herzl.[21] Similarly, in seventeenth-century England, during the convulsions of the Civil War, fiercely millennial sects of Fifth Monarchy men and Ranters sprang up to proclaim the end of the old dispensation and the advent of the new in an England cleansed of tyranny and papism. Their message coincided with the rise of an English nationalism, particularly among the Levellers, which spoke of the Englishman's birthright and the restoration of his Saxon privileges now that the 'Norman yoke' had been broken.[22]

If there is coincidence in timing, there is also much similarity in the social composition of nationalism and millennialism. Both appeal to the disprivileged.[23] They draw their recruits from the mass of villagers hardest hit by colonial exploitation. They attract those at the margin of society, both social and geographical. They represent the cry of despair for centuries of economic neglect and political oppression, and a reaction by the peripheral hinterland against the centres of wealth and power. Indeed, today's 'autonomist' separatist movements in Britain, France, Spain and Canada may be seen as the latest expression of this revolt of the neglected periphery.[24]

And here we come upon an even closer link between the two kinds of protest. For the failure of the one is a cause for the emergence of the other. When the tense expectations of millennialism are disappointed, a more realistic assessment of the situation is made. Defeat brings a greater interest in the actual mechanics of the transition to the golden age. Action is no longer simply compensatory, no longer simply an emotional relief in a situation of political impasse. The new secular knowledge brought by contact with more advanced societies lends the succeeding nationalist protest greater menace and effectiveness. The last vestiges of the cyclical conceptions underlying millennialism give way to a more 'Promethean' outlook, in which man's creative capacity for meeting challenges and effecting change is prized. The old passive religious conceptions are replaced by a political expression of social grievances, with nationalism marking the first stage of this new political awareness.[25]

Indeed, the very origins of nationalism in Europe can be traced back to the politicisation of ancient millennial traditions. From the visions of the Biblical prophets, and the monastic chiliasm of the Essenes, through the apocalypse of the Book of Revelations and the millennial speculations of a Calabrian abbot, Joachim of Fiore, in the late eleventh century, there emerged a peculiar Christian tradition of chiliasm and religious revolution.[26] According to Joachim, the existing world was corrupt, despite Christ's first coming; soon it would be swept away, and with it the Pope, Church, and kings, to be succeeded by a Third Age of universal love.[27] From Joachim of Fiore, the same antinomian message was carried by Franciscan Spirituals in Italy, Brethren of the Free Spirit in western Europe, Anabaptists in sixteenth-century Münster and Fifth Monarchy men in seventeenth-century England, into the central stream of European philosophy. It emerged in the rationalism of Descartes and Spinoza, reappeared in Kant and in the romantic outpourings of Lessing and Fichte, and thence entered into the mainstream of nationalism. The expression has changed over the centuries, but the vision remains. There is always the same message of perfection in this world and attendant perfectibility of man and society. Today the message is couched in the language of social progress and national redemption, but this is no more than a secularised version of Joachimite chiliasm, with its messianic belief that virtue and terror can establish the kingdom of justice on earth.[28]

MODERNIST THEMES

Now it is one thing to assert that the messianic impulse is an element in all national revivals; quite another to equate that impulse with millennialism, and hold that it is at the root of nationalism or the primary factor in its genesis. In what follows, I shall confine my attention to the main errors of this view, in the hope of suggesting some alternative hypotheses about the origins and nature of contemporary nationalism.

If we take first the arguments from covariance, we shall find that the correlation between millennial and nationalist movements is in fact too negative to sustain their temporal connection. On the one hand, large numbers of millennial movements – in the European Middle Ages, in the Pacific islands and in Africa – were not succeeded within a significant time-span by a nationalist movement in the same area, and in many cases the nationalism, when it did emerge, arose in another area. Thus the predominantly Italian millennial movement of the Franciscan Spirituals in the thirteenth century was not succeeded by an Italian nationalism for several centuries, and similar with the Münster Anabaptists in Germany.[29] True, the Hussite movement did possess certain ethnocentric overtones, but a genuine movement of Czech nationalism did not emerge until four centuries had elapsed. The various millennialisms of the 'Cargo cults' again did not engender a definite nationalism, although they carried strong anti-colonial overtones; and similarly in Africa, a number of millennial movements like the Harris or Matswaist sects were not followed by a nationalism built on their foundations. Indeed, cases like the Matswaist or Lumpa sects actually came into conflict with the nationalist movement and the newly independent state.[30]

On the other side, a great many nationalist movements were not born out of millennialisms. Thus a great divide of two centuries and of different social and geographical milieux separate the millennial movement of the Jewish messiah-figure, Sabbatai Zvi, in the 1650s from the Zionist movement. Similarly, several centuries divide the religious ethnicism of Joan of Arc from the nationalism evinced at the time of the French Revolution, or the messianic fervour of sixteenth-century Swiss Protestant reformers from late eighteenth-century Swiss nationalism.[31] In many cases it is difficult to find any millennial movement preceding the rise of nationalism: there is little to be found in India or among the Tatars, none in Belgium, Norway, Egypt, Rumania, Greece, Japan, Armenia or Argentina, to take some random examples. Indeed, the vast majority of nationalisms show no antecedent millennial connection.

What we sometimes find are cases of frustrated nationalism producing, as it were, millennial movements. This seems to be the
explanation of the Mau Mau movement, of the Saya San rebellion
in Burma, which followed the first nationalist campaigns of the
GCBA, and possibly of the Kimbanguist outburst among the Ba-
Kongo.[32] Only in the most backward areas, among remote peoples
like the Oirots and the Nyasas, can we find the progression from
millennialism to nationalism that these theories postulate; and their
nationalisms tend to be primitive and fleeting affairs. Even the
millennial upsurges in the English Revolution of the 1640s follow
the growth of a powerful English national sentiment dating back
to the time of Henry VIII and Elizabeth; and interestingly enough,
that sentiment, though widely diffused, did not find expression
in a large-scale nationalist movement after 1660.[33] In so far as
there is any link at all, millennialism appears to be the product
of an antecedent nationalism rather than vice versa.

There is finally the argument that traces European nationalism
back to its 'roots' in Christian millennialism. But here we must
observe that an important gulf separates the last great outbursts
of that chiliasm in the seventeenth century from the first nationalist
movements at the time of the French Revolution. This century
and a half witnessed the spread of the Enlightenment, the rise
of the absolutist state, the waning of religious authority and the
growth of urban trade and mercantilism. The period had its rebels
and dreamers, but they had little desire to hark back to a millennial
tradition which had proved such a failure in the past, and nor
did a Christian Europe show greater revolutionary zeal or produce
more rebels than, say, the Ottoman empire or India in the same
period. Rebellion was much more common in the late eighteenth
century; but this had nothing to do with a millennial tradition
that had somehow been imbibed into European philosophical discussions. Indeed, to imagine that Cartesian disputes could have any
effect on these later rebellions, or possess any connection with
either millennial or nationalist movements, is to assign to philosophical ideas a far greater force and influence than they warrant.[34]

There is therefore very little covariance between millennialism
and nationalism. Equally, the gulf that separates their respective
ideological characters and effects is just as great.

For, to begin with, nationalism generally appeals to more edu-

cated and propertied urban strata than does millennialism. There
are some cases of peasant nationalisms, where the intelligentsia
appealed to the peasants rather than to other groups, as in China
or Cuba; but even in these cases nationalism emerged first in
the cities. In the great majority of cases, nationalism is an urban
movement of the 'middle classes', in the sense that it gains its
first adherents among the middle strata in the cities, is organised
by the city in the countryside and continues to be dominated
by city cadres, even where it opens up branches in the villages.
The occupational groups that are most frequently represented in
the nationalist movement are civil servants and officers, lawyers
and journalists, teachers and other professionals, some of the entrepreneurs and the lower and middle clergy.[35] All these groups continually throw up ambitious and fairly well-placed men and women,
who attempt to break into centres of power and privilege monopo-
lised by ancient noble or ecclesiastical families or representatives
of the ruling foreigner. This is not to say that nationalisms may
not also take up, or utilise, the grievances of the peasantry or
the newly urbanised proletariat, as Tilak and Gandhi did in early
twentieth-century India. But, as they soon found out, this strategy
brought losses as well as gains, for the demands of the new adherents
necessitated a social and economic platform that threatened to
alienate the better-off and older supporters of the Congress Party.
Rarely does a nationalist movement jettison its main bastion of
support among the loose coalition of lower-middle and new élite
strata from which it gains its original recruits. Hence, although
nationalism becomes a 'classless' ideology in the sense that its
ideals are applicable to every social stratum, and are sufficiently
malleable to suit every interest, it starts out as a 'middle-class'
movement against aristocrats or colonisers, and may never seek
to turn into a 'mass' or multi-class movement. Hence it is misleading
to see in nationalism a force that necessarily binds élites to their
masses; that may be the rhetoric of nationalism, but the reality
is often quite different. Nor, by a similar token, should we equate
the social constituency of nationalism with that of millennialism,
whose appeal is, as we saw, directed to the peripheral disprivileged
and not to the aspirant urban strata.[36]

But not only is nationalism a movement of the urban and professional strata: it is even more fundamentally a programme of the

educated, of those who have been exposed to modern, secular, particularly western, science and culture. Those who would seek too close a link between chiliasts and nationalists overlook the role of the Enlightenment, and, more important, of enlighteners. In every society, contact with western thought has thrown up a stratum of rationalists and enlighteners, whose whole *raison d'être* is centred on their burning desire to lift the cultural level of their society to parity with the West. Secular, western education acts therefore to accentuate the gulf between the Europeanised élites and the vast majority of peasants or proletarians. Entry into the guild of the enlightened, with their special problems of culture contact, is in fact fairly restricted, whatever the pronouncements of apologists. The leisure, opportunities, abilities and incentives for acquiring a western-style education beyond a mere veneer are distributed in such a manner that the bulk of the population in backward countries must be perpetually excluded. And the very emphasis that nationalism places on the virtues of a civic education for communal participation tends to aid only the most ambitious and determined among the children of the underprivileged.[37]

The argument that nationalism, like millennialism, unifies and mobilises the population must also be qualified. In one sense, nationalism, with its heavy emphasis on communal activism, does stir up strata into political activity where before there was passive acquiescence. But the unification sought by nationalists differs considerably from that desired by chiliasts. The latter aim for a brotherhood among the elect who believe in the kingdom and its coming, whereas nationalists seek to unite people of the same culture into a single territorial unit. But neither territory nor ethnicity as such figure much in millennial dreams. With a few exceptions, like the already nationalistic BaKongo or Jews, ethnicity and territory played a decidedly minor role in millennial outbursts. The 'chosen' are an elect of God, not an ethnic chosen people. In many cases, millennial movements straddle ethnic boundaries and even political territories. Where the return of the ancestors is sought and identified with the new Jerusalem, it is a tribal rather than ethnic–cultural tradition that is being invoked. Besides, for all who wait in tense expectation of the apocalypse, the future's heavenly light will destroy the past with all its materialist ties of territory and descent.[38]

It is otherwise with nationalism. History and ethnic tradition play a major role in nationalist thought; while the need for a sovereign homeland is one of the movement's main demands. From the earliest days, nationalisms make a fetish of ethnic ties, of folklore, ancestral soil, language, religions, customs and alleged descent, if only to reassert and reforge on a higher territorial plane the fraternal sentiments of solidarity that lack of communications, localism and sectionalism had eroded and fragmented.[39] If one is going to create a genuine sense of belonging to a community of people whose size, dispersion and heterogeneity militate against any sense of solidarity, and if some ancient and half-forgotten ethnic ties or territorial memories can be salvaged and given new life and meaning, then ethnicity and territory will naturally turn into the main foci of mobilisation and unification. Indeed, so important is the need to create historic roots and a sense of homeland, that nationalists will strain scholarship to invent an ethnicity and political history of which only shadowy memories linger on.[40] Hence, while millennialism turns its back upon past time and present space in its wholehearted and fanatical zeal for a transfigured future, nationalism specifically seeks to resurrect a distant past which can help it shape that future, and sets out to rectify the present inequitable political and territorial arrangements. In other words, nationalism attempts to present a total picture of communal development, and to tie together the community's past, present and future.

This brings us to the most interesting and controversial differences between the two kinds of movement: their basic ideological outlooks. That there is a melioristic strand in both millennial and nationalist movements is undeniable; and equally undeniable is the zeal, passion and self-denying activism of their fervent new morality. Both are, in their different ways, revolutionary movements, if by 'revolution' we understand a social change in which an old order is overturned and replaced, within a short time-span, by another order. But when we begin to inquire into the reasons, goals and methods of such revolutionary activities, the differences come to outweigh this general emotional similarity. And it is these differences that undermine both the 'secular heir' and the 'triple progression' theories of millennial nationalism.

The chief difference between the two movements' goals concerns the place of our present world in their schemes. Millennialists will have nothing to do with our world; it is innately corrupt and damned. Nationalists, on the other hand, accept the present dispensation, at least as a starting-point. Hence the pessimistic, eschatological visions of the chiliasts make a strong contrast with the earthier, more limited claims of the nationalists, despite their often florid rhetoric. It is true that Mazzini, Mickiewicz and Arndt waxed lyrical about the soteriological qualities of a reborn Italy, Poland or Germany; and there is no doubt that an older religious, though not necessarily millennial, tradition was influential in guiding and formulating these ideals.[41] Nevertheless, the actual demands of the nationalists, and their subsequent actions, demonstrate that creating the nation-state falls far short of awaiting the day when the old world will be overthrown and the Kingdom of Saints established for a thousand years in its place. Whatever the momentary flights of lyrical fancy of some ideologies, the vision of nationhood that they actually propose is strictly of this world, as well as in it. Its message is a wholly secular, intramundane, hope for social and political liberation from 'alien' tyranny and corruption. It is not the world as such that is corrupt or doomed, but only the foreigner, the invader and the coloniser. Once such 'deformations' have been swept away, the community can find itself again and its historic wounds can heal, as it begins to realise its authentic energy and discover its true identity.

In these sentiments, nationalists reveal themselves as basically at home in the world. An optimistic, if cautious, sense of wellbeing also informs their attitudes to the future. They feel confident that they can harness for their own collective ends the energetic morality of self-reliance, which is so much a part of the industrial ethic of competition and individual advancement under capitalism; so that, where millennial visions reject on principle every worldly ethic, nationalism 'annexes' them. They become grist to its mill; and, like Marxism, nationalism makes use of them in order to transcend the conditions of their environment. 'Nation-building' is nothing if not an affirmation of this world.[42]

But, and here we touch on the heart of the matter, millennialism at its core is a cry of despair. The world is doomed, it says; and man without the Saviour-God, or His Anointed, cannot rise above his material surroundings. A few lucky souls, if they repent in time, may yet be saved; but man and his creations, society and its philosophies, will be consumed at the last trumpet. Today, perhaps, the 'kingdoms' of Münster or Andalusia may seem like microcosmic prototypes of the just and free society on earth; but the actual participants saw things altogether differently, as their actions of terror and despair tell us. Did not the Andalusian anarchist workers declare their opposition to marriage till the new world be instituted?[43]

There is then no chronological or typological progression from millennialism to nationalism. Their outlooks reflect utterly different values as well as divergent social conditions. It may be the case that 'as the *dominant* form of protest, millennarism always gives way to secularised forms, and therefore becomes marginal, and usually more pacific and otherworldly' (italics in original). It may also be true that in general millennial movements occur 'among strata and groups with the most "archaic", to use Hobsbawm's term, consciousness. They will decline with the modernisation of even these groupings: they will persist the more culturally and socially backward a region'.[44]

But this says nothing of the role of nationalism in such a modernising progression. It does not explain how the transition is effected from the 'archaic' state to the 'political', and even less why it should be nationalism that becomes the dominant form of protest. But nationalism is much more than an ideology of anti-colonialism, or a dislike of the foreign presence. It aims to build a nation, to construct a world of nations, each free and self-governing, each unique and cohesive, each able to contribute something special to a plural humanity. Nationalism therefore sets out to criticise the existing state of affairs from within. It regrets the lack of freedom, the lack of community, the loss of identity; and against this it prescribes the urgent need for choice, planning, participation and auto-emancipation. In the end, nationalism is a philosophy of collective self-help for those who share the same history; and its critique of society is a critique of social and political dependence.[45]

But chiliasts are not interested in critiques of society and politics. Dreaming of their abolition, they flee both. So fervent is their mystic flight from the travails of this world, so complete their underlying Manichaean pessimism, that they can only believe in the imminent and total destruction of this realm of imperfection and darkness by the Deity. Only a few movements allow more than a minor, a waiting, role for man's own efforts to free himself. Such deity-dependent mysticism, unless it turn inwards to passive pietism, must be self-defeating in any terms; for its hope, born of such uncomprehending despair of the world, must soon be dissipated.[46]

Urban status; secular, civic education; a common ethnicity and territory; collective self-help; optimistic world-affirmation: these are the chief concerns of nationalists and the stuff out of which nations are 'reborn'. The myth of nationhood is both practical and romantic, a project of social engineering as much as a cultural voyage. Millennialism is neither, and knows little or nothing of such themes. It erupts in epochs and areas where such matters are not pressing. When the latter become important, they crowd millennial grievances out of the picture and overshadow their dreams. And though a 'messianic' element has entered into nationalism's message, it is both less important and owes more to non-millennial sources than some would have us believe.

NEO-TRADITIONALISM, REFORMISM AND ASSIMILATION

If millennial dreams are not the major source of nationalist myths and concerns, are there other traditions of thought from which it has drawn its sustenance and its typical themes?

I should like to suggest three alternative spiritual traditions on which nationalism has drawn, two of them religious in character, the last classical and mainly secular in inspiration. Of the religious traditions, one was puritanical and often fundamentalist, the other defensive but reformist, sometimes with a tinge of rationalism. From the first have sprung a number of 'neo-traditionalist' movements and regimes, notably in Islamic countries; and these have contributed a strong xenophobic element, and have succeeded in influencing the secular nationalism of the leadership in several new states. Reformist and evolutionary religious ideas and activities have helped to promote educational reforms, and have thereby provided a second important source of inspiration, especially for middle-class liberal nationalisms. The third, classical, tradition played a more direct role in Europe than outside. In non-European countries classicism was mediated through the experience of colonialism, many administrators being steeped in the ancient classics, or committed to Enlightenment paganism. In this atmosphere, it is hardly surprising that some of the more optimistic spirits among native élites should embrace the cosmopolitan ideal of a single, though inevitably western, civilisation. When these people found their enthusiasm for westernisation was not reciprocated by western peoples or their rulers, many of them transferred their almost 'messianic' ardour back on to their subject and often despised native communities, lending the resultant nationalism an 'atheistic' and rationalist fervour.

These then are the traditions which have provided nationalism with its chief sources of inspiration, and I should like to discuss each briefly.

Neo-traditionalism

'Neo-traditionalism' influences nationalist ideology and activity either directly, through its fundamentalist movements and regimes, or indirectly, through the need for secular nationalist leaders to tap the energies and emotions of the 'masses'. In the latter case, a hitherto modernist, secular ideology is compelled to take on an atavistic, even fundamentalist, hue to accommodate the existing state of social consciousness of the peasants or immigrant workers.

Examples of neo-traditionalist movements can be found in Islamic and Buddhist countries. One of the best-known is the Muslim Brotherhood. At the height of its popularity in Egypt in the late 1940s, the Brotherhood is said to have had up to one million followers.[47] Its ideology is puritanical, militant, fundamentalist and populist. It rejects both the corruptions of Sufism and the rationalism of Islamic reform, and in the manner of Wahhabite tradition places Islam and Islamic precepts above every other loyalty, including the Arab nation. The Brotherhood wants to bring to the masses a true, uncorrupted form of Islam. For these reasons, it has organised programmes of social welfare, seeks strict cultural censorship and control over women, insists on severe punishments for infringing Koranic commandments, and rejects foreign capitalism.[48] The 'fascist' and totalitarian aspect is even more prominent in the Brotherhood's organisation, with its 'clans' and 'families', a series of groupings within its cells, its secret circles dedicated to the leader, Hasan al-Banna at the time, and its vesting of sole authority in the movement and its leader. For the Muslim Brother, it is his movement and his Leader, not the consensus of the community, that defines loyalty and commands his obedience.

The attempt to link the Brotherhood and its Pakistani counter-parts, such as the more élitist Jama'at-i-Islami or Allama Mashriqi's Khaksar paramilitary populism, with earlier Christian millennialism is more doubtful.[49] Such fundamentalist movements are better viewed as restorative, aiming to revive a religious rather than a national community through strict adherence to tradition coupled with mass tactics and organisation and a mass social programme. Such movements, like al-Afghani's pan-Islamic crusade, are neither millennial nor nationalist, though they resemble both in certain respects. But they do help to spread a political climate favourable to the growth of nationalism, and they can influence the latter towards a more traditionalist outlook.[50]

Analogous movements appeared within the Buddhist and Hindu traditions in the early part of this century. Again, these neo-traditionalisms were neither genuinely millennial nor specifically nationalist in themselves, although they promoted nationalist ends. In 1921, for example, the *pongyis* or political monks of Burma organised themselves in the Sangha Sametggi council, and began to hold key posts in political parties. Under the leadership of U Ottama, the *pongyis* transformed the traditional Buddhist quest for deliverance from suffering into a campaign to end social and political evils, notably foreign rule; and they proved very effective in politising the rural population and organising a mass Buddhist movement.[51] They were not interested in the setting up of an independent Burmese state *per se*, but their use of religious traditions provided an incipient Burman nationalism with its first, religious, issue, the Buddhist ban on wearing shoes in pagodas, and for a time undermined the more modernist nationalist leadership of the GCBA.[52] Moreover, their mass Gandhian techniques and support for the Khilafat anti-British movement, while not specifically nationalist itself, both contributed to and influenced the direction of the rising secular nationalism towards traditionalism.[53]

Equally important has been the use of traditions by westernised leaders like Tilak and Gandhi in early twentieth-century India. Tilak's appeal to the cults of Shivaji and Kali were not merely attempts to manipulate atavistic mass sentiments.[54] Tilak understood that only through a Hinduism that was close to the needs of the rural masses could India be truly unified and revitalised. He was therefore quite prepared to transform the austere message and ethos of the Bhagavad Gita into a summons to activism and 'disinterested' terrorism, if he could thereby mobilise the Hindu masses against both Brahmin leaders and the British.[55] In Japan, too, the advisers of the Meiji emperors after 1868 argued that only by 'retraditionalising' the masses could they be mobilised for public ends. It was therefore necessary to revive the Shinto cult to instil both emperor worship and mass loyalty to the new entity, the Japanese nation-state.[56] Perhaps this is why, also, a succession of often agnostic or Christian Arab nationalists, from al-Yaziji and al-Afghani to Nasser and Michel Aflaq, have accorded Islam a special place in the Arab pantheon and have sought to reconcile loyalty to the religious community, or *umma*, with Arab national sentiment.[57]

In short, 'neo-traditionalism' in countries as far apart as India, Japan and Egypt has formed a vital ideological point of reference and a powerful influence on the rise of nationalism. In few non-western areas can a secular nationalism afford to ignore or override the pre-industrial attachments of the rural population or their newly urbanised counterparts. Indeed, as the more educated and wealthier strata became westernised in the cities, the rural masses sometimes became even more conscious of and attached to their traditions.[58] And where foreign rulers proved obdurate, nationalists found they had to rouse this population and tap its religious fervour or substitute a 'surrogate religion' like communist nationalism, if independence was ever to be won.

Reformism

Movements of religious reform and reinterpretation occupy a special place in the genesis of nationalism. They often precede the birth of national ideals, and share a similar conception. The leaders of the nationalist movement are often drawn from the same social constituency as the reformists, and there are parallels in matters of organisation. One might even be tempted to view nationalism as the secular heir of religious reform rather than of millennialism.

But that, too, would be equally simplistic. Both nationalisms and reform movements are too complex and ambiguous, and too varied, to allow us to invoke such a monocausal chain. Besides, both reformism and nationalism can be interpreted as consecutive responses to aspects of the modernisation brought by contact with an imperialist and revolutionary West. A more modest hypothesis recommends itself: in terms of covariance and affinity, religious reform movements have contributed significantly to the framework, ideals and social bases of *early* nationalisms.[59]

A few examples may illustrate what I mean. In nineteenth-century Germany there was a clear current of 'conservative reform' among both the Romantics and their *völkisch* successors. This current owed much to the revival of an emotional Christianity by Schleiermacher and Fichte around 1800, and to the medievalist cult of Novalis, Tieck and the Schlegel brothers. Pantheist or deist Christianity, with its emotional reinterpretations, created the climate for a return to the 'organic' Gothic past, an enthusiasm that even Goethe shared in his youth. This in turn helped to produce the early Romantic nationalism of Müller, Fichte, Arndt and Jahn, with its populist harking back to medieval models of social unity.[60] Later these same religious reinterpretations stimulated the racial nationalism of the *völkisch* writers. After 1850 an emotionalised and Germanised Christianity became increasingly identified with the Eddic and Nordic religion of the pre-Christian German tribes. We find this equation in the racist effusions of Wagner, in the heterodox and evolutionary *völkisch* speculations of Paul de Lagarde, and in the mystic *Volk* spiritualism of the popular Julius Langbehn.[61] In a not dissimilar manner, some Slavophile conservatives in Russia adapted their Orthodox religion to Romantic and Hegelian evolutionary ideas. This led them to reject the official doctrines of Tsar and Church and to develop a view of Russian society as an organic unity based on special Russian spiritual values infused with a humanised Christianity. Only by adhering to these spiritual values, which were embodied for the Slavophiles in the peasant masses, could Russia avoid the atomisation and social conflict that disfigured contemporary western societies.[62] In Dostoevski's visionary writings, the cult of monastic Orthodoxy and the suffering of the noble peasant is taken to extremes; but other more prosaic Slavophiles, like Khomyakov, Aksakov and Strakhov, were equally committed to this conservative religious reinterpretation of the role of the peasant community in regenerating and redeeming Russia.[63]

A similar trend from conservative reformism to secular nationalism can be found in Egypt, where the Salafiyya movement of Rashid Rida around 1900 tried to return to a purified and original Islam, freed of accretions and obscurantism.[64] By encouraging the study of Arab history and unity, it tended to promote the rise of nationalism. Similarly, in Africa the secession of 'Ethiopian' churches, notably the Methodists, from the mission churches was essentially a movement of conservative reform. It altered liturgy and prayers to suit an African environment, but left basic theological tenets intact. Even later, when syncretist cults arose and identified these tenets with African ancestor worship, the importance of the Ethiopian movement for an emergent nationalism lay rather in its assertion of the African right to control its own congregations, and its support for African culture in its own right.[65] In both these cases, religious and cultural reforms helped to promote a secular nationalism.[66]

There are also more radical varieties of religious reform. In India, for example, the westernising reformism of Roy led to the formation of the Brahmo Samaj by Chandra Sen. This organisation condemned idol worship and polytheism; indeed, its extreme rationalism provoked Dayananda Saraswati to found a rival Arya Samaj in 1875. The latter was also intolerant of Hindu superstition and polytheism, but aimed to create a purified national religion by reference to the Vedas and the Varna.[67] Both organisations were anti-Brahmin and socially reformist, and both accepted a compromise between western education and eastern ideas and ritual. Their debates contributed much to the climate of early Congress nationalism.[68]

Similar tensions within the Jewish reform movement of the mid-nineteenth century, between radicals like Holdheim, Friedlander and Abraham Geiger and conservatives like Tiktin and Zechariah Frankel, also helped to prepare the reception of Zionism in central Europe.[69] Many of their discussions centred on the use of Hebrew in prayers, the return to Zion and the nature of the Messiah. At the same time, Jewish historiography was being revived by Jost, Zunz and Graetz; and together with the Hegelian notions of Nachman Krochmal, they suggested an evolutionary interpretation of Judaism, which in turn influenced early Zionists like Luzzatto, Smolenskin and Moses Hess.[70] Even in the remote areas of Tatar and Turkish peoples around Kazan, in the Crimea and in central Asia, the religious reformism of Marjani and Gasprinki bred a social and cultural reawakening, which contributed greatly to pan-Turkism and Tatar nationalism in the 1890s.[71]

The affinity between reformism and early nationalism is both ideological and social. Both movements utilise an evolutionary framework. Reformists view man as increasing his value as he moves towards fuller comprehension of the Deity and his purpose in history; in similar vein, nationalists envisage a ceaseless striving for national autonomy and identity, an awakening to real community and solidarity.[72] Both are therefore optimistic, without being apocalyptic. They lay store by dignity, education and self-purification, aiming to create the 'new man' who is self-reliant and free. They share an ethic of self-help and self-respect, and both aim to integrate indigenous values with western science.[73] Both movements have accepted the rationalist ethos and competitive nature of modernity, but aim to harness it to more elevating, collective ends.

There are also social affinities. Reform movements prefer stable denominations or loose associations to the close-knit sect or cell of either millennial or communist movements. Examples of these looser organisations would include theological seminaries; coteries of writers revolving around journals, like the Pochvenniki in Russia, who assembled round the journals of the Dostoevskii brothers, *Vremia* and *Epocha*, or the journalists of Rashid Rida's al-Manar in Egypt; and social reform societies like the Brahmo Samaj or the Young Men's Buddhist Association in Burma.[74] Nationalists, too, often operate in loose, experimental and even segmental organisations. In a crisis, of course, the movement will demand a more unquestioning obedience, but in less turbulent times the nationalists utilise overlapping, often conflicting vehicles to suit their purposes. They will then congregate around scholarly societies, propaganda journals, political rights groups, parties, and congresses such as the Chibbat Zion committees in Russia, the Kuomintang, or the Rassemblement Démocratique Africaine, a loose congress for all west African countries.[75] Only in periods of extreme repression will nationalists organise themselves in small guerilla bands or terrorist cells, often as an auxiliary arm of the umbrella political organisation. As in reformist denominations, the full nationalist organisation is sovereign. In theory, its delegates are representative, its officials elective. In practise, however, those with the means and expertise tend to dominate, and even isolate themselves from the rank and file.[76]

These élitist tendencies in nationalist and reformist associations are a function of the similar criteria of membership. Education is the main determinant of position within both types of movement, education coupled with zeal for the cause. In the case of nationalism, this education is more purely western and secular, but in both cases it is secular education rather than birth or wealth that throws up a new stratum of aspirants for power and privilege, men who are rejected both by their fossilised native hierarchies and their imperial western rulers. The resulting stratum of the professional intelligentsia forms the main social base of both religious reform and early nationalist movements.[77]

This is why we asserted earlier that nationalisms are movements of the enlightened, urban middle strata, not of the impoverished peasantry or the underemployed proletarians to whom millennialism appeals. It is only later in the development of the nationalist movement that, in certain circumstances and in some cases, the nationalist leadership may attempt to broaden their social base by an appeal to the lower-middle strata or even the workers and peasants, and in doing so are often compelled to resort to the 'neo-traditionalist' current discussed above. In the genesis of nationalism, however, the role of secular education, and the uses of education for propaganda, are paramount. Indeed, in one sense the 'nation' itself is the institutionalisation of secular education, and resembles a ladder of continual exertion for self-improvement and mobility through education.[78]

Here, too, we find a causal link with early nationalism. For the tension between reason and revelation that besets religious reform movements inevitably leads to an accommodation with secular thought and with the individual's right to reinterpret the tradition for himself. In the end, rationalism may easily triumph and bring with it the dissolution of all tradition and religion. The attempted reform of traditional religion ends by dissolving it altogether. To avert that threat, the more conservative reformists appeal to ethnic history as the touchstone of a living communal tradition, which will still be valid and meaningful in a technological and capitalist era. Hence the very failure of religious reform becomes the entry-point for an historical nationalism. Religious reform has secularised and democratised the native tradition; to save it from extinction, it now endows it with an historical and social meaning. The people of a religion now becomes the religion of a people, of a living community, of a nation.[79]

Assimilation

Apart from these religious sources of nationalism, there is also a secular tradition that has contributed to the nationalist synthesis. It is a tradition that stems ultimately from classical Greece and Rome, was rediscovered in the early Renaissance, and became highly influential in the late eighteenth century in Europe and America. Essentially pagan and civic, this classical *'polis'* ideal defined the norm of a political community and its appropriate type of government.[80] Its appeal for eighteenth-century intellectuals lay in its promise of an immediate and invigorating solidarity, which seemed so regrettably absent in the contemporary absolutist states.[81] The eighteenth-century 'neoclassical' cult of virtue was both cosmopolitan and territorially bounded. It preached moral and political regeneration of the existing 'nation'-states – France, Switzerland, America, Poland, Prussia, Austria, Spain, even England – through the civic virtue and communal patriotism of their educated classes; yet in the same breath it affirmed the universalism, even cosmopolitanism, of their moral ideals. The cult of rejuvenation through the political virtue of the ancients knew no boundaries, and was the exclusive property of none. Yet the union of citizens, the political community, in and through which such a purification and regeneration could emerge, was not the civilisation of 'Europe' or the 'West', but the solidarity and fraternity of ancient and recognised political entities with their distinctive languages, customs and religions.[82]

This tension within the neoclassical tradition was one factor in the rejection of those who wanted to 'assimilate' into an undifferentiated 'western' civilisation of rational progress. For whatever the lofty dreams of the philosophers, even they had to recognise the considerable political and cultural differences within that overall civilisation, and to commend a particular 'national' variant of progress to the would-be world citizen. Many would-be assimilators had courageously broken with native tradition and received religion. Deists or agnostics, they had come to feel that man alone, by his unaided efforts, could surmount the acute problems of human and natural suffering that the God of traditional religions had appeared unable or unwilling to eradicate. But, after the Lisbon earthquake in 1755, the Enlightenment entered a more serious and moralistic phase, in which sceptics and unbelievers cast around for models of human purpose and solidarity as a means to prevent or minimise the effects of conflict and disaster.[83] They found them increasingly in the austere city-states of antiquity and the tribal rites of the Bible, among the Spartans, early Romans and the Jews under Moses.[84] In such a stoic climate, cosmopolitan ideals began to lose their attraction. Non-Europeans who wished to 'assimilate' into a European civilisation were soon enjoined to forget their cosmopolitanism and embrace the regenerated national community in which they happened to reside or with which they were linked, as Korais and Alfieri were with France, or to return to their native lands to regenerate their fallen and corrupted kinsmen.

As the nineteenth century advanced, and with it the ethnic insults that accompanied imperial conquest and colonialism, an increasing number of educated non-westerners retraced their steps to their native lands in disappointment at the rejection of their 'messianic' cosmopolitan hopes.[85] They had hoped to assimilate as individuals into European civilisation; now they transferred their ardour on to their disdained community, and sought a means of bringing it up out of its ignorance and degradation and into the mainstream of western civilisation in which they still fondly believed. The westernisers, from Herzen and Belinsky to Herzl, Nehru and Ataturk, brought their secular messianism to the task of mobilising their community, modernising its institutions and educating its personnel, to 'catch up with the West'. They see their task as carrying through a revolution of national development, in which the nation functions as arena and stepping-stone to the goal of joining a single global civilisation. They have not really abandoned their faith in the rationalist goals of the Enlightenment; yet circumstances force them to realise that faith within the restricted compass of their nation-state. Here, too, they only reflect the contradictions inherent in the neoclassical tradition, which furnished the basis and *élan* for a middle-class democratic nationalism.[86]

MESSIANIC ELEMENTS

From each of these three traditions – the neo-traditionalist, the reformist and the neoclassical assimilationist – nationalism has drawn, and continues to draw, inspiration and sustenance. From the puritanical traditionalism of the first source, nationalism has grasped the importance and profundity of mass religious sentiments, which it seeks to convert to the service of the nation. Neo-traditionalism, however, has its dangers. Its blind fanaticism and easy submission to a leader's will, together with the xenophobic hatreds it generates, can also feed the fascist and racist movements that have flourished in our century. I shall consider some of these movements, and their links with nationalism, in later chapters. From the second, reformist, tradition nationalism has taken its sense of the role of ethnicity and history, and the need to adapt that history to the changing conditions of a sceptical and scientific age, without loss of uniqueness. Here, too, there have been problems, as the more advanced liberal democracies failed to grasp the changes in ethnic consciousness within their boundaries, a theme to which I revert later. Finally, from the neoclassical, secular ideal of assimilation, nationalism drew its initial concepts of popular sovereignty and citizenship within a recognised territorial 'homeland'. Today, it continues to take much of its inspiration from the political passion and activist fervour of the *polis* tradition. Translated on to a world stage, this 'messianic' ideal of political revolution is today embodied, above all, in the communist nationalisms of the Third World, which warrant therefore more detailed study.

Each of these traditions, and with it the nationalist synthesis, has undergone considerable transformation in our century. As the populist element of nationalist ideology grew stronger, as ever larger numbers of people in different walks of life entered the political arena, the forms and guises in which nationalism appears have become more varied and protean. There are today 'separatist' nationalisms, 'racial' nationalisms, 'communist' nationalisms, 'fascist' nationalisms, 'liberal' nationalisms, 'conservative' nationalisms, 'traditionalist' nationalisms and 'pan' nationalisms. And yet, despite this proliferation of titles, the nationalist element within these variants is always immediately recognisable, and, with a few significant exceptions, always dominant. In the struggle between nationalism and its rivals for a hold on the minds and hearts of contemporaries, the peculiar fusion of utopian and practical elements that nationalism embodies has continued to ensure its primacy, and today it seems to have re-emerged, in the West and in the Third World, with renewed vigour and force. Where the earlier millennial movements' messianism has proved a handicap throughout their history, the peculiar 'messianism' of nationalism, which is so thoroughly practical and attainable, has given it the edge over its rivals.

Wherein lies the particular 'messianism' of today's nationalisms? It has nothing in common with that of either millennialism or communism. The older millennial belief saw in the arrival of the Messiah the advent of the Kingdom of Saints, the New Jerusalem, the Return of the Ancestors, or the Golden Age of Faith (his exact function varied with each religious tradition). Basically, the Messiah was a forerunner of the last days, announcing the new dispensation which would utterly replace a corrupt world, which God's wrath would consume, and which would usher in for the elect an era of salvation and perfection on earth. In the communist version, there is also an end of days, or rather of 'prehistory', in which capitalism is overthrown and replaced by socialism. As history moves towards its revolutionary climax, the Communist Party, for whom salvation is reserved, throws up its prophet and leader, who fulfil the role of the messiah announcing the impending transcendence of the old order by the new.[87]

But nationalism has no real vision of the final days, nor can it reserve salvation for an exclusive elect once independence has been won. By its own logic, all the nation's members are of the elect, and all outsiders, since they too belong to a nation, are equally 'chosen' in a world of unique cultures. Nor is there any room for a 'messiah'. The movement's prophet and leader, be they ever so honoured or charismatic, are only instruments of the national will. The people are their own messiah, and their ethic values collective self-help. Through their 'self'-realisation, they create their own revolution, in which the community's past, be it in China or Russia, Mexico or Israel, is lovingly restored and refurbished.

For a practical ideology like nationalism, the 'messianic' element is contained in its vision of ethnic fraternity for which it strives. Nationalists believe that a 'messianic age' will arrive only when men and women come to share common values and sentiments, as in a close-knit family. The nation is such a 'family' writ large, being comprised of so many actual families sharing common memories and experiences and so producing collective emotions and ideals, in which each individual will 'realise' and rediscover his true self. The programme that nationalism proposes for realising this nostalgic, even primitive, 'myth' is more in accord with a technological and rationalist epoch. In practice, the nationalist movement seeks to create a nationally conscious and cohesive élite, to diffuse the national message to other strata, to define given populations as nations, to eject foreigners and win the right for native peoples to control their own affairs, and finally to create a world in its own image, a world of theoretically independent and equal nation-states. Despite local difficulties and periodic emendations, this is a programme well on the way to fulfilment. Its very practicality is surely one reason for nationalism's continuing success.

Nationalism has avoided the temptation of ideologies to produce an eschatology. It draws its power from real feelings about modern cultural groups, feelings that are widespread; and hence it is firmly rooted in the social landscape of the modern world and its values. This is not to deny nationalism's utopian yearnings, only to underline its optimism and its practical ability to surmount tragedy through collective effort.

The image of millennialism is one of mystic flight from a doomed world. The chiliast yearns for its abolition, that God's elect may enter the new terrestrial kingdom of absolute justice: 'For behold, I create new heavens and a new earth; and the former shall not be remembered, nor come to mind.'[88]

The image of nationalism is that of restoration and renovation, of return from spiritual exile to the promised land. The past has not been in vain. Out of its sorrow and tragedy the nation has rediscovered itself and seeks its rebirth. In its old homeland it will build its former life anew: 'and they shall build the waste cities, and inhabit them; and they shall plant vineyards and drink the wine thereof'[89]; 'And the ransomed of the Lord shall return, and come to Zion with songs and everlasting joy upon their heads: they shall obtain joy and gladness, and sorrow and sighing shall flee away.'[90]

CHAPTER 3

The Fascist Challenge

In the study of fascism two opposing views have generally prevailed. The first regards fascism as the sombre offspring of Europe's struggling nationalisms, their final expression and logical culmination. The alternative view defines fascism as a strictly twentieth-century phenomenon, a species of pan-European totalitarianism during the interWar years – nazism being the extreme manifestation of modern collectivism and mass democracy. By implication, this view treats fascism and nazism as quite distinct ideological movements from nationalism and standing in no particular relation to the earlier movement.[1]

Neither view appears to do justice to the often complex relationships obtaining between nationalism and fascism. The 'totalitarian' thesis is right in pointing to essential differences in outlook and method between the two movements, but it tends to underrate the close empirical interweaving of nationalisms and fascisms during the interWar period and to neglect the influence of *fin de siècle* pessimism. The 'evolutionary' view, on the other hand, fails to comprehend the important difference in the two movements' goals, does scant justice to nationalism's original formulations, and underplays the role of novel social and intellectual elements in the late nineteenth and early twentieth centuries. In this chapter I shall attempt to trace out some of the complex interrelations between the two kinds of movement, first by considering each separately, before going on to examine their parallelisms and differences. Only then will it be possible to establish their empirical links and to undertake a more detailed analysis of the differences between German nationalism and nazism. Finally, I shall outline some of the novel elements in the late nineteenth-century European world that gave rise to the new movement of fascism and endowed it with such a different character from the earlier nationalisms that it incorporated and exploited.

INDUSTRIAL TRIBALISM

Probably the most widely held view of fascism considers it to be a culmination of the more usual nationalisms. This is generally the position of opponents of nationalism and fascism. To them these movements are simply part and parcel of a pernicious river of intolerant chauvinism, collectivism, racism and egotism. There are really two versions of this liberal denunciation: the older view simply saw nationalism as an enlarged and updated form of tribalism, which it also regarded as the core of fascism. Thus nationalism became

> an irrational, a romantic and Utopian dream, a dream of naturalism and tribal collectivism, [appealing to our] tribal instincts, to passion and prejudice, and to our nostalgic desire to be relieved of the strain of individual responsibility which it attempts to replace by a collective or group responsibility.[2]

In similar vein we find Kedourie arguing that:

> it was then no accident that racial classifications were, at the same time, linguistic ones, and that the Nazis distinguished the members of the German Aryan race scattered in Central and Eastern Europe by a linguistic criterion. In doing this, the Nazis only simplified and debased the ideas implicit in the writings of Herder and others.[3]

More recently, liberals have linked their evolutionary view of nationalism and fascism to social and economic processes and treated such movements as successive symptoms of the growing strains of mass industrialisation and democratisation.[4] In this vein we find Seton-Watson saying that nationalism is a 'phenomenon of a certain stage of human history' and as such neither good nor bad, but rather like 'a coin on one side of which appear the venerable features of Garibaldi, on the other the obscene figure of the Commandant of Auschwitz'.[5] And Kornhauser attributes the rise of mass movements like fascism and communism to the instability and vulnerability of 'mass societies' like the Weimar Republic, which became such easy prey for extremist demagogic movements and totalitarian takeovers.[6]

In the liberal 'evolutionary' view, then, fascism is closely identified with earlier nationalisms, for both movements are able to tap 'tribal instincts' and prejudices of the oppressed masses, whom the dislocations of massive industrialisation have uprooted and disoriented. As Bracher remarks, 'At its highest pitch, nationalist ideology appeals to mass insanity, assuming the force of a collective psychosis in which the annihilation of the enemy spells one's own success and salvation.'[7]

Two sources have fed this evolutionary view of nationalism and fascism. The first was the 'crowd psychology' of McDougall and Le Bon, which also influenced Freud's later work.[8] According to these theories, fear of the group is the most powerful bond between individuals in society. Crowds are highly suggestible, rumour is contagious and frequent, while non-conformity is rare because of the fear to stand outside the group. Some studies of crowd behaviour in the revolutionary 'assemblies' during the French Revolution would appear to confirm these speculations about the role of group fear and 'mental contagion' in spreading revolutionary ideas.[9] Hitler's well-known techniques of mass suggestion and orchestrated hysteria are a case in point, for they played on the helplessness of demobbed soldiers and unemployed workers, and were timed for moments when men were stripped of their habitual attachments and affiliations, and had temporarily lost their identities in the crowd.[10] Both Nazis and French revolutionaries needed to elaborate a new vision of true unity, to restore a threatened collective status and identity, and this meant constructing an image of the anti-type whose presence threatened that unity, be he the 'rootless cosmopolitan' Jew or the 'feudal' traitor and *émigré* Royalist.[11] As we move towards more psychological formulations, the differences between fascism and nationalism become increasingly blurred. In the extreme psychiatric view, men are assumed to fear the novel and unfamiliar, and therefore to cling to the old routine which the protective power and security afforded by the State ensures, like an omnipotent father. And from the fear of the new and a need for security is, politically, but a short step to the generation of delusions of grandeur and of international persecution.[12]

The other source of the evolutionary liberal view is the new emphasis on the processes of industrialisation, and its attendant 'strains'. While nationalism is associated, according to this view, with an earlier capitalist phase of industrialisation, fascism emerges in the 'post-capitalist' or 'pluralist' phase, when industrialism has become fully entrenched. For only then do the strains of modernisation detach sufficient individuals from their traditional milieux to provide the shock troops of mass movements; and only then do the anxiety, hostility and fantasy that industrialisation generates require people to identify and root out collective enemies.[13] An army of *déclassé*, detribalised and detraditionalised men and women becomes available for protest; demanding a share in government, they clamour for security and reintegration.[14] And where the existing democratic order cannot meet their demands, they turn to any demagogue, and any extremist movement, that promises the millennium on earth.[15] A nationalistic fascism is just such a movement, its worship of the Leader a new 'industrial tribalism' of the *déclassé*.

For all its popularity and plausibility, the 'industrial tribalist' thesis contains several flaws.

To begin with, its ethical animus against fascism and especially nazism leads its proponents to condemn wholesale any ideology that bears some resemblance to fascism. This inherent moralism in turn breeds a familiar tendency to read back fascist elements into much earlier nationalisms, which are then treated as so many seedbeds of the later type of movement. Now, important historical links between nationalism and fascism *can* be traced in particular cases; but to select only those elements of earlier nationalisms that appear to resemble fascism, ignoring their very different aims and context, is as unhistorical and misleading as the similar exercise of pointing to superficial tactical similarities between communism and nazism, without relating them to their opposed assumptions and situations.

Ideologically, too, 'industrial tribalism' involves an élitist attitude to the 'masses' and 'mass action', which echoes curiously the fundamental irrationalism on which fascism based its creed. By citing nationalism and fascism as examples of group fear, crowd suggestibility and collectivism in an industrial era, the defenders of liberal pluralism appear to share the same fear of participant democracy and technological change that spurred *fin de siècle* irrationalism and became fascism's intellectual point of departure. To regiment and control mass movements and collective violence was a major goal of fascism: a similar élitism can be discerned in the liberal fear of fascism and nazism; a similar, if more muted, distrust of radical mass democracy.

Besides, the assertion that nationalism and fascism are 'crowd phenomena', which is the heart of this thesis, is open to serious challenge. With the exception of Italian fascism and nazism, most fascist movements were fairly small until they took power in the State and could utilise state machinery for their ends. In origins, fascism and even nazism follow the pattern of most modern movements: they start from small circles of ideologues and agitators and only gradually broaden their appeal, depending at all times upon a dedicated core of activists. The same applies to earlier, or later, nationalisms: these so-called 'mass movements' turn out to be surprisingly small-scale affairs, measured by the percentage of total population involved, or even by the percentage of upper and middle strata.[16]

Finally, the role of 'industrialisation' (assuming that a clear-cut definition of this process can be reached) in this thesis needs to be queried. 'Industrial tribalism' assumes that a single cause must everywhere produce similar results and that this particular cause, mass society and industrialisation, was in fact operative. But both assumptions are clearly untenable. The first ignores the role of the very different cultures and political traditions in various European countries, which profoundly modified the impact of industrialisation wherever it appeared in any force. The second forgets that many nationalisms, and even some fascist movements, arose before such industrialisation had arrived or impinged on the area, before there was any heavy industry, a large-scale commodity market or a force of wage-earners. One has only to think of early nineteenth-century German or Greek nationalism, or the fascism of Croatia or Slovakia this century, to realise that, while *some* kind of social and economic change must be present, it need hardly take the form of 'industrialisation' and mass democratisation, which proponents of the 'industrial tribalist' thesis have in mind. Nationalism, like fascism, often made its appearance in agrarian societies, although because fascism emerged later it tended to overlap much more often with the onset of mass industrialisation. Such relationships have again to be traced out empirically, without the preconceptions of the 'industrial tribalist' thesis.[17]

THE CONCEPT OF THE NATION

A more systematic and realistic view of the relations between nationalisms and fascisms must set out from the actions and statements of leaders and followers of the two kinds of movement. The aim of this inductive exercise must, in the first place, be the discovery of the common components between the examples of the two kinds of movements, to understand the basis for their self-styled definition. Of course, both nationalists and fascists differed among themselves, not only over specific goals, but over the weight to be assigned to different elements and values in their 'doctrine' and practice. Nevertheless, closer study can reveal some recurrent themes and activities that mark off all nationalist movements from other types of movement like fascism and communism: and similarly, though a good deal less rigorously, with fascist movements. If this is the case, then we can establish the general features of nationalism and fascism and show that they do in fact refer to definite realities and beliefs and do not simply connote 'collectivism', 'tribalism' or some other vague term of abuse. And if we can establish their features and referents, we can then go on to show how they are related, conceptually and sociologically.

Rather than attempt a formal definition of nationalism or fascism, I shall start by recalling the main goals that inspire nationalist movements. There are three such goals: citizen autonomy, territorial unity and historical identity. Together they go far towards defining the peculiar version of the 'nation' and of 'nationhood' as an ethnic fraternity that lies at the core of nationalist ideology.

By 'citizen autonomy' I refer to the familiar idea that the community consists of theoretically equal citizens, who possess the right to be free and self-governing and whose first duty is the defence and wellbeing of their community. This is the doctrine of national autonomy whose full form is the French revolutionary conception of popular sovereignty. Its classical expression remains that of Sieyès: 'The nation is prior to everything. It is the source of everything. Its will is always legal. ... Nations on earth must be conceived as individuals outside the social bond, or as is said, in the state of nature.'[18] An even earlier statement of this 'neoclassical' ideal of civic patriotism appeared in Switzerland in 1775, when Füssli asked and answered three questions about citizenship and community:

What is the duty of every citizen regarding the protection of the fatherland? To sacrifice willingly and joyfully his life and property to it. What do we call the aggregate of civic duties? The political virtues. What do we call the man who endeavours to practise political virtue with the greatest possible perfection? A true patriot.[19]

And much later, fifty years after the event, Jefferson recalled the Declaration of Independence in the following words:

May it be to the world, what I believe it will be . . . the signal of arousing men to burst the chains under which monkish ignorance and superstition had persuaded them to bind themselves, and to assume the blessings and security of self-government.[20]

The fundamental idea underlying this feature of nationalism is not simply the belief that men are happier if they govern themselves, but the more 'heroic' and dynamic one that communities possess laws of their own being, which demand full self-expression and freedom from external constraint. Individuals ought, therefore, to sacrifice freely their personal interests and welfare for that of the whole body of citizens so that these inner laws, this internal energy and force, can realise itself in the world of action. This is the ethic of autonomy and heroic self-sacrifice that neoclassicists in America, England, Switzerland, Italy, Germany and especially France expressed so powerfully in literature, philosophy and the visual arts, and which is, as we saw, one of the most potent ingredients of the late eighteenth- and nineteenth-century nationalisms.[21]

A more concrete and readily identifiable aspiration is the demand for territorial unity and cohesion. In its simplest form this required all ethnic members to be gathered into the same area, that is a contiguous territorial 'homeland'. As the cases of the American colonies and Bangladesh demonstrated, contiguity is a vital element: indeed, the more compact and physically protected the territory selected the better, as is the case with Switzerland, Iceland and, in its Andean protection, Chile. But the idea of cohesion has a social aspect as well: the territory serves as a secure location, a recognised oasis, for the social experiment of forging or strengthening the ties of 'nationhood'. In so far as it is permissible to speak of 'nation-building' as an ideological goal, then a contiguous territory is a *sine qua non* for that self-proclaimed task. And that, in turn, means relegating, or even suppressing, local or provincial sentiments and ties so as to create a territory- or continent-wide loyalty and sense of solidarity. 'We ought to generalise our ideas and our measures,' said Noah Webster. 'We ought not to consider ourselves as inhabitants of a particular state only, but as Americans, as the common subjects of a great empire.'[22] Similarly, the centralising Jacobins waged a bitter ideological struggle against the so-called 'federalism' of the Girondins which, they thought, failed to eradicate sufficiently the separate identities of the various French provinces.[23]

There was also a more romantic element in this attachment to a single unified territory – the 'organic' idea that communities require their 'own' soil in order to express themselves and their inner being truthfully and abundantly. It is a sentiment felt most acutely by the exile, who sees no hope for diaspora communities, like Ben-Yehudah in the Pale of Settlement in 1880, when he wrote of the Jews' return to Israel: 'The nation cannot live except on its own soil; only on this soil can it revive and bear magnificent fruit, as in the days of old.'[24]

The 'organic' analogy played a greater role in the third main nationalist demand, to discover and imbue the citizens with a sense of their historic identity. Here the goal was more inward and cultural, the aim being to revive or recreate a lost or threatened 'personality' through the study of the community's past, its customs, language, religion and folklore. Although the French Revolution did possess such an 'ethnic–historical' dimension, it was in Germany, Poland, Greece and Italy that these preoccupations became dominant.[25] This coincided with the 'pre-Romantic' reaction against French cultural hegemony, following the Rousseauan 'return to nature' current of the 1760s and 1770s.[26] It also owed a good deal to various 'historicist' revivals in literature, criticism and the arts, such as the discovery of Ossian, the *Edda* and the *Nibelungenlied*, as well as to renewed interest in Homer and the Bible as sources for an archaic, primordial age and for ethnic origins. The late eighteenth and nineteenth centuries saw a proliferation of such historical cults, ranging from the Celtic, Norse and medieval-Gothic revivals to the Roman, archaic-Greek and Biblical; by the twentieth century, the folk cult as the fulcrum of identity quests had spread to the Slavic lands, to Japan's Shinto cult, to the rediscovery of the Vedas in India, and to the Sun Language theory of Ataturk.[27]

What lay behind this new quest for historic identity? A clue is provided by Friedrich Schlegel's praise of the Thuringian castle of Wartburg near Eisenach, the site of the *Minnesänger* contests and of Luther's completion of the New Testament translation. 'At such a sight,' he wrote, 'one cannot help thinking what Germans once were. . . . Since those days, men have settled in the valleys and along the highways, eager for alien customs and alien money, and the castles on the heights stand deserted.' Like Schiller, Schlegel came to see the Germans as a universal people with a spiritual mission; and in his poem *An die Deutschen* (1800) he ascribed to German heroes in every cultural field the task of rescuing a decadent Europe. In doing so, Schlegel opposed all cultural assimilation: 'The original moral character of a people, its customs, its peculiarities, must be regarded as sacred.'[28] And in 1815 Arndt wrote that: 'The Germans have not been bastardised, they have retained their original purity and have been able to develop slowly but surely according to the everlasting laws of time; the fortunate Germans are an original people.'[29]

The return to history and purity of language, so dear to German nationalists, was fundamentally a moral quest, part of the moral regeneration and purification that was a necessary counterpart of the aspirations for autonomy and social cohesion. In Germany as elsewhere, the nationalist cure for social lethargy and social divisions was a moral and political revolution, a demand for a reborn consciousness of the self, the true, purified ego, freed of alien, unoriginal traits. Such a self could only be discovered in past ages which had revealed the genuine moral character and qualities of the community, now so sadly encumbered and distorted.

These, then, are the main, recurrent aspirations of nationalists the world over. They are not the only goals, of course. Nationalists also lay stress on a cult of the will, a belief in heroic struggle for the community. More recently, they have made economic autarchy a vital concern. In Latin America, especially, the virtues of economic self-sufficiency, and the need for protection against price and commodity fluctuations in the world market and *vis-à-vis* American or multinational corporations, have become a major plank in the nationalist programme of regeneration.[30] And, of course, there is the ever-present nationalist demand for international status and 'dignity' which quite often involves political confrontations or even outright expansion.

Nevertheless, when one looks at these demands closely, they can be seen to spring out of the original three nationalist aspirations as so many corollaries. At different times and places, the corollaries may be accorded primacy, so producing the bewildering variety of nationalist movements' aims, which makes a search for an all-encompassing definition of nationalism so elusive. But they should not deflect attention away from the underlying goals, which define for us the vision of the 'nation' held by nationalists everywhere, as an autonomous, united community with a clearly recognised identity. Nationalism, accordingly, becomes an ideological movement for the attainment and maintenance of the autonomy, unity and identity of a social group, some of whose members conceive it to constitute an actual or potential nation.[31]

The Cult of Violence

Even more ambiguous and slippery a concept than nationalism, fascism, as its etymological derivation from the lictors' axes proclaims, refers in the first place to the authority of the State as such. Mussolini was quite clear about this:

> The foundation of Fascism is the conception of the State, its character, its duty, and its aim. Fascism conceives of the State as an absolute, in comparison with which all individuals or groups are relative, only to be conceived of in their relation to the State. . . .
>
> The State is the guarantor of security both internal and external, but it is also the custodian and transmitter of the spirit of the people, as it has grown up through the centuries in language, in customs and in faith. And the State is not only a living reality of the present, it is also linked with the past and above all with the future, and thus transcending the brief limits of individual life it represents the immanent spirit of the nation. . . .[32]

What fascists in the Mussolini mould desired was the abolition of the parliamentary system with its divisive class basis, and the substitution of a new hierarchy of an élite surrounding the Leader, and the unified masses, within the overall framework of state authority. Fascism's classless society was also strongly hierarchical, men being ranked according to their service to the State and Leader. Similarly, a number of fascisms adopted Mussolini's formula of the 'corporate state', in which managers' corporations sat together with, and led, workers' trade unions. But in the last resort, corporatism was secondary to the principle that the State embodied a spiritual force, as Mussolini wrote in his well-known article on fascism:

> the fascist state . . . is form, inner law and discipline of the whole person. It permeates will and intellect. Its principle, the central inspiration of the human personality dwelling in the civic community, penetrates to the depths and settles in the heart of the man of action as well as of the thinker, of the artist as well as the scientist: as the spirit of the spirit.[33]

The State, however, though it embodied a higher principle, was in the end only an instrument and vessel. Even Mussolini came to accord primacy to the Party or Movement. His law equating expulsion from the party with national treason and demanding the traitor's removal from political life amply demonstrates this.[34] As he put it, 'The party will make politics on a big scale, the state will represent the police on a big scale.'[35] Yet it was not the organisational party as such that provided the core of fascism, or the object of its endeavours. It was rather a style of political activity that the Party embodied, and a *weltanschauung* underlying that style.[36]

We may call that style a cult of violence and the underlying philosophy a form of Darwinian 'vitalism'. Fascism openly glorified the warlike instincts: 'never had the world been so ferocious,' wrote d'Annunzio.[37] The ideal *homo fascista* for French fascists like Brasillach or Drieu de la Rochelle was the man of force, who triumphs over the weak and finds personal fulfilment in fighting for his group and thus determining history. He is, in short, a hero.[38] That is why fascists emphasised youth so much and why so many fascist leaders were young.[39] It is also why fascists were so contemptuous of bourgeois morality, which they identified with the older generation, although in practice they supported family and national bonds. The ensuing political style is activist, dynamic, aggressive but also collectivist. More than this, politics becomes a spiritual activity. That is how it was regarded by the leader of the Rumanian Iron Guard, Horia Sima, who wrote that: 'We must cease to separate the spiritual man from the political man. All history is a commentary upon the life of the spirit.'[40]

The underlying 'philosophy' expresses a nihilistic mood, a rejection of the European tradition, cultural as well as political. In their attack on bourgeois decadence, fascists reject not merely parliamentary democracy and liberalism, but also the 'materialism' of both capitalist interests and Marxist doctrine. In glorifying the untamed instincts, fascism repudiated not merely reason and tolerance but even the more humane emotions. The fascist hero is a brutal realist. He is both loyal to comrades and Machiavellian to outsiders. He is virile and energetic, but always in the service of the cause and the Leader. Indeed, the Leader epitomises both the political style of the 'new man' of fascism and the 'instinctual' or vitalist philosophy that inspires that man. For when every other value has been rejected, what remains but brute force and primeval instinct?

This 'nihilistic–vitalistic' syndrome could, of course, be easily allied to racist ideas. The Darwinian struggle for survival and supremacy that unbridled instinctualism unleashes finds a perfect arena in the struggle for racial domination on the part of biologically determined communities of power. The mental world of the fascist is filled with notions about social units as power-communities in a ceaseless life-and-death battle for mastery, in which biological analogies are so suggestive and natural. We must, however, avoid equating fascism with racism. Many fascisms, notably in central and eastern Europe, were more or less violently racist; but others in western Europe were silent on the racial question, at least until the later thirties, especially in Italy, Belgium and Holland. In Spain, too, the early Falange was relatively free of anti-Semitism, and some French fascists, though anti-Semitic, held that their German counterparts were exaggerating the racial issue.[41] In other words, the struggle for supremacy and the triumph of the strong and instinctual could be played out by states and nations; it did not necessarily entail a racial conflict.

What all fascisms shared, apart from worshipping the State, force and the vital instincts, was a hatred of Marxism. Marxism was seen as dividing the community and placing class conflict above the unity of the community and its war with other communities. Class conflict increased man's alienation from his community. It further eroded his organic roots and excluded the bourgeoisie from the community, to which fascists wished to return it. Above all, Marxism was a materialist conspiracy, which denied man's spiritual vitality and his deeper instincts in order to cater to his 'interests'.

In contrast, fascism embraced those 'magic' elements that modern society seemed to have banished or forgotten. It provided occasions for displaying a lost solidarity through rallies and processions involving, once it came to power, thousands of single-minded 'new men' vociferously proclaiming their devotion to the Leader and Party. Above all, it united the community for the inevitable and much-sought war against its enemies.

NATIONALISM AND FASCISM COMPARED

It is sometimes said that fascism is more of a mood or style than a doctrine or movement; and it must be conceded that, by comparison with nationalism, let alone communism, fascism lacks theoretical coherence and clarity. However, it would be a grave mistake to write off fascism as no more than a political tone or social mood: the dynamic of the Iron Guard, the Falange or the Fascisti, let alone the Nazis, has deeper roots and a more clear-cut and forceful outlook, which can usefully be compared with that of nationalist movements. The comparison can be made along a series of dimensions and issues: I shall focus attention on the conceptual and emotional contrasts and parallelisms, the divergence in attitudes to communism and socialism, and to racism and anti-Semitism, and their respective social composition, before turning to the historical relationships between the two kinds of movement.

Conceptions and emotions

The basic conceptual similarity lies in the central object of both movements' labour – the 'nation'. At the same time, nationalism and fascism view the nation very differently.

As we saw, nationalists conceive the nation to constitute an ethnic community distinguished mainly by a separate history and language, whose members are regarded as free citizens possessed of common rights and duties in a definite, circumscribed territorial 'home'. The aim of the nationalist is to foster this community, its sense of solidarity and its autonomy.

Fascism, on the other hand, tends to view the nation in instrumental terms, as a 'power-house', a repository and weapon for the exercise of will and force. The 'nation' embodies the spiritual *élan vital* of the group, and may assume the form of the State, as in most western fascisms, or the race, as in the central or eastern European varieties. For fascisms, the concept of citizenship is at best an irrelevance, at worst a misleading bourgeois fiction. History, too, serves a purely instrumental function. The aim is not even to secure an identity through moral regeneration, though some fascists may well have been originally attracted to the movement by its usurpation of nationalist motifs on this score. History, for fascists, is simply a storehouse of examples of the triumph of strength over weakness, of Machiavellian force over decent scruple, of intellectual aggression over reason and moderation. As for the territorial homeland beloved of the nationalists, this must give way for every self-regarding fascist to the overriding quest for *lebensraum* through conquest and enslavement.[42]

As a result, the 'nation' in fascist eyes ceases to be an object of endeavour *per se*, a project to be renewed and realised: instead, it becomes a category of the vitalist outlook and the subject of the cult of violence. No longer simply a body of citizens seeking their autonomy and identity in a secure homeland, the fascist 'nation in arms' becomes an authoritarian élite of warriors engaged in a biologically determined struggle for survival and domination.

An important consequence of this narrowing of the meaning and goals of nationhood is fascism's relative inability to combine with other ideologies, and this despite its lack of intellectual coherence. Whereas nationalism has managed to interpenetrate with quite varied and, in principle, opposed ideologies like communism and liberalism, fascism's range of combination has been limited to imperialism and populism (with which, of course, nationalism frequently combines). The reason is that nationalism is a good deal more flexible and less totalitarian in its aspirations and outlook than fascism. Its goals are more concrete and limited, and can be dovetailed with more all-embracing ideologies, as happens with the 'national communism' of China, Cuba and Yugoslavia, or the 'liberal nationalism' of interwar Czechoslovakia or the American War of Independence.[43] Fascism, on the other hand, was a total revolution: it involved a complete commitment, the creation of the 'whole man', and claimed the right to monitor and guide every aspect of society and even of the individual's life. As such, it was necessarily much more exclusive than nationalism ever sought to be.

Emotionally, fascism and nationalism share a good deal of common ground, although there are some vital differences. Both types of movement are activist and 'dynamic', both aim to create the 'new man', both emphasise youth, vigour and service to the community. Agricultural settlement and cultivation of the soil plays an important part in nationalist thinking, as one would expect of so territorially conscious a movement; and few nationalisms have not extolled peasant mores or life in a regenerating nature.[44] Fascisms, too, devote some attention to the soil: Quisling's early romanticism envisioned the good society as a simple association of peasant farmers, while even the early SS viewed farming and settlement by Germans as a noble and necessary task.[45]

Nevertheless, the emphasis and attitude to each of these aspects is different in nationalism and fascism. For example, nationalism subordinates activism to its goals of building fraternal solidarity and ethnic autonomy in the homeland, whereas activity, dynamism and *esprit de corps* of the 'movement' itself are central for fascisms. Again, nationalism's attitude to youth and physical vigour is touched with ambiguity because of its concern with historical scholarship, with the whole body of citizens, and with the deeper springs of moral identity. Fascism knows no such inhibitions. Of course, it too seeks to control and direct youthful vigour and violence for communal ends, but it also elevates the brutal, youthful, realistic 'whole man' above the weak, lethargic masses. It can be said that the selection and training of such a power élite is a principle goal of fascism, but rarely appears in nationalisms. There is a parallel difference in nationalism's and fascism's attitude to war and violence. Nationalists certainly exalt the struggle on behalf of the community. Those two early documents of French nationalism in painting, David's *Oath of the Horatii* (1784) and Delacroix's *Liberty Guiding the People* (1830), are full of martial vigour and the struggle against tyranny. But they do not extol violence as such; their battles are fought on behalf of republican liberty against a potential or actual oppressor, are imbued with a spirit of self-sacrifice, and are not unmindful of the tragic effects of vindicating one's rights.[46] Both are a far cry from the violent futurism of Marinetti, which Mussolini at one point hailed, and which emphasised constant movement and activity for its own sake.[47] Nor is there that glorification of brute instinct and aggression in nationalism which led fascists to extol militarism as such. In all these respects the emotional focus of nationalism differs greatly from that of fascism, which tends to displace on to one of the means emotions that nationalism reserves for the ends alone.

Racism and anti-Semitism

Neither racism nor anti-Semitism are necessary ingredients of either nationalism or fascism, despite their elevation by nazism. On the other hand, fascism is much more prone to racial notions and anti-Semitism than nationalism.

Racism is generally absent from the original formulations of nationalism by Burke, Rousseau, Jefferson and Herder. It played a small part in the thinking of Fichte, and a somewhat larger role in the exhortations of Jahn and Arndt after 1806. It was not prominent in Italian, Czech, Greek or Norwegian nationalisms, and references to 'ethnic purity' did not often carry racial overtones. Language and history were the prime objects of purification in eighteenth- and nineteenth-century nationalisms, as they remain for the most part today; and the sense of 'ethnicity' implicit in most nationalist utterances is cultural rather than biological. This does not mean that nationalisms have not practised ethnic discrimination, only that such discrimination is based upon cultural rather than physical criteria.[48]

As for the Jews, nationalism followed on the whole the precept of Clermont-Tonnerre in the Assembly debate on Jewish emancipation of 1789, to give to the Jew as individual everything, to the Jew as Jew nothing.[49] And European Jews have been only too willing to pay the necessary price for emancipation, at least until the modern form of anti-Semitism appeared in central Europe in the 1870s, and have fought loyally in the armies of their respective fatherlands. It was only in the later nineteenth century that some nationalists in Germany, Austria, France and Rumania, who combined conservative ideals with populist methods, began to adopt a racially inspired anti-Semitism in place of the old religious kind, particularly (but not only) in areas either where the Jews formed a numerous minority, as in Rumania and Poland, or where they appeared to be salient and influential, as in some sectors of German or French society. It is at this point, the moment of Dreyfus and Maurras' Action Francaise, that cultural grounds of discrimination begin to be combined with biological ones.[50]

Nor should we confuse racism with anti-Semitism in discussing the fascist approaches. We have already noted a contrast between 'western' *étatiste* fascisms and 'eastern' racial movements; but even within the western camp there were some striking variations. In general, racism was either rejected or relegated in the 'western' cases until 1936: Degrelle's Rexists and the Flemish paper *De Daad* actually repudiated racist anti-Semitism, and de Mussert's Dutch nazism passed over the question in silence despite the sizeable Jewish populations in Belgium and Holland. Only later did Oswald Mosley add a racial anti-Semitic dimension to his propaganda and action, particularly when he found that marches through the Jewish East End could enhance his movement's sense of struggle and dynamism.[51]

Perhaps the greatest range of expression on racism and anti-Semitism is to be found in French fascism. In the early 1930s, men like Drieu de la Rochelle ridiculed Nazi ideas of a racially distinct German people and of eugenics. After 1936, when Leon Blum's Popular Front came to power, French fascists became more anti-Semitic. Yet it was only after 1940 that they became converted to the doctrine of blood, and even as late as 1942 Marcel Déat distinguished between honourable, patriotic Jews and racially harmful ones. France's anti-Semitic tradition should not be equated with racism; for in France it was perfectly possible to exclude the Jews on pre-eminently cultural, rather than biological, grounds.[52]

In practice, the difference has been fundamental. It was in the central and eastern European countries, where biological racism triumphed, and where fascism was a revolution aiming to liquidate the existing state rather than transform it as in the West, that a policy of physical segregation and extermination of Jews and Gipsies could be implemented; and it was in Germany and Austria, where racism was most virulent, that this policy was conceived.[53] This suggests that in these countries it was neither nationalism nor fascism that provided the impetus to the new anti-Semitism, though fascism undoubtedly contributed to it. Rather, it was the racial doctrine of social Darwinism itself that re-ignited the fires of anti-Semitism upon a new basis of 'science' and 'observation', from which it was impossible for Jews to escape through loyalty, conversion or even flight, as in former days.

In comparing the reaction of fascism and nationalism on these issues, we must conclude that fascism has far fewer ideological or emotional defences than nationalism against the incubus of racism and anti-Semitism, once these have appeared in any force; but that, as the present South African regime indicates, it is possible for a racist ideology to operate outside the context of a fascist movement or regime. As so often in social and political life, there is no strict correlation between fascism and racism or anti-Semitism. At the same time, there is an obvious affinity between its exaltation of power over weakness and the salient fact of Jewish powerlessness before the Second World War. As a target for the cult of violence, the Jews could not have been improved upon as a fascist category, especially in eastern Europe.[54]

Socialism and communism

One of the cementing and defining features of fascist movements is their hatred of Marxist communism. Nationalism, on the other hand, has proved itself quite adaptable to every variety of Marxism, arose much earlier, and shows few signs of this hatred. With regard to socialism, the position is more complex. Both fascism and nationalism can and have combined with non-Marxist socialisms, and especially with populistic socialisms. At the same time, fascists are much more critical of what they consider to be the 'materialism' of socialism, approximating here to the position of traditional conservatives.

For fascists and nationalists, economic questions are secondary. Their interest is in cultural, political or spiritual matters. It is from this standpoint that fascism, in particular, attacks the hypocrisy of bourgeois society and the power of monopoly capitalism. Both Doriot and Déat thought that big business, the monopolies and trusts, were wiping out the small business of the traditional middle classes and must be regulated and controlled, in the manner of Mussolini's corporatism. Their enmity to capitalism was an expression of their alienation from bourgeois industrial societies in the West, and from what they held to be its corrupting materialism and unbridled individualism. At the same time they commended private property and small-scale business so long as it served the communal interest and the State. To that end it was frequently necessary to compromise with big business, although some French fascists were critical of Hitler's acquiescence in the role of the big German cartels.[55] Despite these compromises, and the dropping of socialist radicals who might impede the movement's success in its battle for power, many European intellectuals and professionals were attracted to fascism for idealistic, and anti-capitalist, reasons. It was only in victory that the real power basis of fascism came to the surface, and the anti-capitalist idealism of the intelligentsia and small business gave way to an élite philosophy of power of the party technocrats and a ruthless, monopolistic control by the Leader.

This movement from anti-capitalist idealism to ruthless power technocracy is aptly illustrated by Codreanu's Legion of the Archangel Michael. Founded in 1927, this revolutionary populist movement managed to capture 15 per cent of the vote in the Rumanian elections of 1937 (or about half a million votes). Its strength was concentrated in certain poor and anti-Semitic peasant counties, and it succeeded in attracting many peasants and workers. Codreanu and his associates were inspired by the historical affinities and romance of isolated mountain and forest retreats and free villages (*razas*) of Moldavia, and they took a genuine interest in peasant problems and later in those of the worker. Zealous and puritan in tone, the Legionaries parted company from Cuza's more reactionary anti-Semitic National Christian League, and instead attacked the evils of bourgeois society with its corrupt values. In a sense, Codreanu's Legion started as a case of revolutionary populist nationalism, with an anti-Semitic dimension, but preaching the use of terror to create the 'new man', and insisting on radical, collective discipline in their fight against the *status quo*, the Legionaries succumbed to the power élitism inherent in their methods. Revolution and populism took second place to a power struggle against competitors and persecution of opponents.[56] This then is an example of fascism with a strong social-reform component, anti-Marxist yet revolutionary and socialist (though opposing the concept of class struggle), starting out from a romantic nationalism but becoming increasingly a cult of violence and power élitism, and preaching the rightful superiority of the strong 'new man'. Elements of such élitist 'social nationalism' can be found in some developing countries after the Second World War, though usually without that commitment to violence *per se*, to instinct and crude dynamism, or to the naked use of power in the interests of the superior in strength.[57]

The Rumanian case illustrates the more general trend for fascism to appear as the main rival of Marxism, echoing its criticism of existing 'bourgeois' society, but from a national and non-materialist standpoint. Hence the bitterness of its conflict with Marxism. Nationalism, however, is not motivated by a critique of 'bourgeois' or industrial society as such, but only of the cosmopolitan, standardised, imperial form that it takes, its failure to allow for cultural diversity and ethnic autonomy. Nationalism does not attribute these ills to a socioeconomic formation but rather to a politico-cultural constellation. Hence it does not regard itself, nor need it be regarded, as a rival of Marxism or socialism, and it can well ally itself with any social doctrine that accords its cultural and political demands their due, whether conservative or Marxist.

On the other hand, fascism may well overlap with social democracy, despite the latter's repudiation of the fascist instinctualist and brutalist philosophy, and the well-known political opposition between the two in Germany, Spain, France and Italy. For where there are no (or weak) socialist parties to represent the peasants and workers, which was the case in Rumania and even Hungary, a social-revolutionary fascism comes to fulfil this role.

Social composition

At the sociological level, distinctions between fascist and nationalist movements are especially difficult to pin down. One must first separate the leadership from the followers and then distinguish successive historical epochs and culture areas of the far broader spectrum of nationalist movements – a task clearly beyond our scope, and one for which adequate data are lacking. However, certain preliminary general comments can be made.

The leadership of both kinds of movements draws heavily upon the intelligentsia, the secular, westernised stratum of professionals and intellectuals whose life-styles and status, as well as their livelihoods, are based upon recognition of their diplomas and academic qualifications, and who are concerned with the application and dissemination of techniques and ideas. Nationalist leaders, however, have tended to be recruited from more upper-middle-class sections of the intelligentsia and from those professions like journalism and the law which are well-established and demand a fairly high level of education. Scholars, writers, doctors, artists and engineers, as well as officers, have also played a large part in the nationalist leadership.[58] Fascist leaders, however, tend to be less well educated and come from lower-middle-class backgrounds, as was the case with Hitler and Himmler – or with Codreanu, Mota and Papanace, who originated from the newly urbanised lower-middle-class intelligentsia, being sons of small-town teachers, peasants and priests.[59] At the same time, this class distinction cannot be pressed far, since in more recent times leaders of nationalist movements outside Europe have tended increasingly to come from the same semi-educated middle strata as many fascist leaders.

What is more to the point is the difference in social constituency of the two movements. It is true that both attract adherents from a wide social spectrum and so, in Kornhauser's terminology, are 'mass' rather than class movements. Closer analysis, however, reveals that nationalism appeals to upper-middle-class and middle-class groups like merchants, officers, bureaucrats and the technical and professional strata, whereas fascist movements gain their following from the lower-middle and working classes. Thus in Germany over 30 per cent of the Nazi Party membership were manual workers, and 21 per cent were white-collar workers, with 12.6 per cent peasants and 17.6 per cent professionals, merchants and artisans.[60] In Hungary, too, Szalasi's National–Socialist coalition had a large contingent of manual workers – some 40 per cent of its membership;[61] while in Austria, the semi-fascist Heimwehr movement drew heavily for support on the peasants, although lower-middle-class and ex-officer groups formed the leadership.[62] And in Spain, the Falange had much lower-class support.[63]

These differences in the social composition of typical nationalist and fascist movements must induce doubts about the well-known characterisation of fascism as an extremism of the centre. Indeed, Lipset's whole 'class' approach underplays other vital social factors in the genesis and appeal of fascism.[64] While it is true that, in Italy, smallholders, artisans and shopkeepers tended to support Mussolini and the later neo-fascist MSI, and in France Doriot and the later semi-fascist populism of Poujade, the same cannot be maintained for the underdeveloped, largely agrarian eastern European societies.[65] What stamps fascism in the East is the student and youth character of the movement, its appeal to educated but alienated young men, disgusted with the weak compromises and corruption of the political system.[66] This was very much the case with Poland's intellectual youth, and in Rumania – as we saw; but it also occurred in a similarly underdeveloped 'western' society – Spain – where the movements of Jose Antonio and Ramiro Ledesma were led by educated young men in their twenties.[67] Of course, youth and student following is also a characteristic of some nationalisms, such as the Carbonari or Macedonian IMRO, again occurring in underdeveloped societies. Mazzini's insistence on youth in his Young Europe organisation, and the general nationalist emphasis upon inculcating the young with the idea of national regeneration through education and sports, has led Kedourie to dub nationalism as a 'children's crusade' against their parents.[68] At the same time, nationalism aimed to attract many older men and women – scholars, professionals, merchants, priests – whereas fascism made the exaltation of youth one of its chief goals and justifications, associating youth with strength and ferocity.

A similar ideological emphasis accounts for another organisational difference from nationalism, the role of the Leader. Of course, nationalist movements have their revered founding fathers, their Fichte, Palacky, Alfieri, Herzl, Afghani and Banerjea. They also have their organisational leader, their charismatic man of action – a 'Father' Jahn, Garibaldi, Masaryk, Ben Gurion, Nasser, Ataturk and Gandhi – as well as particular party leaders.[69] Such men become part of the nationalist pantheon and, in time, of the national heritage. Rarely, however, are they unchallenged in their lifetime; rarely are their pronouncements treated as binding law for the movement and nation, except where they have also established a personal dictatorship. But that is something over and above their nationalism; it does not flow from the doctrine or movement. With fascism it is different. The cult of violence, the doctrine of the new man of superior force and instinct, demands a personification, a concrete embodiment, to serve as an example for adherents and believers. Il Duce, the Führer, were institutions over and beyond their own charismatic qualities. In the extreme case they demanded and received a Byzantine submission based on party discipline and on the élite philosophy of power and violence, which marks them off as a quite separate phenomenon from the more loosely organised, less disciplined, more heterogeneous nationalist movements with their shifting and often divided leadership and their lack of a leadership mystique. The development of that mystique is one of the key elements in replacing a nationalist movement by fascism.[70]

The analysis of social composition and organisation of the two kinds of movement is necessarily inconclusive. The main characteristic is a very considerable overlap: both nationalism and fascism recruit leaders, and many followers, from somewhat different sectors of the 'middle classes', nationalism attracting more established, better-off, better educated groups – although we should add that it can also appeal to peasants and even workers in certain situations.[71] Fascism adds a more lower-middle- and working-class catchment and an emphasis on youth *per se* and on the will of the Leader, which are usually absent or underplayed in nationalist movements, but can emerge in less developed areas.

One other difference is worth noting. Nationalism often appeals to professionals, traders or officers, whose avenues of mobility are blocked and whose access to wealth and prestige is hampered by the restrictions and discriminations of the *ancien régime*.[72] Fascism, on the other hand, tends to attract the *déclassé*, the downwardly mobile and threatened. The demobbed soldier and ex-officer, the shopkeeper or artisan undercut by technological advance and big business, the indebted small farmer, the underemployed intellectual, unemployed and recently urbanised workers – all experience a sense of insecurity and loss of position which in turn breeds that anxiety and aggression that opportunistic fascists were so adept at exploiting and venting upon defenceless scapegoats. Such downward mobility and its attendant anxiety need not necessarily be a function of economic progress as industrialisation theory would maintain. It can result from any sudden and rapid change, such as the introduction of mass democracy, large-scale urbanisation or war. In fact, the combination of downward mobility with prolonged warfare and democratisation has proved even more potent in the genesis of fascism than industrialisation.[73]

HISTORICAL LINKS

Purely historical considerations reinforce the basic picture of differences between nationalism and fascism that I have drawn, but fill it out by revealing the complex connections between them in the later nineteenth and early twentieth centuries.

Nationalism's initial appearance is usually dated to the latter half of the eighteenth century.[74] At this period a new and clear-cut doctrine of national sovereignty and self-determination emerged, and for the first time it became a primary aim of political endeavour to achieve 'nationhood' or to maintain it. True, early intimations of a concept of national identity can be found in seventeenth-century Holland and England, while the rise of national states reaches back to the thirteenth, and a sense of ethnic solidarity was well-known in antiquity.[75] But such ethnocentrism should not be confused with nationalism, nor the rise of dynastic states with the growth of national sentiment. Secularism and bureaucracy have transformed ethnic solidarity, raising it to a more abstract, political plane, free of the religious images in which it had so long been embedded, while democratic aspirations transformed the old dynastic states into genuine 'nation-states'.[76]

The first powerful expression of European nationalism occurred during the French Revolution where, significantly, it combined with liberalism to overthrow both enlightened despotism and the aristocracy.[77] From that time on, nationalism entered into a series of varied alliances with other ideological movements, ranging from conservatism in Russia to extreme radicalism in Italy.[78] During the course of the nineteenth century it achieved a quite distinct profile and set of aims, long before fascism appeared on the scene; so that this century-and-a-half lead compels us to treat nationalism as a completely independent movement from fascism, both analytically and historically.

But might fascism, albeit different in many respects, be legitimately viewed as a later phase of nationalism – a new adaptation

and even transformation of nationalism to the realities of an industrial era? This version of the 'evolutionary' view has much to
commend it: it concedes fascism's novelty; it accepts the impact
of the very different twentieth-century conditions; and it can point
to the detailed historical connections and overlap of fascist movements with a pre-existent nationalism everywhere.

The most important of these links is the movement of 'integral
nationalism' forged in a defeated France of the Third Republic,
and especially by Barrès and Maurras' Action Française. During
the abortive Boulangist coup and the Dreyfus Affair, the conservative monarchists and anti-Dreyfusards advanced novel concepts
of the 'nation', utilising both Drumont's anti-bourgeois anti-Semitism and the blood-and-soil notions of racism.[79] Here, too, the
'revolutionary reaction', which is so central a feature of fascism,
made its appearance, with the use of revolutionary methods and
an appeal to the 'masses' in the interests of traditional values
and a return to a mythical, idealised past of rural harmony and
organic national unity.[80] Against the rationalisation of capitalism
and the industrial machine, the 'integral nationalist' formula of
a revolutionary reaction became increasingly popular among the
alienated youth in western lands; while in the less developed eastern
European countries populist nationalisms took an increasingly anti-
western turn in the face of the secular and commercial inroads
of western thought and trade.

This commitment of reactionary nationalists to an idyllic past,
in which the search for an historic identity submerged nationalism's
other aims, was a particularly potent sentiment in Habsburg Vienna,
with its polyglot and multicultural population, and in the western
provinces of the Russian empire, with their large Jewish communities. Here racism and anti-Semitism, fanned by religious hostilities
and economic or cultural competition in the middle strata, could
kindle the revolutionary nationalism of subject ethnic groups and
spread to classes that felt themselves threatened by the new market
economy and bureaucratic machinery that eroded traditional ways
of life. The Jew, in any case isolated from surrounding peoples
by his religion and restricted occupational roles, could be easily
identified as a symbol of the reaction and protest against this
threat. In this way a thwarted but still hopeful nationalism, and
an anxious, reactionary anti-Semitic populism, could temporarily
be fused to form a suggestive basis for the revolutionary creed

of instinctual violence and élitism propounded by poştWar fascism.

But it was the Great War itself that generalised the alienation and dislocations of western societies. Only in the wake of so profound a disturbance could a violent fascism attract a larger audience. The years that followed the Armistice were years of war weariness, in which traditional authority was replaced overnight by new and untried regimes; when mass consumption and standardisation induced cultural pessimism; when youth and the *déclassé* turned away from a 'bourgeois' morality and materialism; when Marxism posed its most radical challenge in Russia; and above all when Russia and the United States first threatened to dwarf Europe and then fell away from it, on either side.[81] In a Europe reeling from four years of internecine warfare, from the decimation of a whole generation and the loss of vitality and self-confidence, the fascist revolution promised the only genuine hope of revival and revitalisation, amid a return to accepted verities and stabilities.

In this sense we may see in fascism an attempted solution to a specific European interWar situation, which the Great War had generalised across frontiers, drawing every country into its vortex. To this extent, fascism appears as a unique phenomenon, in contrast to the far more enduring and global movement of nationalism. Not that there are no 'fascist' components in subsequent nationalisms or postwar regimes. Peron's Argentina, Sukarno's Indonesia, Salazar's Portugal, McCarthyism and Poujadism all contained some elements from the fascist syndrome of interWar years: so have some African and Arab movements. Which only goes to confirm that any social and historical phenomenon is composed of a number of elements in an 'ideal-type' syndrome and that a given element may become detached from its syndrome and enter into another.

But from a historical as well as an analytic standpoint it makes more sense to start from the premise that fascism is predominantly a European phenomenon of the 1918–45 period, before trying to trace out any 'debts' to other ideological movements like conservatism or nationalism. For nationalism is in no way tied to these interWar years, nor to Europe, nor to specific conditions of cultural anomie and mass violence. Nationalism can in fact emerge in a far wider range of economic and cultural backgrounds – in fairly well developed societies like Revolutionary France, in educationally well equipped but economically underdeveloped countries like early nineteenth-century Germany or Italy, and in areas that have few educational or economic facilities like nineteenth-century eastern Europe or early twentieth-century Africa.[82] Nor can we describe early nationalisms as a revolt against monopoly capitalism or against cultural standardisation and mass consumption or against Marxism; for none of these phenomena existed till the end of the nineteenth century. Besides, that essential precondition of fascism, the social Darwinist philosophy of biological survival and selection, did not affect Europe till the late nineteenth century, well after nationalism had blossomed in most European ethnic groups.

VOLK AND RACE

Although similar contrasts and linkages between fascism and nationalism are discernible in Germany, nazism also manifests certain unique features as a synthesis of 'western' and 'eastern' types of fascism. For this reason nazism requires separate discussion.

When the origins of nazism are traced back to Fichtean and Romantic doctrines of German nationalism, it is the *völkisch* conception that is usually singled out. The term '*Volk*', with its mystic overtones of primeval forests and dark tribal instincts, combines ethnocentric, national and racial connotations.[83] In the Romantic period, however, the organicism of the *Volk* principle was mainly cultural, a matter of common speech, common customs and a shared history. This was certainly the image of the *Sturm und Drang* exponents of Herder, Justus Möser and the young Goethe of *Von Deutscher Baukunst*.[84] In the early nineteenth century, too, the cultural interpretation of the *Volk* concept predominated. Wackenroder's revival of the German Renaissance, Tieck's medievalist eulogy of Nuremberg and 'Germany's noble past', Friedrich Schlegel's equation of medieval art and architecture with the true German spirit, as well as the historical researches of such *Germanisten* as von der Hagen and Büsching, interpreted the notion of a German nation in terms of the artistic, literary and political heritage of the Germanic peoples, which they wished to preserve from contamination by alien cultures.[85] Novalis and Fichte also saw Germany's preeminence as largely spiritual, with the nation being a 'bearer and pledge of earthly eternity'. In similar vein, August Wilhelm Schlegel,

Friedrich's brother, followed the Swiss historian, Johannes Müller, in elevating the recently discovered *Nibelungenlied* to the status of a German Iliad, while Romantics like Arnim, Brentano and the Grimm brothers emphasised the historical role of folk poetry and tales in Herder's footsteps.[86]

In most German writings of the early nineteenth century, we encounter nothing more than a passionate cultural nationalism, or in the case of Fichte and Adam Müller a rousing political nationalism. To see in this 'deep schism between German and Western political thought, and the emergence of a special German sense of destiny with anti-Western overtones', the 'ultimate cause' of Germany choosing the road to nazism appears, in the light of comparative analysis, a more retrospective than causal–historical hypothesis. With a few exceptions, there is nothing that points towards nazism even in the Romantics' statements that Bracher adduces in support of his contention.[87] The familiar comparison of western with German culture, the spiritual pre-eminence assigned to the latter, the fear of assimilation and cultural impurity – all this is echoed in several other nationalisms which, because they have not been succeeded by fascist movements, are never treated as 'seedbeds' or 'precursors' of fascism. Perhaps the best-known example of such anti-western reactive nationalisms is the Slavophile tradition, the messianic pan-Russian conservatism of Aksakov, Grigoreev, Strakhov and Dostoevskii.[88] Here too we encounter that elevation of Orthodox Slavic genius, of Russia's special destiny of backwardness, and the exhortation to preserve her monastic purity which, *mutatis mutandis*, we found in the German Romantics on whom the Russian Slavophiles drew.[89] Outside Europe, the Indian experience furnishes a parallel in the bitterly anti-western Hindu nationalism of Tilak and Gandhi, Banerjea and Aurobindo, which succeeded the earlier westernising 'liberal' nationalism of Congress. Again we find the familiar contrasts of western technology and eastern morality, of the West's shallow materialism and India's spiritual richness and profound understanding.[90] In fact, this is simply part and parcel of the tension between different nationalist goals, in a situation where a precarious sense of nationhood must be strengthened so as to regenerate the community and achieve unity and autonomy.

To a limited extent, the German case did differ from others, in a tendency to slide from a strictly cultural, usually linguistic, definition of 'Germanness' to a racial one stressing common physique and descent. At first, this trend was quite secondary. We meet it in Arndt's emphasis on the 'dark forces of the age' and on the Germans constituting an 'original people' who 'preserved the purity of their blood' without being bastardised. Similarly Friedrich Ludwig Jahn, the influential founder of the Turnerschaft and Burschenschaft, the gymnastics and student leagues, believed racial purity to be essential to creative nationhood. He attributed Rome's fall to racial intermingling, and in his seminal work, *Deutsches Volkstum* (1810), Father Jahn founded the idea of a Reich upon a state animated by the *Volk* and its *Volkstum*.[91] But even Jahn and his pupil Wolfgang Menzel, who proclaimed Odin as the 'innermost spirit of the German people, the driving power which made the German people supreme in world history', subordinated the racial factor in the end to be an overall cultural conception of the national problem, in which the main enemy is France and French civilisation.[92] The conflict of cultures and *ethnie*, rather than biological races, remains the central focus of their interpretation of world history.

Early nineteenth-century cultural nationalism is attuned to the chances of a genuine anti-monarchical, liberal revolution, to the new markets of the *Zollverein* and to the growing influence of the urban middle classes. But the failure of the 1848 revolutions increasingly dissipated these liberal impulses and subordinated them to the power of the Prussian *Machtstaat*, the authoritarian bureaucratic–monarchical state extolled by Hegel and von Ranke. True, this idea too was not new. Fichte and Adam Müller had preached the absorption of the individual by the organic state in the early nineteenth century, though in Fichte at least the conception retained an element of Jacobin revolutionary fervour.[93] But it was only in the aftermath of Bismarck's victories of 1866 and 1870 that most of the bourgeoisie and intelligentsia came to accept the conservative–authoritarian vision of state centralism.

This period also saw the first intimations of those crucial components of fascism, the glorification of military might and the 'nihilist–vitalist' outlook. While Arndt's and Jahn's calls to arms were still directed towards a heroic self-sacrifice for the good of the community, Treitschke began to exalt militarism as an end in itself and preached the subjection of the individual to state authority, however aggressive and 'immoral' its policy. Concurrently, Wagner's vulgar anti-Semitism and his Christian Germanism was heavily imbued with a sense of futility and destructive urges. Failure in the 1849 Dresden uprising and consequent exile turned his revolutionary impulses to the artistic potential of a reinterpretation of the primordial forces and demons of the Nordic *Edda* and *Nibelungenlied*.[94] Such a barbaric mythology, he felt, supported the claims of the 'German' *Hohenstaufen*, and formed a potent antidote of passion and anarchic instinct to the evils of capitalism, law and abstract reason of French and Jewish 'intellect'. Wagner sought a 'dejudaisation' of German art and society, and in his operas glorified anarchic passion and destructive lust; thus in *Tristan* he expresses the belief that 'night and death redeem man from the turmoil and burden of daylight and life', and in *Die Walküre*, Wotan heroically wills his own destruction:

> I must leave what I love; I must murder what I woo; deceitfully I must betray whoever trusts me. . . . What I built I must break down! I abandon my work. One thing alone I demand, the end, the end![95]

Wagner's Bayreuth ethos, and its cult of Nordic barbarism, was a portent. In it we find the first crucial steps away from the older romantic, cultural nationalism towards a revolutionary 'blood and soil' instinctualism. The most important of these steps is that of genetic determinism: the assertion that every German is everlastingly bound to his nation and can never renounce his identity, because his is an inescapable destiny, subject to dark, primeval forces beyond his control. Later this determinism will be given 'scientific foundations': but its presence is unmistakable in Wagner's emphasis upon submission to historical fate.

A second step was taken in the Bismarck era: the creation of a mythical anti-type, the Jew who stands for everything un-German, cosmopolitan, rootless, materialist and contaminating. The earlier romantics had not singled out the Jews despite the survival of Christian anti-Semitism. If they had a single enemy it was France, and the reason was cultural, not racial and biological. A final step is the glorification of the hero as a man of instinct, a warrior prepared to die: for what? So as to destroy every existing value, all 'civilisation', and to found a new order, new men of power and brutal passion. Thus the 'will-to-power' will find its Leader and its élite, and the citizens of the nation will become the masses of the race.[96]

It was only after the economic crisis of 1873 and the arrival of the new racial anti-Semitism of Marr and von Glogau that these 'irrationalist' seeds could bear fruit. The intellectual foundations had been laid in the 1850s by Gobineau, Broca and Robert Knox. The latter's statement that 'With me race, or hereditary descent, is everything; it stamps the man' and his belief in the inevitability of race warfare was elaborated in a variety of social Darwinist biological–racial schemes of world history, centring on the 'Aryan' cult of Paul de Lagarde, Julius Langbehn, Vacher de Lapouge and Houston Chamberlain.[97] In Germany, especially, it served to justify Lagarde's and Langbehn's beliefs in a German religious mission, her need for *lebensraum* in the East, the superiority of her inherited *völkisch* characteristics, and her need for an élite state based on race and the 'power of the blood'.[98] Similar sentiments were responsible for the agitation of extremist anti-Semitic sects and pan-German leagues, led by Marr, Ahlwardt, Heinrich Class and Otto Boeckel. Their radical anti-capitalism and anti-Marxism fastened on the Jews as 'parasites', 'predatory beasts' and 'contaminators' of modern society, a racial–radical outlook that had little in common with Adolf Stoecker's more traditional Christian Social Party and its religious anti-Semitism. The ill-fated attempt to unite the conservative nationalist parties with these radical racial sects illustrates the wide gulf separating them, as well as the superficial links and mutual political utility between traditional nationalism and an emerging racial populism.[99]

The immediate origins of Hitler's brand of fascism must be sought in his Austrian precursors after the stock market crash of 1873 and the burgeoning of Czech nationalism had shaken the position of the German-speaking middle classes in the Habsburg Empire. These threats, together with the spectre of Marxist socialism, gave the racial, pan-German, socialist anti-Semitism of von Schönerer and Lueger's Catholic 'organic' anti-capitalism a large Viennese audience and paved the way for the formation of anti-Marxist workers' parties devoted to the German interest. One of these parties, the Sudeten socialist Deutsche Arbeiterpartie (DAP) for the Munich DAP, formed after the War by Anton Drexler and Gottfried Feder, and transformed by Hitler in 1920 into the Nazi Party.[100] But such parties of railway workers, though they provided a potential lower-class base, required a directive ideology, a social and political programme, to achieve the fascist success; and that ideology and programme was provided, in the first place, by the Germanic Order and Thule Society (founded in 1912, reconstituted in 1918), with its racial-*völkisch* ideology, 'Aryan' rites and its élitist social appeal.[101] More generally, the early Nazi programme was a logical, practical precipitant of the new racial–biological 'explanation' of history, coupled with the nationalist militarism and cult of violence to which four long years of war had habituated Europe and which some, unable to put it aside, transferred into the domestic political arena. Biological militarism had been preached before the war – by Langbehn, Guido von List, von Schönerer and especially by the renegade monk and editor of a racialist periodical called *Ostara*, Adolf Lanz von Liebenfels. (The super-race theory of his *Theozoology* of 1901 with its battle of blond, strong 'Arioheroes' against the impure 'inferior races', ending in their sterilisation and liquidation, was a potent influence on the immature Hitler in Vienna in 1909.[102]) But only after the War had diffused this spirit of inter-group violence and given a semblance of credibility to the social Darwinist conception of history could racial fascism finally emerge.

THE NAZI REVERSAL

The fully elaborated Nazi ideology of the 1930s consisted of a mélange of commonplace notions. At its dynamic core stood Hitler's overpowering fear of a German physical decline and extinction and his belief in the everlasting struggle for existence of biological species. Out of this fear arose a simplified and conspiratorial scheme of world history, modelled on Lanz's battle of Arioheroes and inferior races, designed to uphold the German race and its position among other races. Savage geopolitical warfare was Hitler's cure for the nagging doubts about German potential: '"The only thing that will ensure a people its freedom of existence", he wrote in *Mein Kampf*, "is sufficient space on this earth."'[103] And that entailed a perpetual war of siege and annihilation against all inferior races, who threatened the life-force of the German race as it was embodied in the Aryan race nuclei, the 'culturally creative primeval force'.[104] Identified with the Party and later the SS, such Nordic nuclei would constitute an aristocratic élite of race-conscious and racially 'good' elements, and would therefore wield absolute power in Hitler's envisaged race state, so as to preserve its racial purity and its world position. Hitler and Rosenberg submerged the individual entirely in the 'ties of race', to whose protection they devoted all their energies, out of a deep conviction that otherwise the 'Jewish virus' would destroy mankind by causing him to 'transgress the laws of nature', i.e. of the struggle for survival.[105] War, annihilation and selective race breeding are the tools by which Nazis are to implement their fundamental goals of preserving the masterrace and its purity and dominance – as did the ancient Spartans, or the Japanese or English, in Hitler's estimation.[106]

The components of Nazi ideology had all been developed since the mid nineteenth century, but before Hitler and his associates nobody had managed to fuse them and endow them with so radical and practical a coherence. Among the most important of these themes are:

(1) the supremacy of the State, and a worship of power, discipline and order (hence Hitler's admiration for ancient Rome and the Church);

(2) biological determinism of society, and the struggle for survival;

(3) eugenics and race breeding by cultivating the 'blood' of a national élite;

(4) eternal war for territory (*lebensraum*) and conquest of inferior races;

(5) elimination of the unnatural and defiling 'Jewish virus' responsible for modern emancipation, liberalism, Marxism and capitalism;

(6) the hero as warrior-lord, land-cultivator and ruthless realist;[107]

(7) destruction of Marxism as the final 'Jewish bid for world domination'.[108]

It was not only Hitler who infused a dynamic into such clichés. It was far more the Nazi vision of Germany as the racial core of a new world order, founded on a principle of biological caste-ism and an ethic of primitive instinct. Hitler's desired reversion to the primitive 'tribal' state of affairs involves also a reversal of the usual nationalist vision. Proceeding out of the revolution of nihilism, which, like the dragon from hell, will destroy all the values of modern civilisation, Nordic Germany will arise and march triumphant over the inferior 'racial mishmash' of Europe, as an élite tribe of primordial purity: 'So we have assembled,' Himmler concluded,

and according to immutable laws we march as a National Social-ist, soldierly order of Nordic men and as a sworn community of their clans on the road to a distant future, and we desire and believe that we may be not only the grandsons who fought it out better, but beyond that the ancestors of later generations necessary for the eternal life of the German Germanic people.[109]

In this brutal world of animal species in which, as Hitler put it, 'One creature drinks the blood of another. The death of one nourishes the other. One should not drivel about humane feelings . . . the struggle goes on'[110], and in which there are 'only conquerors and serfs', the nationalist quest for autonomy has become the submission of the citizen to the will of the State and its Führer, its goal of territorial cohesion is turned into an imperialist drive for expansion and *lebensraum*, involving the annihilation of non-ethnic elements, while the discovery of national identity has ceded place to the correct selection and breeding of the racial élite.

The resulting scheme of world order, envisaged by Nazi doctrine, can be summarised as follows. The world is divided, not into theoretically equal nations living side by side, but into racial castes resembling a stratification pyramid. At the top is the Führer, who embodies the inner will of the master-race and, as the supreme warrior-hero, expresses its ideals and real nature. Beneath him, and submissive to his will, come the racially pure, the selected specimens of the German race, who are endowed with superior blood, physique and blond appearance; they are the natural, right-ful lords of mankind, the 'overman' (as the Nazis misinterpreted Nietzsche). It was Himmler's SS that was specially entrusted with the task of extracting 'good blood' and training the racial élite through special racial institutions which would determine genealogy and blood-character, and in élite castles and organisations for developing the necessary outlook and zeal.[111]

Only after this racial 'Aryan' élite come the mass of the Germans, themselves purified of 'defective' elements;[112] and only thereafter the whole racial caste of Nordics, including the Dutch, Scandinavians and English. Beneath them were placed the Latin races, and other Mediterranean peoples. At the base of the system Hitler and Rosenberg placed the Slavic 'helot' races who were to serve the master-race in the conquered eastern territories. They were to live apart in degrading conditions and were expendable.[113] Finally, the Jews and Gipsies, being 'non-peoples' and 'racial vermin', were to be exterminated.[114]

It would, however, be a mistake to assume that the guiding 'horizontal' principle of biological caste-ism and racial purity entailed a static framework: far from it. The perpetual conflict of master and subject races continued within this stratified caste system, for the German Aryans and Nordic races were always under threat of decline or of rebellion from below, and world salvation of the Aryan 'race nuclei' depended upon achieving an absolute sovereignty, which was always in doubt.[115] Nevertheless, the main 'racial revolution' (for Hitler the only true kind of revolution) could be executed: the elimination of the 'wirepuller of the destinies of mankind', as Eckart conceived the Jewish role in history; the liquidation of what Hitler calls the 'world poisoners of all peoples, international Jewry'.[116]

In its underlying assumptions, such a racial caste-ism reveals the basic patterns and spirit of general caste principles, though with some significant modifications. We are faced with a system of hereditary groupings, in a scheme that envisages a total segregation between the racial units, occupational specialisation of races and a rank order governing their interrelations.[117] In spirit, too, the Hitlerian New Order resembles other caste systems in being animated by a sense of pollution and impurity. On the other hand, there are important differences with other 'caste situations', and even more so with the unique Indian 'caste system'.[118] In particular, the caste units of Hitler's system are felt to be in perpetual conflict for supremacy, and the sense of pollution is focused upon an active agent, which instigates the 'corruption', and which explains and subsumes every social ill. Moreover, there is no other-worldly religious legitimation for the Nazi system of inequality: it is of the essence of Hitler's belief that the Jew is not simply a Christ-killer, or even, as in the older *völkisch* conception, an economic and cultural competitor; rather, he is an active racial disease, a purely secular and physical construct, or rather a spirit become a 'substance of flesh and blood'. The Jew, for Schönerer and his disciple Hitler, is no longer just a rootless cosmopolitan, belonging to a 'pariah' people, to be shunned; and pogroms and expulsion can no longer suffice. Instead, the Jew becomes the incarnation of racial evil, a species of malignant bacillus, the non-race eroding all pure races, the ruin and unseen disease of the Aryan race. The subman is not simply outside society, an untouchable; he is the dynamic bacteriological corrupter of mankind. As such, he must be annihilated lest he destroy not merely the purified élite but the whole 'natural' order of castes.

This, then, is the heart of Hitler's Manichaean 'anti-Semitism of reason' as opposed to the usual anti-Semitism of emotion with its periodic pogroms. And here, too, we have the explanation of Hitler's basic divergence not only from other caste systems and situations but even from other fascist systems, where the sense of pollution is unfocused or embryonic.[119]

Here, too, the fundamental divergence of nationalism and Hitler's fully evolved nazism is revealed with the utmost clarity. Conceptually, caste and nationalist principles are diametrically opposed. The nationalist holds that each nation possesses its own character, virtue, destiny and mission: that was the underlying assumption of Herder, Jefferson, Burke, Rousseau and Mazzini.[120] Fully fledged nazism, on the contrary, sees a world divided into racial strata locked in battle and arranged in a hierarchy of blood and power. To nationalists history, citizenship and the homeland are crucial values: for Nazis these have been overshadowed by hereditary physique and state power, fused in eternal war. According to nationalism, men belong to nations by choice and sentiment, by tradition and common culture: whereas, for the true Nazi they are organs of their racial caste, mere specimens of its blood-and-physique level, their mental characteristics but a reflection of immutable biological traits. Finally, for most nationalists violence and warfare are means to the ends of autonomy, unity and identity: for nazism, war is the fulfilment of man, the true and natural expression of his race instinct, and 'the most powerful and classic expression of life'.[121]

Sociologically, too, nazism differs somewhat from German and other nationalisms in its social composition and organisation. It was the urban and rural lower-middle classes who furnished Hitler's most zealous recruits, together with a strong peasant following.[122] As it grew into a 'mass' movement, nazism also came to appeal to the unemployed worker, threatened by cartels and unions alike, to ex-soldiers and ex-officers, to the very young, and to underemployed members of the intelligentsia and lower-level bureaucrats; but also to some industrialists and business leaders. By contrast, the more traditional Nationalist Party in Germany appealed successfully to the conservative middle classes and landowners, who had a stake in the social order and feared the Marxist threat; and it is interesting that, though the Nazis increased their vote at the expense of the liberals and even the socialists (but not the communists), they did not penetrate conservative Nationalist strongholds except in some areas on the Polish frontier.[123]

Organisationally, nazism differed considerably from traditional nationalisms. Of course, both define themselves as 'movements' rather than just parties: but nazism, like other fascisms, lays special stress on the reality and immediacy of movement and process; hence its greater flexibility and opportunism. Moreover, right from the start, nazism evolved a tight military command structure at the centre, suited to its aggressive tactics and Leader mystique. Nationalist organisations, except in guerilla warfare situations, tend to be less centralised and more unwieldy and display small concern for the enthusiastic and disciplined submission to the Leader. Liturgically, too, nazism transcends the usual nationalist symbolism of flags and oaths, anthems and processions, turning them into the hallowed prehistoric totems of the Leader salute or the swastika. In short, totalitarian controls and an almost 'magical' archaic symbolism transform nazism into a pseudo-military–religious order, far removed from earlier nationalisms.[124]

Taken singly, these contrasts appear to be differences of degree. Taken together and seen as the practical outcome of a definite vision of society, they become fundamental differences in kind. For the final criterion of Hitler's racial fascism is the biological imperialism of the German master-caste, and its final practical expression becomes its eternal war to annihilate inferior polluting slave-races. From the standpoint of such a war of 'world salvation', petty nationalism becomes a mere tool, useful perhaps to win over embittered Ukrainians or insecure Saarlanders, but of little ultimate consequence for Hitler's real purposes, which – as far as the nationalisms of the non-Russian nationalities were concerned – were hardly encouraging. Perhaps the clearest expression of Hitler's contempt for traditional nationalism is found in his last political testament, when he derides the weakness of the Germans who betrayed him to the 'stronger' peoples of the East, and conjoins their doom to his own death. And even in the last hours in his bunker he enjoins his successors to uphold the racial laws and to resist relentlessly the 'poisonous' Jews.[125]

Thus did Nazism incorporate and then reverse the vertical nationalist principles of autonomy and identity, through its own peculiar vision of the biological master-caste and its eternal war of annihilation, while perverting to its own ends the German nationalist tradition.

IRRATIONALISM AND THE GREAT WAR

Nationalism must be regarded as one of the global ideological forces of the whole modern era: fascism and nazism, on the other hand, were largely products of the early twentieth century in Europe. True, fascist components appeared around 1890 and have persisted after 1945, and have sprung up outside Europe. But if we wish to observe a modicum of precision in our use of terms, then we must concede the main tenet of the 'totalitarian' viewpoint, namely fascism's twentieth-century character and incidence. On the other hand, the corollary of this view need not be accepted: nazism and fascism may differ from nationalism, but in the Europe of this epoch they were heavily intertwined with, and politically indebted to, nationalism.

How shall we explain this dual situation? On the one hand, the new factors in post-1870 European society and politics helped to generate a different mood and aspirations, standing apart from those that nationalism could create and satisfy. On the other hand, the new mood and aspirations could be made to appear extensions of the older nationalist ones, to be satisfied by new formulae. In the end, however, the basic difference was likely to reassert itself: the novel factors were rejected or contained, and the new mood and aspirations they generated were thereby dissipated, whereas the underlying factors and aspirations behind nationalism have not so far been contained or dissipated. This is one reason why fascism as a movement has not made much headway in postWar Europe, while nationalism is experiencing a revival today, albeit in a modified 'autonomist' guise, among Western Europe's 'peripheral' *ethnie*.[126]

Four new factors introduced into European society and politics after 1870 are particularly germane to the rise of fascism: the new irrationalist ideologies like élitism and social Darwinism; growing threats to the status and livelihood of urban lower-middle classes and small farmers; the opportunities afforded by democratisation and an increase in the franchise; and finally the Great War itself, a gigantic and prolonged glorification of mass violence as an apparent solution to every ill.

Without the Great War, which itself gave such a fillip to mass democracy in the West and which involved large sectors of the population, it is extremely doubtful if fascism or nazism could have become anything more than fringe sects of lower-middle-class radicals. Similarly, without the depression of 1873 and the recurrent 'crises' of capitalism, the phenomenon of rural and urban *déclassé* could never have become so widespread nor their support for the fringe groups anything more than ephemeral. Again, without the spread of the franchise in the West and democratic demands further east, it would have been impossible for fascists to exploit and agitate among the *déclassé*. Finally, without the peculiar élitist fusion of counter-revolutionary conservatism and radical anti-Semitic populism within the context of social Darwinian assumptions, the fascist solution could never have appeared so attractive and explosive.

As a doctrine of the right of the strong and violent, fascism's anti-positivist revolution must be viewed primarily as a new solution to the old nationalist problem of the decay and decline of community. Nationalism's own solution is essentially practical, though it has psychological and cultural dimensions. Man must rediscover his own historic identity; he must locate and develop it in a recognised, secure territory in solidarity with others sharing that identity; and he must realise identity and fraternity by freely choosing to live according to the peculiar inner laws of that community. Such a solution is activist, puritan, collective and revolutionary; but it proceeds directly out of the main tenets of the Enlightenment, that is the moralising, heroic and sentimental later phase of that movement.[127] It represents a fusion of pragmatic rights with ethnic–historical ties.

Fascism repudiates not only reason and liberalism but also sentiment, that is, the humane dispositions and values that, according to nationalist reasoning, were unable to flourish in the standardisation and regimentation of bureaucratic absolutism and an artificial cosmopolitanism. Nationalism aimed to give concrete political form to the aspirations of both rationalism and romanticism, however uneasy their conjunction: fascism set out to destroy both, and replace the whole western cultural heritage by men and regimes built on brute instinct and primitive appetite.[128] It drew upon the radical critique of that heritage supplied by Nietzsche, but debased and perverted his call for a total transvaluation of western and Christian values, substituting the man of brutality and lack of feeling for Nietzsche's man of courage and daring. This is the final message of Himmler's speech to the SS at Poznan in 1943 on the final solution, with its explicit repudiation of Herder's 'idealist' concern for other peoples' aspirations, and its 'morality' of self-conquest through the abrogation of all hitherto existing morality:

> To have gone through this [the extermination of the Jews] and – except in instances of human weakness – to have remained decent, that has made us tough. This is an unwritten, never to be written, glorious page of our history.[129]

One cannot read this speech, and other Nazi pronouncements on the subject of the 'inferior races', without realising the profound nihilism that lies at the root of the fascist, and especially the Nazi, revolution.

That this nihilism and cultural pessimism became prevalent must be ascribed to the peculiar circumstances that united irrationalist values and ideals to the anxieties, and opportunities, of the *déclassé* in central, southern and eastern Europe. The particular circumstance was the apparent failure of the democratic–nationalist solution to the problem of communal decay and cohesion, manifested first in the Great War itself and the rise of Bolshevism, and second in the failure of Wilsonian principles and the Versailles Treaty to ameliorate the endemic nationality disputes. In fact, the attempt to satisfy simultaneously the nationalist aspirations of so many

European *ethnie*, after such a resort to total war, was bound to bring dissatisfaction with traditional nationalist–democratic programmes, particularly among those who were exposed to the new market forces and irrationalist philosophies and were fearful of the effects of the widened franchise. In the West, massive industrialisation and inflation produced a large class of politically vocal, and downwardly mobile or threatened, small property-holders, squeezed in between the vast cartels and the powerful unions.[130] In the East, large-scale industry and a large proletariat were either absent or were concentrated in a few cities. It was rather urban commercial rivalries, coupled with economic anxieties and secular, democratic aspirations, that threatened traditional ways of life, especially among newly enfranchised strata. In these circumstances, men readily sought out an external agent of decline and anxiety, and easily persuaded themselves that the fashionable western doctrines of violence, race and the élite could solve the problems of inter-ethnic urban competition to which eastern Europe was now exposed.[131]

Until the Great War, nationalism appeared to present the best hope of containing or solving the effects of economic and political change, both in the West and the East. But the example of the Great War induced many of the *déclassé* to draw different conclusions, to jettison the western cultural and political heritage for the nihilistic vitalism of the fringe coteries. Only their evolving fascism now seemed able to regenerate shattered communities and re-establish eroded values and institutions; for this purpose, nationalism and socialism had proved insufficient: hence the attempts to combine both in a 'national socialism', which for the most part parodied and emasculated their principles. In this way, fascism could operate in the name of a 'purified' socialism and a 'true' nationalism, and could feed on the unsatisfied aspirations of both movements, while really making war on both.

The Great War was significant in another way. Not only had it revealed nationalism's intrinsic limitations, but it had shown up the nationalists' failure to prevent the rise of Marxism as a revolutionary and communally divisive force. It became therefore doubly necessary to challenge and transcend nationalism, to transform it into a mass doctrine of the strong and violent. That was the basic lesson of this war of annihilation, the Great War, with its use of poison gas, a lesson Hitler remembered all too well.[132]

Not everyone, of course, felt that nationalism was exhausted. Statesmen continued to operate within a nationalist framework, and the majority of politically uninvolved citizens assumed its continued efficacy with varying degrees of national sentiment. Nationalism was not superseded, either after 1918 or after 1945; for the conditions that favour its rise and spread are of a more general and fundamental kind than those that underlie the fascist phenomenon. Yet, in interWar Europe, nationalism no longer made the political running. Its role was taken by a more strident and dynamic fascism. The fringe sects expanded and set the tone, particularly in the thirties, when they succeeded in making Europe in their own warlike image. The more legalistic and limited demands of nationalists were simply incorporated and then outstripped by those of fascism. Nationalism's legitimation at Versailles, the final recognition of its claims in world politics, left the revolutionary field open for such worldwide 'salvation movements' as Marxism and nazism, whose own solutions to the problems of communal regeneration and decline were infinitely more radical and all-embracing.[133]

CONCLUSION

Fascism and nazism cannot be equated with nationalism. They involve different assumptions and categories and are infused with a distinct spirit and ethos. They tend to appeal to somewhat different sectors of the middle classes, and possess completely dissimilar political styles and organisations. At the same time, they are linked in a number of subtle ways, which spring from their common attempt to provide solutions to the problems of communal decline and revival, and from their shared revolutionary impulse.

Nor is it correct to read back the seeds of fascism and nazism into earlier European nationalisms. Fascism drew on many traditions, of which nationalism was but one, and a rival at that. The vital fact is that nationalism has largely accepted the European heritage and attempted to build upon it, whereas fascism involved a wholesale and deliberate rejection of that heritage. Fascism, therefore, though it borrowed elements from nationalism, represented also a profound attack on the whole nationalist outlook. This is all too clear in the case of nazism. In his analysis of its rise, Parsons rightly emphasised the lack of a liberal tradition, and the rejection of rationalism, in German society. Despite its massive industrialisation, many sectors of German society remained hierarchical and conservative, all too receptive to the demagogic solutions of a Hitler.[134] However, this line of reasoning neglects one important factor – the revolutionary–charismatic element that fed on irrationalism.[135] Fascist nihilism implies not only a rejection of the western heritage, a protest against the 'normal' trend to disenchantment and rationalisation: in the cult of the Leader and the concept of élite blood, it incorporates a truly 'anti-rational', a vitalistic drive, a systematic and disciplined worship of the barbaric, primitive *élan vital*, on which rested nazism's military élitism. Fascism and nazism represent, therefore, an alternative and a challenge to the nationalist European, and world, image of development, and not a continuation of it. Hence its potentialities as an alternative model even today, and hence also its limitations. Whereas nationalism builds on to the European heritage, fascism wishes to destroy it and replace it by a barbaric élitism founded upon the State and the race. Its influence for that very reason is likely to be more fragmented: instead of the full, radical doctrine of interWar years, we are more likely to get pale adaptations or individual elements in various movements and regimes. For the act of overthrowing a long heritage is more arduous than fascists suppose. Nevertheless, the fascist option will remain in the European consciousness as an attempt to cut the Gordian knot in times of national crisis through an act of revolutionary brutalism.

CHAPTER 4

Colour, Race and National Identity

With the exception of communism, the most serious rival of modern nationalism has been the ideology of race and colour. In 1900 Du Bois warned that the problem of the twentieth century would be the problem of the colour line, and indeed we find men everywhere today exalting race and colour, and prepared to fight and die on their behalf. Earlier theories of progress would have found such developments as deplorable as they were inexplicable; of all the ideologies associated with modernisation, racism is still generally regarded as the most damaging and repellent. Moreover, it is often confused with nationalism, and this has led many people to condemn any manifestation of nationalism and to treat nationalism as the first step on the road to war and genocide.

But such a wholesale rejection of nationalism is neither fair nor necessary. It rests on a misleading equation or association between it and racism. We need instead to distinguish the two doctrines, and ask ourselves: (1) why is nationalism so frequently confused with racism? (2) how far does it encourage racial or colour ideologies? and (3) to what extent can colour contribute to national identity and revival? For, if the first of these questions reveals the distance between nationalism and racism, the answer to the second may tell us how nationalism can, in certain circumstances, become transmuted into racism; while the third question, by reversing the causal chain, may suggest why race ideas have become so popular today, and how colour can 'substitute' for missing cultural attributes of national identity. Together, the answers to these questions may help to clarify some of the dangers and utility of the racial and colour factors in the processes of national modernisation.

NATIONALISM, RACISM AND ETHNOCENTRISM

To understand why nationalism is so often confused with racism, we need to compare their main ideological features.

Nationalism may be defined in various ways, but here I shall be concerned mainly with the ideological movement for the attainment and maintenance of autonomy, cohesion and individuality for a social group, some of whose members conceive it to be an actual or potential nation. A nation in turn may be defined as any social group with a common and distinctive history and culture, a definite territory, common sentiments of solidarity, a single economy and equal citizenship rights for all members.[1] In both definitions, of course, it is the ideal type of the nationalist vision that is delineated. In practice, few nations or nationalist movements conform to these ideals, yet all nationalists strive for them.[2]

Like other ideologies, nationalism fuses a theory of society and politics with a prescription for action and change. It weds a cultural account of politics to an activist ethic. The supreme goal for a nationalist is 'national identity' or 'nationhood', a visionary state of authentic self-expression and fraternity in which an historic community realises its unique qualities. The search for nationhood is a long and arduous struggle for self-regeneration. It requires both cohesion and autonomy: the growth of deep bonds of emotional solidarity, and the exercise of the citizens' rights of sovereign participation in decision-making. Though mankind, for the nationalist, is 'naturally' divided into unique culture-communities or nations, yet human beings must continually strive to preserve, deepen and fully understand their world of nations. They must jealously guard their sovereign independence, strike deep roots in their native soil, and immerse themselves and their personal identities in that of their own historic community.

These ideals of citizenship and independence, of fraternity and the homeland, and of an historic identity, which are of such concern to nationalists, play only a minor role in racist thinking.[3] For racism may be defined as a doctrine that divides the world into racial castes locked in a perpetual struggle for domination, in which the allegedly physically superior are destined to rule the inferior and form a racial élite. A racial caste, in turn, can be defined as any social group that is held to possess unique hereditary physical traits which allegedly determine all the mental attributes of the group.[4] Again, these are ideal-typical, and subjective, definitions; they are based upon the beliefs of often small coteries, however influential, and are rarely, if ever, to be found to correspond to an actual situation. In fact, possibly only the Nazis can be described as pure racists.

At this juncture there often arises a confusion over the use of the term 'race'. Physical anthropologists from Blumenbach onwards have frequently divided the human species, *Homo sapiens*, into broad racial categories – Mongoloid, Negroid, Caucasian, Australoid, American Indian or Hottentot – on the basis of pigmentation and other physical traits.[5] Recently the research on blood group gene frequencies in different populations has been combined with more traditional trait typologies to yield a larger number of 'races' or Mendelian 'sub-species'.[6] But there is still no agreement on the number, names and main characteristics of such 'races' or 'sub-species'. Indeed, the frequencies of genes in the blood groups of neighbouring populations are often very finely differentiated, and in any case they obey the rule of 'methodological nationalism'; that is, they are measured in terms of national data-gathering units.[7] The result, of course, is that on the one hand a number of national groups may yield similar gene frequencies and share identical physical traits, and on the other a given national unit may display marked genetic or physical differences within its population, as demarcated by state boundaries. Moreover, differences in frequencies of blood group genes do not generally correspond with those associated with other physical traits like skin colour, head shape or hair type. Besides, with the advance of contact and civilisation, the unity of the human species is outgrowing its genetic differentiation. As Dobzhansky puts it, 'Civilisation causes race convergence, due to gene exchange, to outrun race divergence. In this sense, human races are relics of the pre-cultural stage of evolution.'[8]

Whatever the current state of scientific research on the question of racial–genetic differences, the anthropological concept of racial classification has to be sharply distinguished from everyday social and political usages of the term 'race'. Such a distinction is not easy to uphold, because the social usage of 'race' has often resorted to the much more tentative anthropological findings of the time for 'scientific' support. In itself, the social usage of 'race' is anything but tentative or scientific, and its purpose is quite different. What it aims to do is to describe and explain ethnic and national differences, by defining ethnic groups as biological units, and explaining their world relationships in hereditary–physical terms.[9]

Of course, men have always remarked upon their physical differences, and have often extolled or scorned the variety of customs, cultures and physiques that divide them into social groups. Rarely, however, before the mid nineteenth century did they attempt to reduce this variety to a single, physical cause, or regard physical differences as immutable. Even more important, until the last century there was no attempt to derive all the mental attributes of the individual or group from his physical or genetic make-up, or to erect a theory of interstate relations on the basis of immutable and culture-determining physical types.

But it is just such a theory of intergroup relations that 'racial Darwinists' set out to furnish. They argued, in the first place, that the individual was little more than a (more or less 'pure') specimen of his group's physical type. His mental and cultural characteristics derived wholly from the organic properties of his biological group. As a consequence, individual wills were simply expressions of the group will and instinct, and failure to conform was evidence of physical deficiency, in the more extreme versions of this outlook. It followed secondly that if some individual specimens mirrored the group type more faithfully and vigorously than others, then they ought to be encouraged by a suitable process of selective reproduction, and conversely that impure specimens ought to be discouraged. Hence one of the racialist's main concerns became the attempt to perfect nature through eugenics, both to breed 'purer' ethnic groups, and later to create a racial élite. In this respect, racism conforms to the pattern of other ideologies that seek to intervene in the process of natural history, and supplement or hasten evolution through engineered change.

The final aim of all racial breeding was the formation of a segregated 'master-race', a world racial élite possessed of the finest of mankind's physical traits. But in practice this meant only that, within the dominant ethnic groups, the racially strongest specimens were to be encouraged to reproduce at the expense of the weaker or the mixed specimens. Another social mechanism was required to sort out the dominant ethnic groups, and finally the master-race. Nature's chosen mechanism was of course struggle and warfare; and in this, as in all else, nature had to be assisted in its selective task through a perpetual struggle for racial mastery, to test the group's natural fitness and to evolve a natural hierarchy of racial castes. Individual absorption in the group, eugenics, perpetual warfare and the creation of a natural hierarchy of racial castes become for the racist moral imperatives, for nature had ordained that racial supremacy carried with it the right of domination.

Clearly, the racist doctrine outlined above bears very little relationship to the ideas of nationalists. Yet the fact remains that the two ideologies have been, and still are, frequently confused or associated. Why is this? Partly because both doctrines were evolved in western and central Europe within about half a century of each other, and partly because they referred, in Europe at least, to the same kind of social grouping – the national community – albeit in very different ways. But the main reason for the confusion is the relationship, often complex, that exists between ethnocentrism and ethnicity on the one hand, and nationalism or racism on the other. For both racism and nationalism refer back, ultimately, to the same basic unit, the ethnic group and its traditional correlate, ethnocentrism.

Now the central elements of ethnicity, from which both racism and nationalism set out, concern the origins and history of a social group, its possession of a common culture, and the presence of sentiments of social solidarity. An ethnic group can indeed be usefully defined as any social group whose members claim a common origin, share a common history and culture, and possess feelings of mutual solidarity, which mark them off from other groups. The normal accompanying attitude of ethnic groups is founded on the belief, on the part of its members, that their community is the centre of the world and the sole standard of truth and justice. Hence ethnocentrism may be defined as the belief by its members in the centrality, rightness and superiority of their community, and a corresponding denial of value to other communities.[10]

Throughout history, the ethnic community has been one of

the main kinds of social organisation, and its normal attitudes
have been ethnocentric. In antiquity, we can distinguish such
politically effective and homogeneous communities as ancient
Egypt, the Hittites and Persians, and also large numbers of
politically insignificant and remote 'tribes' like the Lullubi or
the Picts, known to us from the pages of classical authors from
Herodotus to Strabo, and from inscriptions of imperial conquerors
like Tiglath-Pileser III or Darius I.[11] It is, naturally, difficult
to know how far such remote groups regarded themselves as
the sole bearers of truth or value, or the real centre of the
world; but certainly these sentiments were to be found among
relatively small and politically second-rate powers like the ancient
Greeks (before Alexander) and Jews, and later among medieval
Arabs and Burmans, and in China and Japan.

Now the ethnocentrism of all these ethnic communities, great
or small, near or far, was essentially a cultural, even religious,
sentiment. Very rarely was it biological in content, and never
primarily so. True, Tacitus despised the 'oriental' peoples, and
Juvenal the clever Greeks;[12] Tacitus praised the primitive noble
Germanic tribes, not only for their love of freedom and agrarian
ways, but also for their robust physique.[13] Horace, too, scorned
the luxury and effeminacy of Cleopatra's eastern hordes in their
civil strife against Octavian's virile Italian, or western, half of
the Roman *imperium*.[14] The Greeks, as is well known, laughed
at the unintelligible barbarians; the Chinese deemed it fitting
that unruly western tribes should submit to their sway; and
Arab traders despised their Negro slaves.[15]

Yet, in most of these cases, the basis of prejudice was cultural
rather than physical. Though our authors and groups remarked
upon and scorned the physical traits of their opponents or slaves,
it was really their lack of certain values or qualities that they
themselves prized, which they detested – the 'unintelligibility' and
'servile nature' of barbarians and Persians, or the 'lack of manli-
ness' of eastern peoples. Similarly, for Arabs, Chinese and Burmans,
lack of true religion among their subject minorities or slaves
was the prime motive for their contempt; to be without the
true faith was to lack civilisation. So until the modern era,
racial differences, though noticed, remain secondary in the genesis
of ethnic prejudice, serving mainly to reinforce pre-existing cultural
fears.

To a large extent, nationalism has kept the cultural basis of the earlier ethnocentrism, but has given it a new political framework and modern concepts. In evolving a more general theory of world political relationships, nationalism has had gradually to drop the older beliefs in the absolute centrality, rightness and superiority of one's own ethnic community. In an increasingly interdependent world, it has become simply impossible in the long run for particular ethnic states to operate as if other ethnic states possessed no value at all, or were beneath contempt. As isolation gave way to trade and exchange of ideas and techniques, as problems of economic development became central to the élites in each nation-state, so other communities and states came to serve as guides and models; and evolution, as well as revolution, became 'international'. Even where ethnic purity was sought inside the boundaries of the new states, the new nationalism could hardly afford the luxury of older ethnocentric attitudes when it came to dealing with a world of nations and superpowers. The solution, therefore, for the national quest was to strengthen the cultural basis of the community, while dropping the old ideas of centrality and superiority.

In contrast, racism has developed out of ethnocentrism in the opposite direction. It has emphasised the ideas of centrality, group rightness and superiority, but dropped the cultural basis of ethnocentric prejudice. Instead, it has elevated to first place ethnocentrism's rather secondary physical prejudices, and where before such prejudices were haphazard and ephemeral, racism now gives them a consistent and theoretical basis. Moreover, it is no longer just the outside appearance of foreign tribes that evokes epithets of opprobrium; racism believes that external traits mirror internal 'blood' types, which in turn carry the instincts and vital energies of the race. Not only, therefore, can an individual not exchange his community of birth for another; the caste hierarchy itself becomes rigid and impermeable, for the *élan vital* and instinctual forces of each community are radically dissimilar and in conflict with those of other ethnic communities. And so racism turns the old ethnocentrism into something immutable and all-determining, and in the final analysis, the concept of ethnicity becomes one of racial élites struggling for supremacy against the pollution of inferior races.

RACIAL CHALLENGES TO NATIONALISM

So far we have seen that, for all their differences, racism and nationalism are frequently confused or associated together because both ideologies derive ultimately from the same ethnocentric root. Both movements arose in Europe, nationalism in the later eighteenth century, racism in the first half of the nineteenth century.[16] Indeed, during the nineteenth century, the terms 'nation' and 'race' were used interchangeably to refer to ethnic communities. It was only towards the end of the nineteenth century that racial Darwinism succeeded in separating the concept of race (and racism) from that of the nation (and nationalism), and in applying it not only to European ethnic groups and minorities like the Jews, but also to whole categories of peoples outside Europe.

The confusion between the two concepts and ideologies has persisted to our time, partly because both have emerged side by side in Latin America, Asia and Africa, though in attenuated form, and partly because certain Third World ideologies have appeared to be speaking the language of race, while seeking nationalist goals. But closer examination of non-European nationalisms today shows that a pure racial doctrine or movement, such as appeared in Nazi Germany, is rarely espoused outside Europe.

Thus in Latin America the main forms of anti-colonialism have been a 'state' or 'territorial' nationalism, aspiring to independence for the former provinces of the Spanish and Portuguese empires and to economic and political integration and protection against foreign economic interests, and a rather weak movement of co-ordination and co-operation among the nation-states of the continent, which falls well short of a 'pan' movement of unification and continental integration.[17] The concepts of racism in these ethnically mixed societies has been notably absent, despite the existence of considerable prejudice. This prejudice, however, seems to have been largely cultural, even in pre-independence times. Thus in Mexico, European Spaniards tended to look down on American Spaniards or '*criollos*' not so much because of their racial 'impurity' and mestizo origins, but because they spoke a provincial dialect of American Spanish and had become corrupted by contact with heathen superstitions.[18] Nevertheless, the fact that skin colour, hair type and facial features gave rise to elaborate sub-categories among the ever-growing Mexican mestizo group shows some concern for purity of racial origins, though never enough to prevent passing or miscegenation on a large scale. Today, racism is officially spurned by the ruling Partido Revolucionario Institucional, heir to the socialist–nationalist revolution of 1910–17, though it is coupled with some anti-western pride in Aztec origins.[19]

Racial ideas have also appeared, and more forcefully, in Peru and Brazil, in the first country in conjunction with a populist nationalism, in the second as an impediment to an integrative nationalism. In Peru, José Carlos Mariátegui argued in the 1920s that the Indians of the sierra were the basic ethnic group of Peru, 'the cement of the nationality', and coupled ethnic populism with a demand for socialist agrarian reform.[20] This *indianismo* was taken up by Haya de la Torre's Apristas and developed by one of their adherents, Luis Alberto Sanchez, into an ideology of Indian renaissance, which inspired artists and writers in all the Andean republics as well as Mexico.[21] In Brazil, on the other hand, 'developmental nationalism' spurned the *sertanismo* or Indian nativism that had emerged in the 1890s;[22] Jaguaribe, in particular, fixes Brazilian nationalism firmly to bourgeois modernisation which has no room for past national characteristics of an ascriptive kind, or for the static oligarchic, bureaucratic or even proletarian elements that impede Brazil's integration and development.[23] But among these elements there is a continuing racial prejudice against Afro-Brazilians, especially in the large urban, industrial regions of south Brazil; it seems, if anything, to be on the increase, despite official condemnation by Church and State, and the Indian policy of the government.[24] Economic competition between poor whites and Negroes in Rio and Sâo Paulo, which fuels this racial prejudice, is exactly what the 'developmental nationalists' hope to overcome through their 'project' of creating a truly unified Brazilian nation.[25]

In Asia and Africa, the interrelations between nationalism and racism are even more complex and paradoxical. To begin with, nationalism has manifested itself in both continents on at least three levels: the ethnic or 'tribal', the state or territorial, and the 'pan' (cultural or continental). Thus, in Asia and the Middle

East, Tamils, Moros, Nagas, Kurds, Mizos and Palestinians mani-
fest an ethnic nationalism, similar to that which inspired Poles
and Rumanians, Norwegians and Basques in Europe. In Africa,
too, ethnic nationalism has become increasingly important and
turbulent; the Ibo, Kikuyu and Somali are well-known examples,
but at one time or another many of the larger and more unified
'tribes' have entertained aspirations for autonomy, territorial cohesion and cultural identity, among them the Ewe, BaKongo, Mongo,
Luba, Soli, Luo, Zulu, Yoruba, Hausa, Ganda, Fang, Ashanti
and Lunda.[26] In most cases, such cultural 'sub-nationalisms' were
quickly checked by the leadership of new states whose dread
of ethnic 'balkanisation' has reinforced their commitment to the
second or 'state' level of African nationalism.[27] State or territorial
nationalisms have also triumphed in Asia; thus Malaysia contains
three ethnic communities, Lebanon two, Burma and Indonesia
several, and India's Hindu ethnic group is subdivided into at
least fifteen linguistic communities, some of which have manifested
signs of national self-assertion.[28] But like their African counterparts – in Nigeria, Ghana, Tanzania, Zambia, Kenya, the Congo – the territorial nationalists in ethnically mixed Asian states
have so far prevailed over centrifugal ethnic nationalist secessionism, with the exception of Bangladesh.

There is a third level of nationalism in Africa and Asia:
the superstate or 'pan' movement, which seeks to unify a number
of culturally similar or geographically contiguous states into a
larger political community. That was one of the initial inspirations
behind pan-Turkism, pan-Arabism and pan-Africanism. Though
unsuccessful in this political aim, these movements have had
a marked cultural and ideological influence, since they appeal
to strong emotions of historic solidarity, shared memories and
myths of common origins. Like pan-Germanism, pan-Slavism and
pan-Negroism, the Asian and African 'pan' movements have both
reinforced the new states and their territorial nationalisms, and
at the same time undermined their *raison d'être* by submerging
their nascent individuality in a larger, all-encompassing historic
identity. Indeed, 'pan' movements need not be cases of simple
nationalism: pan-Islamism utilises modern methods for quite traditional goals and operates on behalf of the *umma*, the congregation
of believers, rather than the secular (Arab) nation.[29]

Instances of racial prejudice and belief occur mainly at the ethnic and 'pan' levels in Africa and Asia. Racial hostility turned into race riots in Malaysia, and into pogroms of Ibo in the Hausa and Fulani regions of Nigeria. In Lebanon, intercommunal strife exploded into civil war, while the Philippines, Iraq and Sudan witnessed long wars of religious and ethnic minorities against the government of the majority. Linguistic communal strife has bedevilled India, and Burma has had to fight protracted wars against its Shan and Karen minorities. In Ceylon and Indonesia, Tamil and Chinese minorities have experienced considerable hostility, while even in Japan the Eta or Burakumin ethnic caste, though hardly distinguishable culturally, have continued to suffer social discrimination.[30]

Most of these 'racial' hostilities turn out, on inspection, to be largely cultural in inspiration, and indeed, more often than not, updated versions of a traditional ethnocentrism made more intense by the competitive, impersonal atmosphere of expanding cities.[31] They owe very little to racist beliefs, much less to any theory of racial Darwinism. The antagonistic minority may be thought inferior and an impediment to national integration, but rarely as a source of pollution or physical threat to the group's vital forces. Nor is the minority regarded as a biologically immutable unit, whose physical traits determine its mental make-up, even if physical repulsion can heighten cultural antagonisms, as appears to have been the case between Hutu and Tutsi in Rwanda and Burundi, or between Fulani rulers and Hausa subjects in Zaria.[32]

A more theoretical racism can be found at the 'pan' level of nationalism. Pan-Turanianism, the precursor of pan-Turkism, sought to unite all Turkic-speaking and Finno-Ugric peoples; linguistic affinity was treated as the index of alleged common ethnic origin. Hungarian scholars like Arminius Vambéry linked Magyars, Finns and Mongols with Turkic peoples into a single 'Turanian' ethnological unit and located their origins in 'Turan', the area of central Asia to the north-east of Persia.[33] Pan-Turanianism sprang out of the fears of pan-Slav claims against Turks and Hungarians; pan-Turkism, its successor, was much less defensive, its racism much more physical and pagan. Gokalp, Tekin Alp and Enver Pasha glorified in the conquests and exploits of pre-Islamic Turks who, for them, numbered in their ranks

the Mongol conquerors, Genghis Khan and Hulagu.[34] Interestingly
enough, pan-Turkic racial nationalism, with its emphasis on physical training and militarism, preceded by nearly two decades
the much more limited Turkish 'state' nationalism propounded
by Kemal Ataturk, who renounced pan-Turkist dreams of uniting
all Turkic-speaking peoples in order to create a modern nation-
state in Anatolia.[35] On the other hand, pan-Turkism itself was,
in part, a militant reaction to the ethnic nationalisms of the
Ottoman Empire's Christian subjects; we can easily discover in
it all the hidden fears of a declining ruling ethnic community,
beleaguered and defeated.

In turn, a reactive pan-Turkism inflamed a secular pan-Arab
nationalism among the Empire's rebellious Arab subjects, even
though its seeds had been planted in late nineteenth-century
Lebanon and among a few Arab scholars in Europe.[36] Later,
under Axis influence, some of this pan-Arabism acquired a racial
tinge, just when the secular 'state' nationalisms of Syria, Jordan,
Iraq and Egypt were flourishing. Yet emphasis upon ancestry
or physique never played a large part in pan-Arabism; its role was
taken by the Arab language or Islam, even in Axis-influenced Iraq.[37]
Indeed, most of this pan-Arabism is really a species of traditional
Islamic ethnocentrism in a modern and anti-Zionist garb.[38]

In Africa, the 'pan' level of nationalism also acquired a racial
component, but for various reasons here the position was quite
different. In Africa 'race' in the specific sense of 'colour' has
provided a vital key to the lost past, and at the same time
symbolised a present humiliation.[39] Moreover, for Nkrumah, Pad-
more, Kenyatta and the other early post-independence leaders,
pan-Africanism furnished a cultural rationale for both anti-colonialism and 'state' nationalism. It enabled the new leaders
to ward off the threat of balkanising ethnic 'tribalisms' through
an overarching cultural identity, and transferred internal ethnic
divisions on to an international and continental stage.[40] This
was achieved, as Legum contended, through an ideology of 'race-
consciousness' rather than 'racism', or an attempt to assert the
equality and dignity of the African race as a whole with other
non-African races, rather than its biological superiority or centrality.[41] How far such an ideology should be termed 'racial', in
the European sense, is a question to which I shall return.

African ethnicism or pan-African race-consciousness bears little resemblance to the racial Darwinism that was rampant in Europe at the end of the nineteenth century, and even less to Nazi racism. By the mid nineteenth century Europe already possessed several strong ethnic nationalisms – in Germany, Ireland, Poland, Serbia, Italy and Hungary. But it was only after the failure of the 1848 revolutions, and the rise of racial Darwinism, that 'pan' nationalisms began to gain adherents in Germany and Austria, and in the Slav countries. Pan-Slav ideals were nurtured by German Romanticism and Hegelianism, and elevated the Russian motherland and state to a point where it appeared to threaten German interests, and challenge western hegemony.[42] With writers like Danilevski and the Slavophiles, we encounter an extreme nationalism with a marked racial flavour, particularly in the assertion that a youthful and vigorous Russia must, as a biological necessity, destroy a decadent West.[43] Such biological metaphors and racist beliefs became widespread among European intellectuals from the 1850s onwards: we meet them in authors as diverse as Wagner, Charles Kingsley, Matthew Arnold, Galton, Pearson, Barrès, Freytag and the early Gumplowicz.[44] They were an essential element in great power rivalry at home and overseas, and were widely accepted by élites and ruling classes, especially in Germany and Austria. Indeed, Nazi race concepts owe a particular debt to both the pan-German racist anti-Semitism of a von Schönerer or Heinrich Class, and the cosmic and *völkisch* mysticism of Paul de Lagarde, Eugen Diederichs and Guido von List.[45]

In Europe alone, then, did racism enjoy a continental vogue for a certain period of time, and in Europe almost alone did racism succeed in engulfing and replacing the more traditional forms of nationalism. The sole exceptions to this generalisation were to be found in Japan during the 1930s, in the activities of the Ku Klux Klan, and in South Africa; and while the case of the Klan owes little to any nationalism, the Japanese and South African cases show clear European influence superimposed upon a strong ethnic nationalism of isolated or beleaguered communities.

This suggests that, while threatened ethnic or 'pan' nationalisms can provide fertile ground for racism, they need not necessarily do so; nor need racist beliefs emerge from a prior nationalism.

Moreover, it becomes increasingly important to distinguish a continuum of positions stretching from nationalism through a racial nationalism, and a nationalist racism, to a pure racism at the other extreme, as follows:

Nationalism	Racial nationalism	Nationalist racism	Racism
Jacobin France	Anti-Dreyfusards	1930s Japan	Nazism
Norway/Greece	19th-century	Iron Guard	Ku Klux Klan
Eastern Europe	Germany	South Africa	
Ghana/Zambia, etc.	Pan-Turkism		
India/Burma, etc.	Pan-Slavism		
Brazil/Chile, etc.	Négritude		

Despite the inherent slipperiness of ideological concepts, we need to distinguish those cases where a nationalist movement utilises racial dimensions to heighten its appeal from other cases where a predominantly racist movement makes use of national sentiments and ideas. In the first case, the racial nationalism promotes the 'nation' and adds a racial component to distinguish the nation more sharply from its neighbours; in the second, the nationalist racism subordinates the nations to the 'race', placing nationalist goals in the service of a racial élite. These are, again, ideal-type formulations: in practice, it is a matter of judgement where one places, say, German or Turkish movements in the nineteenth or early twentieth centuries, whether one judges them to be 'racial nationalisms' or 'nationalist racisms'. But, clearly, to cross this line has profound implications for policy and action, not least for ethnic minorities in these states.

What emerges is the popularity of nationalisms, and to a lesser extent racial nationalisms, and the paucity of racisms, whether nationalistic or pure racisms. Of course, there have been many more instances of sporadic racial hostility, yet, only a few cases of outright racist movements, superseding nationalisms. The question that naturally arises is why did some 'pan' or ethnic nationalisms succumb to this racism?

The answer to this question varies with the period of history and the continent concerned. In Europe the countries in which racism flourished at the end of the nineteenth century – France,

Germany, Austria – had all undergone traumatic social changes, and dramatic alterations in their political status. In the case of France and Austria, there was the sting of defeat and the fear of dismemberment. A recently united Germany, on the other hand, despite its military victories, remained profoundly uncertain of its internal solidarity and its international acceptability. After the First World War, defeat would fuel German insecurities, and provide the opportunity for racism to utilise and then displace an unsatisfied nationalism.[46] In Russia, too, defeat in the Japanese War would strengthen the anti-Semitic racism of the monarchists and Black Hundreds.[47]

Quite apart from these international factors, social forces helped to propel the movement towards a nationalistic racism. In Germany, for example, early nineteenth-century nationalism, when it began to acquire a racist flavour, was still steeped in hierarchical, medievalist notions of a fairly religious kind. It was at first in the name of a Christian Germanism that Jews were excluded from various student societies.[48] Similarly, the early nationalistic formulations of Müller and Schlegel tended to extol the autocratic state and the medieval estates.[49] Even in mid-century, the nationalism of Treitschke was *étatiste* and conservative in its militarism, despite the vehemence of its claims. It was only after Bismarck's victories and the onset of massive industrialisation that a new lower-middle-class populism, fanned by demagogues who preached a political or racial anti-Semitism, began to challenge the older conservative state nationalism.[50] Though it found a very willing ear among the bourgeoisie and industrialists intent on colonial expansion, this new 'Great German' populist racism appealed especially to the recently urbanised lower middle classes in Germany and Austria. The movement from a conservative racially tinged nationalism to a radical nationalistic racism represents therefore a social shift in favour of the recently emancipated and politicised lower middle classes in the expanding cities and small towns, especially in separatist Bavaria and Austria. To these people, economic and cultural competition from conflicting ethnic groups could be conveniently explained in terms of a Jewish 'conspiracy', the Jews themselves being increasingly regarded in racial Darwinist terms as a biological 'predator' rather than as the 'perfidious' religious community of traditional Christian doctrine.[51]

In France, too, the position of the Jew as an 'indigestible' ethnic minority was transformed from that of a religious confession to one of an eternally alien enclave. At the beginning of the century, Napoleon had convened the Sanhedrin to separate Jewish ethnicity from Judaism, and had demanded that the Jew surrender his national aspirations and ethnic status for French citizenship and freedom of worship.[52] At the end of the century, Drumont and Maurras restored to the Jew his ethnic status, with a vengeance. It was no longer religion that defined his Jewishness, but his culture and his blood, elements that would always prevent his assimilation into French culture and the French 'race'. In this act of redefinition, the radical Right may have been supporting the anti-Dreyfusard monarchists, the Army and Church, but they were also advancing a new racial nationalism which could so easily slide into a nationalistic racism, such as was later to emerge in Action Francaise or the theories of Drieu de la Rochelle and Déat.[53]

The French drift into a racial nationalism, and the German and Austrian movement of populist racism, could have acquired momentum only in certain very specific conditions. Chief among these were the imperialism of the great powers of Europe, and the prestige of western science, particularly biology and anthropology. Economic and political competition overseas not only sharpened intra-European antagonisms, but also fed the persistent ethnocentrism of White nations, which were experiencing growing internal cleavages as a result of rapid economic change. Notions of imperial mission and the White Man's burden could alleviate internal cultural strains, and compensate for the restrictions placed on European rivalry within Europe itself. That rivalry, by its very intensity, bred a new siege mentality among the defeated or latecomers to the colonial power game. Frustration and encirclement in turn encouraged a belief in the importance of manpower and population numbers as an index of power and prestige. Possession or increase of a large population led naturally to the desire for an enlarged territory to feed and settle them, hence to the acquisition of colonies, by force if necessary, and the annexation of lands already occupied by members of the ethnic group who happened to live outside the nation-state's boundaries. Finally, there arose the belief that such boundaries were themselves mere accidents of dynastic or traditional contrivance, to be altered by that universal arbiter of communal destinies, war.[54]

A final legitimation and explanation for such beliefs and desires was furnished by the new sciences of physical anthropology and biology, and the prestige that Darwin's discoveries appeared to confer on them. The warring European nation-states could now be understood as so many biological species or races engaged in the natural struggle for domination. They became fixed and unalterable. Their membership was no longer a matter of residence or political choice, not even of belonging to the same culture and sharing the same language. All that counted now was an assumed type of physique and blood group, binding the individual to his group and effacing his individuality. By the end of the nineteenth century, the criterion of citizenship for a racist had shifted, first from a territorial and political to an ethnic one, and then to a criterion of biological heredity, while the old sense of ethnic superiority, at once cultural and defensive, had become an aggressive and militarist racial expansion.

In Europe, at any rate, this decisive shift began as a reassertion of traditional values, a conscious return to the codes of an agrarian warrior aristocracy. It is no accident that one of the earliest racial explanations of national history occurs in the Comte de Boulainvilliers's defence of noble Frankish privileges, or that the much more influential and global theory of the Comte de Gobineau over a century later also linked racial with aristocratic decline.[55] Only in the latter half of the nineteenth century did the new lower middle classes in the expanding towns adopt a counter-revolutionary ideology that was both anti-capitalist and anti-urban. In the myth of a seamless and organic racial élite destined to rule inferior races, the two strata most exposed to the ravages of industrial capitalism – a declining landowning aristocracy and a threatened lower middle class – could find a comforting ideology of communal hope, and a promise of social restoration.

Outside Europe, the two areas most affected by industrial capitalism, Japan and South Africa, were also the most prone to racist ideologies. In both cases, an isolated or defensive nationalism reacting against the challenge of superior technology and power bred a myth of racial superiority which overshadowed at times the nation itself in the interests of a system of racial categories or castes.[56] But whereas Japan's nationalist racism was turned by the fascist movement of the 1930s towards expansion, South Africa's had to confront an ethnically heterogeneous population inside its borders, a fact that has led it to evolve an ethnic policy that modifies its overall racial framework.[57] In other parts of Africa, Asia and Latin America, we have encountered some racially tinged cases of nationalism; and especially in the case of the 'pan' movements, these have been very largely the work of small coteries of the intelligentsia, itself a fraction of the population. In some cases, they arise from doubts about cultural identity, such as the conflict between Spanish and Indian in Latin America, or between Turkish and Islamic in Anatolia. In other cases, it is bound up with the special problem of colour, a question that merits closer examination.

COLOUR AND PAN-AFRICAN IDENTITY

So far I have considered only the nationalist contribution to a racism, which in some cases challenged and engulfed its nationalist rival. But there is another side to the question, the racial contribution to nationalism; and it is the role of colour in defining and reviving national identity that highlights the 'positive' aspects of race, especially in Africa. In the ideology of Négritude, in particular, which was classified as a case of 'racial' nationalism, we find expressions of a race consciousness that has preceded and fuelled the nationalist revival, and beyond that promoted conditions necessary for modernisation and development.

In dwelling on the so-called 'positive' aspects of race, I do not for a moment deny the 'negative' consequences. Colour, which on one level is simply an indicator of 'race' and a term for a syndrome of physical traits, has always served to distinguish, divide and exclude. In the competition for scarce resources, especially in modern cities, distinctions of colour can identify groups that it is desired to exclude or relegate much more easily and unequivocally than language or religion. But not only does it define the outsider; it also imprisons men within a despised category, and becomes a badge of discrimination. Colour can also in itself distance groups from each other. It inculcates a fear of the unknown and unpredictable. It suggests a set of roles whose features are unfamiliar, and whose expectations are inherently unknowable. By grouping together large numbers of depersonalised individuals, it stimulates exaggerated and groundless fears which identify and create an 'anti-type' of corruption and malice. Such for example was the horror of the 'Yellow Peril' in the late nineteenth and early twentieth century.[58] Here we watch the effects of the modern equation of power, numbers and colour, which turns on the capacity for categories like 'colour' to mass together immense numbers of dehumanised, and later demonised, individuals and conceive of them as a malignant force. Colour, of course, is by no means the only physical syndrome that can be utilised for this purpose; the Nazis' Nuremberg Laws alleged distinct blood groupings and physique to identify a 'Jewish' *Gegentypus* and to promote the dehumanisation and demonisation of the Jew.[59] But colour, despite passing and miscegenation, has proved the most salient, general and definite syndrome with which to categorise, mass and hierarchise vast numbers of men and women, and thereby to deprive them of their individuality and humanity. Moreover, the traditional associations of colours, especially of white and black, to signify good and evil, desirable and undesirable qualities, have immeasurably enhanced the role of colour as mankind's chief differentiator today.[60]

While the 'negative' aspects of race and colour have been frequently described and analysed, and their association with an earlier, preparatory nationalism assumed or more rarely documented, the 'positive' role of colour has received much less attention, at least until the advent of Black Power and the cult of ethnic roots.[61] In fact, there are cases where race or colour consciousness has preceded the rise of nationalism and the processes of 'nation-building'. Probably the best documented example is the pan-African movement, which shows how race consciousness can 'prepare' a so-called 'progressive' nationalism and provide the motivation for modernisation in Africa.

In the absence of many cultural attributes of community, colour can serve three main collective functions: it can define and identify the group; mobilise and unite its members; and help to revive a lost national identity. All three appear, under present world conditions, to be prerequisites for any self-generated and self-sustaining programme of scientific modernisation or economic development, since together they ensure a minimum of group cohesion and dignity for the African 'colour nationalisms'.

The first of these functions, that of group definition, is simply the converse of colour's distantiating role. Just as colour can point up dissimilarity and distance, so it may also reveal similarity and proximity. Just as those who do not share the colour sign are the 'unknown' and 'unidentified', so those who do become the 'known' and 'identified'. Between those who know and can identify each other, there can be no role uncertainty, no ambiguous expectations. On the contrary: they are members of the 'family' whose tastes, attitudes and perceptions one can expect to share. In this respect, then, colour provides a sign of similarity and identity.

Second, colour helps to dissolve local fragmentation and to unify the identified and defined. This is particularly apparent where group conflicts polarise members of different colour communities. The need for self-defence, for organisation and leadership, in the face of threat or attack inspires a desire for some rationale for the community, some set of justifications and explanations for their need to unite and mobilise. Where discrimination is intense, colour can provide a rationale that cuts across smaller, local ethnic communities, as for example in South Africa. And because colour tends to categorise large numbers, it can inspire feelings of strength through unity and mobilisation, as with an army on the move, abolishing traditional local units and values.

Finally, colour can revive a 'lost' or threatened identity, or indeed help provide a new identity, in two ways. First, it can boost morale through the sight of vast numbers of chromatically similar human beings united in purposive activity. Their very mobilisation, as all movements have discovered, inspires confidence. But more importantly, colour can be utilised to achieve a movement for 'status reversal'. Where before 'black' had signified for everyone all that was vile and corrupt, now the reverse is true: black is pure, black is noble, black is beautiful. All that is required to achieve this reversal of perceptions and attitudes is an act of purification; by purifying the group of all the foreign ways and customs and appearances, which had obscured the community's true nature and genuine blood, a new liberated man will arise to challenge and overcome his oppressors, and 'realise' his specific excellence and identity.

In all these ways, 'racial' or colour nationalisms in Africa conform to the universal logic of all nationalist movements, with their essential mechanism of 'power through purification'. The only difference from the more straightforward cases of ethnic nationalism is that, whereas the latter utilise history, language and religion to purify and discover the community's identity and inner power, African 'racial' nationalisms must start out from physical forms and pigmentation, and invest these with moral and aesthetic meanings. Where, as in Africa, languages and religions are many, and history hard to recover, race and colour become the sources of inner purity and strength, and the cultivation of correct feelings and perceptions about colour the only road to self-realisation and power.

Already in the 1860s Africanus Horton and Edward Blyden drew attention to the need for racial pride and self-respect. One source of their interest in race was to rebut the racist theories then current which placed the Negro midway between the European and the ape. Horton called on his anatomical knowledge to prove that, in brain capacity, height, skeletal weight and thickness of bones, the Negro was the equal of the white man.[62] He went on to maintain that the 'Negro race' would 'in course of time, take its proper stand in the world's history', and to point to the Russians as an example of how a people, through contact and good government, might leap in a century into civilisation.[63] There was also the familiar attempt to derive European science and literature from Africa, to list a gallery of 'great Africans' and to show that all nations must have their moment of prominence, once self-government is granted.[64]

An even more important forerunner of pan-Africanism's racial or colour nationalism is the idea of 'racial integrity' propounded by the West Indian Edward Blyden in the later nineteenth century. Already, as a teacher and minister in Liberia in the 1860s, Blyden was urging educated Africans to 'cultivate pride of race. . . . We must have faith in the Negro race,' he declared, adding:

There is something within us, a God-given principle, ever whispering to us the lessons of self-government, and telling us of our sublime origin and high destiny; and during all that dark and dismal might of oppression, and unnumbered woes, that principle remained uncrushed, retained its vital activity; and this day every Negro, on every plantation, in every humble cabin hears its secret whispers. Surely we Liberians should hear and harken to it. If any man, who has lived in Liberia two years, cannot come to believe in the ability of the Negro race, under favourable circumstances, to maintain an organised, regular and adequate government, that man has mistaken his country. . . .[65]

After he had fled to Sierra Leone in 1871, Blyden began to speak for all West Africans in racial terms, preaching race segregation and biological purity and insisting on Africa's special contribution to world history.[66] Citing the Slavs, Germans, Italians and Greeks as European 'races' 'striving to group themselves according to their natural affinities', Blyden argued that 'there is no people in whom the desire for race integrity and race preservation is stronger than in the Negro':

Argument may be necessary [he wrote] in discussing the methods or course of procedure for the preservation of race integrity, and for the development of race efficiency, but no argument is needed as to the necessity of such preservation and development. If a man does not feel it – if it does not rise up with spontaneous and inspiring power in his heart – then he has neither part nor lot in it. The man who needs conviction on this subject, had much better be left unconvinced.[67]

To the end, Blyden preached love of race as a religious duty. In a lecture of 1893, in Freetown, Blyden adapted Herder's belief in diversity as a divine institution to the African scene, and declared:

But the duty of every man, of every race is to contend for its individuality – to keep and develop it. Never mind the teachings of those who tell you to abandon that which you cannot abandon. If their theory were carried out, it would, with all the reckless cruelty of mere theory, blot out all the varieties of mankind, destroy all differences, sacrifice nationalities and reduce the human race to the formless protoplasm from which we are told we came.
 Therefore, honour and love your Race. Be yourselves, as God intended you to be or he would not have made you

thus. We cannot improve upon his plan. If you are not yourself, if you surrender your personality, you have nothing left to give the world. You have no pleasure, no use, nothing which will attract and charm men, for by suppression of your individuality you lose your distinctive character.[68]

Even these short extracts show that Blyden's defensive African ethnocentrism does not really distinguish between race and nationality, and that the element of colour provided Blyden and his followers with a symbol of identity and group definition.[69] Heavily influenced by his personal dislike of mulattos and by current theories that attributed cultural diversity to the 'influence of race and climate', Blyden opposed the spirituality and fraternity of pure, traditional Africans to the highly materialistic, urban and wealthy civilisation of the West.[70] The African's sympathetic harmony with nature and communion with God pointed to the probability that

Africa may yet prove to be the spiritual conservatory of the world. . . . When the civilised nations, in consequence of their wonderful material development, shall have had their spiritual perceptions darkened and their spiritual susceptibilities blunted through the agency of a captivating and absorbing materialism, it may be that they have to resort to Africa to recover some of the simple elements of faith.[71]

For all his insight into the regenerative power of colour in creating a national identity, Blyden remained essentially conservative and defensive. It was Casely-Hayford who, during the First World War, pointed to the unifying and mobilising force of colour. In his book on the West African prophet Harris, Hayford concentrated on the charismatic appeal and mass following of an itinerant preacher,[72] and in his autobiographical novel *Ethiopia Unbound* (1911), Hayford extended Blyden's ideas of race development, by calling on European-educated Africans to represent the traditional African and his values.[73] Hayford also appreciated Garvey's mass 'Back-to-Africa' solution to the problems of American Blacks, while deploring his violent methods. Yet it was only after 1945 that the populist aspect of colour could emerge successfully.

From the late nineteenth century, the nascent racial nationalism of pan-Africanism had been fed by a wider, and more overtly colour-conscious pan-Negroism espoused in the West Indies and America.[74] The New World added a more agonised tone, and an aesthetic component. Reacting to the humiliations of slavery and Southern race prejudice, American ministers like Crummell and Bishop Turner poured scorn on white and assimilationist attempts to forget or decry Negro racial unity or equality, in the teeth of an enveloping white racism. 'The only place I know of in this land where you can "forget you are colored" is the grave!' cried Crummell,[75] while Turner's controversial assertion that 'God was a Negro' foreshadowed Garvey's and the Black Muslims' rejection of white American society.[76]

The aesthetic note is struck by John Edward Bruce's declaration of 1902 that 'I am a Negro and all Negro. I am black all over, and proud of my beautiful black skin.'[77] Du Bois struck the same note when he showed how Blacks laugh at themselves and fear to see themselves as the white world has caricatured them. 'Let us train ourselves to see beauty in black', he urged;[78] and in his essay on the 'Criteria of Negro Art', he claimed that the Negro people can contribute new varieties of beauty in a world of ugliness, because

we have within us as a race new stirrings; stirrings of the beginning of a new appreciation of joy; of a new desire to create, of a new will to be; as though in this morning of group life we had awakened from some sleep that at once dimly mourns the past and dreams a splendid future; and there has come the conviction that the Youth that is here today, the Negro Youth, is a different kind of Youth, because in some ways it bears this mighty prophecy on its breast, with a new realisation of itself, with new determination for all mankind.[79]

That note is found again in Langston Hughes' poetry:

I am a Negro;
Black as the night is black,
Black like the depths of my Africa.[80]

Black
As the gentle night,
Black as the kind and quiet night,
Black as the deep and productive earth. . . .
      . . . .
Beautiful as the black night. . . .
Black out of Africa,
Me and my song.[81]

In the French school of Négritude, centred on *Présence Africaine*, it becomes even more central. Senghor reverses the white standards when he writes:

Woman nude, woman black
Clad in your colour which is life. . . . .
Your beauty strikes me to the heart
As lightning strikes the eagle.[82]

So does Césaire, in his seminal *Cahier d'un Retour au Pays Natale* (1939):

Mercy! mercy for our omniscient, naive conquerors.
Hurray for those who never invented anything,
hurray for those who never explored anything,
hurray for those who never conquered anything,
hurray for joy
hurray for love
hurray for the pain of incarnate tears.[83]

And the Guyanan poet Leon Dalmas brings together both moral and aesthetic elements when he asks to have his 'black dolls' back, so as

to feel myself myself
a new self from the one I was yesterday. . . .[84]

The origins of the Négritude movement revealed another facet of racial nationalism; its interest in ethnology and African tradition. It was fed by two sources: the primitivism of the Harlem

New Negro Movement of the 1920s, with its rediscovery of the
African cultural heritage, and the rural romanticism and exoticism
of the Haitian Jean Price-Mars, which appealed to African and
West Indian students and intellectuals in Paris who felt alienated
from their traditions and repelled by western modernity.[85] Irrationalism and romanticism, as Immanuel Geiss points out, brought
some of the formulations of Senghor and Césaire in the early
1930s closer to surrealism and even national socialist anti-intellec-
tualism.[86] Their literary conception of Négritude was, nevertheless,
much more ambivalent. It glorified the African landscape, extolled
African culture and the black woman, and rejected the capitalism
and rationalism of western civilisation; yet it also embraced the
West's humanism, its socialism and its cultural pluralism.[87] What
Négritude announced was the revolt against racial colonialism,
which had taken advantage of an 'indelible peculiarity, the more
or less dark colour of our skin', as Price-Mars put in 1956.
Now, he continued,

> by a magnificent reversal of the things of the world and
> a supreme revenge of the spirit, it is this distinctive sign
> which we rely upon in the twentieth century to confirm, exalt
> and glorify the culture of the Negro peoples.[88]

Indeed, *Black Orpheus* proclaimed Négritude as standing for 'the
new consciousness of the Negro, for his newly-gained self-confidence, and for his distinctive outlook on life, with which he
distinguished himself from non-Negroes'.[89] So that, as Geiss puts
it, 'The quintessence of Négritude is the unlimited positive evalua-
tion given to the fact of being Black – in the New World as
in Africa.'[90]

But, to value blackness is also to exchange derision and slavery
for freedom and dignity; to discover one's brothers through a
common lot of colonial oppression and prejudice; to find strength
through uniting with them; and finally to purify oneself and
realise a personal identity through the newly liberated community.

Hence to conclude that 'the lyrical pan-Africanism of Senghor
and Césaire turns out to be just a new way of compensating
psychologically for the inferiority complex induced by historical
experience' underestimates the social and ideological functions
of colour nationalisms.[91] For all their vaguenesses and hesitations

over goals and criteria, both pan-Africanism and pan-Negroism can only be understood as ideologies of mobilisation and attempted modernisation of some of the politically weakest areas of the world. For centuries, white westerners defined that powerlessness in colour terms. Today colour nationalisms accept the group definition of dependency, but challenge its legitimacy in order to try to reverse the situation. Of itself, such a reversal cannot induce the scientific and technological leap into the twentieth century that we call 'modernisation'. But it constitutes an essential prerequisite. For without a sense of collective dignity and self-esteem, black élites cannot inspire the sacrifices necessary for growth and modernisation, or bridge the gulf that separates them from their peasant compatriots. Only through a myth of 'We are all Africans', and an ideology of Négritude, could a sufficient unity be forged to overcome the dangers of 'balkanisation' that seem to threaten the perpetuation of political dependence and economic underdevelopment.[92]

Unfortunately, the evidence suggests that, even in these indirect terms, colour nationalisms have not proved as successful as their proponents had hoped. Pan-Africanism has not really reduced the social distance and cultural gulf separating the western-educated élites from their rural population.[93] For an ideology of group identification, that would constitute a more serious failing. And yet, the failure may well be only partial. For pan-Africanism and pan-Negroism have managed to identify a horizontal stratum, an Afro-American élite spanning three continents, and to implant the ambition and tasks of leadership. They have provided this élite with an arena and programme for their talents and education, and have created a measure of unity of purpose among the élites of politically least-favoured areas. That in itself is no mean achievement. As a 'transnational nationalism', pan-Africanism underpins their fragmented nationalisms and helps African and West Indian nationalists to concert efforts on some global issues.[94] Hence it has been instrumental in presenting the West with a challenge and claim for the redistribution of global powers and resources, at present so heavily concentrated in a few key centres. Though it has not achieved the political unity or mass consciousness that Nkrumah expected, pan-Africanism remains an essential component of the several 'state' nationalisms of Black Africa, and a justification for future exertions and sacrifices.[95]

Hence, although race and racism generally undermine the nation and nationalism, there are circumstances in which a blend of racial consciousness with national ideals is the sole means for advancing the nationalist cause. In the African case, colour has given that nationalism both form and life. Formally and aesthetically, colour has played the same role as language did in the German or east European nationalist movements. And as they rediscovered their own worth and originality in the beauty and distinctiveness of their languages, so did the Africans recover their dignity in the beauty of their colour and the nobility of their physique. It became just as much a source of joy and pride for them as had the Czech or Greek languages become for those who rediscovered them, and in both cases it was the special and peculiar, the original and unique characteristics of these group attributes that excited and attracted their devotees.[96] And just as the despised vernaculars triumphed over the (French) courtly *lingua franca* of the cosmopolitan European aristocracy, so now a highly pigmented skin, that badge of scorn and shame, became an object of pride and delight, and its oppressed and lowly carrier the repository of everything that was true and noble.[97]

But colour has become something more than a vehicle of beauty and artistic experience. It has become the 'lifeblood' of African nationalisms exactly because it symbolises and sums up the whole history of Black Africans, in a way that detailed chronicles of the rise and fall of African states and empires could never convey. In a sense, colour substitutes for history, as it does for language, not because Africa has little known history (despite Cheikh Anta Diop's researches), but because that history barely touches on the central African and Negro experience of slavery, prejudice and exploitation.[98] The pre-colonial history of Africa may be more or less important, more or less shadowy; the fact remains that it is no longer part of an African consciousness which has been shaped by the radical trauma of colonialism and the slave trade. It is infinitely harder for Africans to reach back to a golden era before the night of their oppression than for Jews to recall the Davidic kingdom before their days of wandering and martyrdom; for the Jew or the Arab, the Bible and Koran, the very prayer-book and customs, enshrine sacred memories of the glorious epoch of independence.[99] Besides, it is skin-colour and physique that have defined the relevant histories to be researched, those of Egypt, Ethiopia, Ghana, Mali, Songhai and Zimbabwe in particular. And as with all nationalisms, the purpose behind that research is always moral and didactic: to inspire in Africans feelings of solidarity and confidence, and in Europeans a healthy respect, for the African contribution to world history and progress, and thus to give the lie to European, white slanders on the black race. African history, therefore, is the history of the black race, and is only meaningful in terms of the unity and dignity of that race.[100]

In this respect, also, pan-African colour nationalism is simply a variant of nationalism, and not a species of racism and racial Darwinism. Although its racial consciousness could easily tip over into a more embittered nationalist racism, pan-Africanism has been almost wholly an ideology of race in the service of nationalism, utilising colour as the means for evoking and recreating a collective national identity.[101] Despite the many temptations towards racism offered by European theories and denigration, the racial element at the core of pan-Africanism is inseparable from the national goals and ideals that it serves and fuels, much as the engine does a car. Whereas nationalist racisms utilise the feelings of nationhood and national identity for racist ends of domination and exclusiveness, of eugenics and segregation, and for the creation of a racial élite as the ruling biological caste to be defended against inferior races, the racial nationalism of pan-Africanism utilises colour to promote citizen autonomy, territorial cohesion and historic identity among all Africans, or even among all people of African descent. Where a long, recorded and relevant history is lacking, where languages are so many or imposed from outside, where religions have become so mixed in their elements, colour and race can boost morale, inspire activity, engender solidarity and help to create a national identity by restoring their dignity and beauty to those who had lived without either for so long.

CHAPTER 5

Communist Nationalisms

It is of course true of every nation that insistence upon nationality is now to be found only among the bourgeoisie and their writers.

Marx and Engels, *German Ideology*, p. 518.

In proportion as modern economic development has proceeded, there has grown a need for all who spoke the same language to be joined together in a common state.

Karl Kautsky, 'Die Moderne Nationalitat', *Neue Zeitung* V,
1887, pp. 402–5.

Of all the ideologies associated with the crises of modernisation, none has proved a sharper critic or stronger rival of nationalism than Marxism. Yet in recent years, no ideology has been so closely intertwined with this same nationalism. In preWar Europe, Marxist-inspired movements vociferously denounced 'antiquated national prejudices', even if in moments of war-fever they reluctantly made their peace with them.[1] In the Third World countries of the postWar era, however, self-styled Marxist movements have often supported the national bourgeois revolution and have betrayed in their midst that 'insistence upon nationality' that the founders of scientific socialism assigned to their bourgeois enemies alone.

We are in fact witnessing a proliferation of Marxist nationalisms and highly nationalist Marxisms which, on the face of it, appear to confound the disparate visions and principles of both nationalism and Marxism. Whether the result be labelled 'socialist nationalism' or 'national communism', there is no doubt that this fusion of Marxism with an emotionally charged anti-colonial or anti-fascist nationalism has generated considerable social enthusiasm and achieved a wide diffusion. In China, Yugoslavia, Vietnam, Algeria, Cuba, Angola, Mozambique and Somalia, this synthesis has produced a powerful and largely indigenous movement able to defeat rivals and take, and hold, power, despite the fact that the sources and theories of the two component ideologies are radically distinct, and despite the temptation offered by alliances with rival great powers to dissolve this unique fusion.

In view of the wide appeal of this 'Marxist nationalism', it becomes important to understand the bases of the fusion between two rival 'salvation movements' of modernisation. This will also enable us to grasp some of the tensions inherent in the symbiosis. We shall examine first the ideological parallelisms and convergences between Marxism and nationalism, which permit such a fusion. Thereafter it will be necessary to expose the social and political conditions that foster so explosive and distinctive a movement. Only then can we determine how genuine and lasting such a synthesis can be, or how fraught with contradictions.

IDEOLOGICAL CONVERGENCE

Modes of alienation

Secular belief-systems or ideologies exhibit an underlying formal structure, comprising:

(1) a social and political analysis of current dilemmas and problems, embodied in a model of existing social structures;

(2) a set of ideals and goals for which all must strive, with a utopian sketch of the future 'golden age';

(3) an analysis of the mechanisms of transition from distorted present structures to the 'true and natural' state of affairs of the utopian vision, together with prescriptions for action to hasten the transition.

Nationalism and Marxism both possess elaborate variants of all three components of this underlying pattern: a model of the distortions of current social structures, a vision of the golden age to come, and an analysis of the route to be taken to get there. The nationalist variant tends to be simpler and vaguer in some respects, but it can be shown to share some important features with the Marxist versions, which provide common ground for the present interpenetration of the two ideologies.

To begin with, nationalism, like Marxism, divides all history into three epochs: that of 'prehistory', including the present; that of the revolutionary transition; and the epoch of 'history' proper. In other words, there is a general concordance in their attitudes to history and time. Both are 'linear' conceptions of history, and both have a myth of a final concluding era of justice and freedom.

In the second place, both ideologies agree in identifying the immediate and current enemy as the most oppressive, the present structures as the most alienating. Of course, oppression and alienation have haunted man from the dawn of 'prehistory'; but it is only today, in the last two centuries, that the real nature of tyranny and exploitation have been revealed, because only now have they become universal and unrestrained. For nationalism the tyrant is 'imperialism', the alien coloniser, the invading enemy, the predatory stranger; for Marxism the bourgeois capitalist embodies all the evils of an exploitative economic system. In his train, the imperialist has brought drab uniformity and servile regimentation of body and soul; similarly, capitalism inevitably entails slavery and alienation of the worker: thus

> all means for the development of production transform themselves into means of domination over and exploitation of the producers; they mutilate the labourer into a fragment of a man, degrade him to the level of an appendage of a machine, destroy every remnant of charm in his work and turn it into a hated toil. . . .[2]

Both ideologies present existing social and political structures as polarised around conflicting interests and values; on the one hand, the occupying or threatening alien and his collaborators locked in battle with the freedom-fighters of an oppressed nationality; on the other hand, the class conflict of propertied capitalists and propertyless proletarians. In between the elect and their oppressors there is no room for intermediate strata, the passive spectator or the collaborator.

Apart from these outward, open enemies, nationalism and Marxism define also an inner, hidden corruption. For the nationalist, it is decay and degradation that dissolve the bonds uniting the members of a collectivity; so that, as Banerjea remarked, moral regeneration by the study of history and language becomes 'the last consolation left to a fallen and degraded people'.[3] The enemy within is loss of identity, self-oblivion, the end of authenticity, which erodes and corrupts the community, dividing and weakening the members and tempting them into cultural imitation and political dependence. It is not necessary to endure physical occupation by outsiders to excite a 'renewal' nationalism; in Meiji Japan and Revolutionary France, the external enemy was a catalyst and rival beyond the seas, but the real enemy was felt as an inner decay, a loss of purpose and identity which allowed a corrupt tyranny of the few to stifle the authentic expression and liberties of the many within the community itself.[4]

Whereas class, regionalism, ethnic heterogeneity, dynastic allegiance or confessional difference can all undermine the original solidarity of the community in the eyes of the nationalist, for the Marxist the origin of internal oppressions must be traced back to the division of labour. For the division of labour first allowed a surplus to be produced, which could in turn be expropriated by a ruling class. In doing so, the rulers based their oppression upon the defence of property and privilege, which became the basis of all subsequent class systems and hence of political power. Thus Marx and Engels assert that

> The various stages of development in the division of labour are just so many different forms of ownership; [and that] With the division of labour, . . . is given simultaneously the distribution, and indeed the unequal distribution (both quantitative and qualitative), of labour and its products, hence property.[5]

With regard to the effects, too, of this dual distortion, Marxism and nationalism reveal some striking parallelisms. Both deal with different aspects of a general alienation and estrangement, in surprisingly similar terms. Exile is the ultimate in degradation for a nationalist, but there is also an inner exile which can be felt in one's 'own land', as with many a black nationalist in his American homeland. This psychological self-estrangement can be found in the literature of Négritude, and is finely caught in McKay's celebrated lines in his poem, *Outcast*:

I would go back to darkness and to peace.
But the great western world holds me in fee,
And I may never hope for full release,
While to its alien gods I bend my knee.
Something in me is lost, forever lost,
Some vital thing has gone out of my heart,
And I must walk the way of life a ghost
Among the sons of earth, a thing apart.
For I was born, far from my native clime,
Under the white man's menace, out of time.[6]

Inner exile is also the theme of one of the most cogent statements
of the Zionist position, Pinsker's *Autoemancipation*. Here the Jews
are characterised as a 'ghost' people, a 'nation long since dead',
who nevertheless 'lived on spiritually as a nation', but are universally regarded as alien:

> We must recognise [argued Pinsker] that before the great
> idea of human brotherhood will unite all the peoples of the
> earth, millenniums must elapse; and that meanwhile a people
> which is at home everywhere and nowhere, must everywhere
> be regarded as alien.[7]

The degradation lies within. The outer oppression mirrors an
inner decay of the people, whether they be physical exiles or
second-class citizens in their own territory.

The Marxist, too, views alienation under a double aspect,
the concrete and the philosophical. Empirically, alienation is
the lot of the proletarian labourer in his work-situation. The
vast system of factory production, with its rigorous, impersonal
discipline and huge concentrations of labour, its repetitive, fragmented toil and lack of any relationship between the worker
and his product, inevitably breeds a profound discontent and
estrangement. Marx considers that the product of man's labour
'stands opposed to it as an alien thing, as a power independent
of the producer. ... It is the objectification of labour', so that
'The more the worker exerts himself, the more powerful becomes
the alien objective world which he fashions against himself, the
poorer he and his inner world become, the less there is that
belongs to him.'[8]

But beyond this concrete alienation of the workplace, there is also a more generalised alienation which includes every projection of man's thought and activity that becomes separated from and external to man, in which 'Actuality is not experienced as it is itself but as another actuality. Common experience is not subject to the law of its own spirit but to an alien spirit.'[9]

Money too is a form of alienation, something external to man. 'By externalising this mediating activity,' says Marx, 'man is active only as he is lost and dehumanised.'[10] And particularly under capitalism, man's activities are inevitably externalised as things or commodities, which enslave man and estrange him from himself.

For Marx, following Feuerbach, had a vision of man's essence, of his 'species-being', which alienation had perverted, in much the same way as the nationalist carried with him an image of the original true and undiluted community, the 'nation'. For Marx, man's own activity, his daily work, had become 'an alien, hostile, powerful object independent of him', which placed him 'under the domination, coercion and yoke of another man', the 'lord of labour'.[11] Man's 'spiritual nature' had been deformed and dehumanised. In similar vein, nationalists lament the loss of belonging and inner harmony of a submerged nation, which results not from alienated labour, but from a breakdown in continuity with the community's past. Where the 'link in the chain' has been broken, men become atomised, rootless, unfree. Their spiritual growth is stunted, their psychic life fragmented. Men become self-estranged individuals in an alien ocean of assimilation leading to ultimate extinction, a defenceless prey to every conqueror and every passing fashion. The inner enemy of identity-less decay has prepared the ground for external enslavement and corroded the will to dignity and freedom.[12]

Mechanisms of the transition

How can man break out of this state of dependence and alienation? That he can do so is never in doubt for either Marxists or nationalists. Both believe optimistically in the justice of the historical dispensation, regarding man's emancipation as a historic necessity. Both claim to know the laws of social evolution. The

nationalist charts the inevitable growth of national consciousness
within his community, which will shake off the members' long
slumber and recreate the nation. The transition from homelessness
to nationhood is a process of self-discovery and self-realisation.
This is the mission of every community. Mazzini was quite
convinced that 'no peoples ever die, nor stop short upon their
path, before they have achieved the ultimate historical aim of
their existence, before having completed and fulfilled their mission'.[13] The Italians possessed such a historic mission and 'a
collective idea to be developed'; they therefore required a unitary
state. Mazzini never doubted that 'A people destined to achieve
great things for the welfare of humanity must one day or other
be constituted a nation. And slowly, from epoch to epoch, our
people has advanced towards that aim.'[14] All obstacles, he declared,
will be overcome by the rising of the people, by the actions
of the secret societies, by 'the blood shed by the martyrs of
every province of Italy'. Evolution will be hastened by revolution,
the gradual awakening by education in national history, the
progress of Italy's innate destiny by the people's desires and
their democratic instincts.

Mazzini's views are representative of nationalism's judicious
blend of an evolutionist doctrine with an activist ethic. The
transition to nationhood is inevitable in the long run; yet it
requires the mobilisation and active participation of the people
in the national movement. A national awakening involves inward
purification. Foreign cultural influence must be swept away, to
allow the rediscovery of a genuine communal identity. Education
and propaganda will make members conscious of their submerged
identity and restore their fragmented solidarity. The link in the
chain must be forged anew, and the people's virtues revealed
in their past must be reconquered. That was the task Douglas
Hyde set before his audience in the National Literary Society
of Dublin in 1892:

> We have at last broken the continuity of Irish life, and just
> at the moment when the Celtic race is presumably about
> to largely recover possession of its own country, it finds itself
> deprived and stripped of its Celtic characteristics, cut off from
> the past, yet scarcely in touch with the present. . . .
> Just when we should be starting to build up anew the

Irish race and the Gaelic nation – as within our own recollection Greece has been built up anew – we find ourselves despoiled of the bricks of nationality. The old bricks that lasted eighteen hundred years are destroyed; we must now set to, to bake new ones, if we can, on other ground, and of other clay. . . .

In a word, we must strive to cultivate everything that is most racial, most smacking of the soil, most Gaelic, most Irish, because in spite of the little admixture of Saxon blood in the north-east corner, this island is and will ever remain Celtic at the core.[15]

Of course, Sinn Fein like other nationalisms was not content with educational propaganda; it was quite prepared to wage the struggle through violence, if need be. In fact, war has frequently been invoked by nationalists as a solvent of odious tyranny and corruption – by Fichte against the Napoleonic invader, by Ataturk against the Greeks, by Mao against the Japanese. A national war of liberation can not only hasten the inevitable transition to nationhood; it, and it alone, can forge a really unified and self-conscious nation after independence has been won.[16]

A similar fusion of evolutionary historicism and militant struggle runs through Marxist formulations and movements. For Marx, the motor of all social development lies in the periodic contradictions between the 'forces' of human production and the 'relations' of class and property within which such production is carried on. There is always a lack of synchronous development between the forces and relations, as man's powers of organising and streamlining production through new techniques outstrips his social structures. With time, the resulting tension spills over into social revolution, as existing property and class structures are overthrown and replaced. Thus technological progress, resulting from the need to satisfy an ever-growing volume of human desires with scarce resources, must destroy capitalism:

The monopoly of capital becomes a fetter upon the mode of production which has sprung up and flourished along with and under it. Centralisation of the means of production and socialisation of labour at last reach a point where they become incompatible with their capitalist integument. This integument is burst asunder. The knell of capitalist private property sounds. The expropriators are expropriated. . . . But capitalist production begets, with the inexorability of a law of nature, its own negation. It is the negation of negation.[17]

Here as elsewhere Marx and his followers emphasised the inevitability of the 'natural laws of capitalist production', and of the 'material conditions' that shape our lives. Revolutions too require the maturation of these material conditions to be effective. Indeed, no movement of the proletariat can succeed until the material, productive conditions make such a revolution inevitable.[18]

And yet only man, only the proletariat, can effect the transition to socialism. Only the class that embodies alienation can dissolve his alienated condition and restore man to himself and to nature. Man is, after all, a self-conscious producer of both life and means to life. He is *homo faber*, and for socialist man 'the entire so-called world history is only the creation of man through human labour and the development of nature for man.'[19] Given the appropriate material conditions, creative man can transcend his limitations through action and revolution; by liberating society, man liberates and reintegrates himself. By breaking the 'fetters' of existing class systems, man overcomes his own self-alienation.

In practice, the very clarity of Marx's thought has sharpened the differences among Marxists between quietists and activists, between those who embraced a more evolutionary notion of history, like Bebel and Kautsky, and those like Lenin who emphasised man's revolutionary praxis and the actions of a vanguard élite. In this respect, nationalism's greater vagueness and inconsistency has served it better.

Communism and nationhood

At first sight, the differences between the nationalist and Marxist visions of the ideal new society appear too great to bridge. Yet, here too, there is considerable overlap and complementarity in their attitudes and images.

Since the division of labour is regarded by Marxists as the prime cause of social ills, its overcoming, and hence the transcendence of a society based upon property and class divisions, occupies the centre of a communist vision. Once men have ceased to be specialists, their actions will no longer alienate man from himself, from his fellow man or from nature. In a communist society, where

> nobody has an exclusive area of activity and each can train himself in any branch he chooses, society regulates the general production, making it possible for me to do one thing today and another tomorrow, to hunt in the morning, fish in the afternoon, breed cattle in the evening, criticize after dinner, just as I like, without ever becoming a hunter, a fisherman, a herdsman or a critic.[20]

In more philosophic vein, Marx describes communism as a process, as the

> positive overcoming of private property as human self-alienation, and thus as the actual appropriation of human essence through and for man; therefore as the complete and conscious restoration of man to himself within the total wealth of previous development, the restoration of man as a social, that is, human being. This communism as completed naturalism is humanism, as completed humanism is naturalism. It is the genuine resolution of the antagonism between man and nature and between man and man; it is the true resolution of the conflict between existence and essence, objectification and self-affirmation, freedom and necessity, individual and species. It is the riddle of history solved and knows itself as this solution.[21]

Only in a communist society, where the division of labour and man's enslavement to it have been overcome, does labour become 'not only a means of life but life's prime want'; and only in such an era of co-operative abundance can society 'inscribe on its banners: "From each according to his ability, to each according to his needs!"'.[22]

In depicting communism as a process of social reintegration and restoration to man's true 'species-life', Marxists approach some of the meanings with which a nationalist invests the concept of 'nationhood'. For it is only in a state of true nationhood that individual men can rediscover their authentic identity within the collectivity, and achieve fraternity and autonomy. Only in the nation can man find full freedom and harmony, and will the good of all rather than his own selfish ends. The nation is the only true entity; for Adam Müller the state embodies an 'intimate association of all physical and spiritual needs'; while the nation he regards as 'a great, energetic, infinitely active and living whole', which fuses all sectors of society into a seamless unity.[23]

Apart from its unity, nationalists single out a number of other vital features of the concept of nationhood. To begin with, a 'nation' is 'natural'. It is, like the family or language, part of the natural order, not manmade and contrived. Thus Rousseau declares: 'The Corsicans are still almost in the natural and healthy state', while Herder holds that national diversity is part of God's plan for nature and places the limited savage above the idle cosmopolite.[24] Second, the nation is seen as an exclusive cultural entity. Rousseau praises Moses, Numa and Lycurgus, the founders of their nations, because 'They all sought bonds that might attach the citizens to their fatherland and to each other, and they found them in particular usages, in religious ceremonies which by their nature were always exclusive and national. . . .'[25] Similarly, Burke held that England's unity and organic growth were assured by her peculiar constitution, history and traditions; together they nurtured a partnership 'between those who are living, those who are dead and those who are to be born'.[26] And Mazzini regarded the nation as

> the association of all men forming a single group through language, certain geographic conditions or the role assigned to them by history, recognising the same principle, conducting themselves under the rule of a uniform law and working for the accomplishment of the same aim. . . . Nationality is the role assigned by God to each people in the work of humanity; the mission and task it ought to fulfil on earth so that the divine purpose may be attained in the world.[27]

Third, individuals can realise their genuine freedom only through the nation. Through toil and sacrifice for the nation, man rediscovers his lost identity and attains autonomy in his actions. In this way, he transcends artifice and tyranny, egotism as well as oppression, the internal corruption and the external enemy.

Fourth, nations are self-sufficient. They embody a genuine life exactly because of their simplicity and self-containment, in which men pool their resources and labour in a rural community. Marx in fact echoes this agrarian idyll in *The German Ideology*; although in practice, like most nationalists, he embraced the ideal of autarchy through industrialisation. And finally, the nation is a territorial unit, marked by a strong sense of cohesion. Its self-sufficiency springs from its roots in the soil, from its compact location and its firm geopolitical anchorage. But over and above this geopolitical unity, the possession of a distinct and recognised territory signifies a social ideal: the striving for a practical solidarity within a given social space. For only when such a solidarity is attained can man be said to have 'returned' home from his inner exile.[28]

While there is no denying considerable differences in context and emphasis, Marxists and nationalists can be seen to share a concern for man's alienation and his reintegration and return to his authentic state of being. Both ideologies adhere throughout to a holistic, naturalistic and libertarian view of man and his destiny. Both are also profoundly historicist and evolutionary in their conceptions and outlook. History unfolds, by leaps and bounds, man's true species-nature, a nature that is human as it is social and collective, and social as it is human. Man can only 'find himself' in and through community. He can only make himself whole and reunite the fragments of his nature by becoming a truly social or collective being, by realising the communitarian essence of his being, and by living in harmony with his fellow men within a self-sufficient community. Similarly, to unite himself with nature, and be at one with his surroundings, man must shed all the accretions, distortions and corruptions that a self-seeking civilisation based upon greed and selfish advantage has inflicted upon him. It requires an act of revolutionary self-assertion and self-transcendence to break loose and rediscover an authentic existence. Freedom and autonomy consist in the realisation of authenticity, and authenticity in turn can be attained only within the community of equals.

Thus nationalism, like Marxism, places its golden age firmly in the future, and not in the past, as is sometimes asserted. The past serves the nationalist as a guide and model, even a measure against which to set the lamentable decay and shortcom-

ings of the present era. But it can never provide a blueprint
for the future. Even the most conservative of nationalists knows
in his heart that he is utilising the past and maintaining it
so that he can build a better future and a more stable one.
And on the other side, Marxists do not ignore the past. Does
not their evolutionary scheme set out from a postulated state
of primitive communism, one based on scarcity and low levels
of production and population? The question is how to incorporate
the social virtues of that state in a modern setting, how to
achieve the era of material abundance which will allow the
building of socialism. For socialism can only be built on the
foundations of the 'total wealth of previous development', and
as the culmination of earlier stages of human prehistory. Socialism
can only be built, Marx repeated, on the foundations of capitalism
and the achievements of the bourgeoisie. The communisation
of production, which had been man's earliest stage and his 'natural'
state before the division of labour, implied a return to this
naturalism but in a higher, more humanised form. The past,
therefore, had to be transcended, not denied.

SOCIAL ROOTS

Delayed development and power dependency

Both in their general structure and in their specific mechanisms,
Marxism and nationalism, for all their mutual antagonisms, display
considerable parallels and convergences. These meeting-points
clearly *permit* a doctrinal syncretism. Current social and political
conditions *propel* both ideologies towards a symbiosis.

Indeed, marxisant nationalisms and nationalist communisms
have now appeared on every continent. Some have been externally
imposed or encouraged; others, however – in Yugoslavia, China,
Vietnam, Cuba, Angola and Mozambique – are largely indigenous
movements, though even here outside help and the general world
situation have played a greater role than is sometimes thought.
Of course, these and the other instances of 'nationalist communism'
are extremely varied in their ideals and methods; they do not
conform to any particular brand of Marxism, be it that of

Marx/Engels, Lenin or Mao. Instead, they have all selected motifs and themes from the Marxist canon and adapted them to their local conditions, after mingling them with a heavy dose of their nationalism. Similarly, their nationalisms owe little to Rousseau's or Herder's or Mazzini's formulations; current nationalist brands have again been evolved to suit specific circumstances. But then, nationalism has always allowed more doctrinal latitude than Marxism, giving it something of an edge over its rival.

For all that, there is a definite family resemblance between the recent movements of left-nationalism, such that their slogans, goals and tactics have become fairly easily recognisable to outsiders, and with the result that they have been able to evolve an international language of discourse between themselves, despite barriers of culture and geography. How has this come about?

It has come about, in the first place, from their common perception of a prolonged and abnormal backwardness in their country or area. It is the prolonged nature of this underdevelopment rather than the condition as such that is one necessary cause of their turn towards a Marxist nationalism. Other Third World countries, like Kenya, Malaysia or Venezuela, also suffer from similar syndromes of underdevelopment; though they have not adopted a version of left-nationalism yet, they may yet do so, if they are to stimulate growth, force savings, mobilise energies and secure the necessary large-scale investment for infrastructural development. So far, their governments have been strong enough to arrest further decline into relative underdevelopment *vis-à-vis* more developed countries. In areas and states where the government has been too weak or divided to counteract stagnation and decline, there has been a leftward shift towards a socialist or communist nationalism. In these cases, the earlier orthodox–liberal or conservative nationalism failed; inefficiency, corruption and lethargy bred impatience and disillusion, especially among more westernised groups and encouraged the trend towards a more radical and effective version of nationalism. This indicates that Marxist-type nationalisms can be viewed as a simple function not of underdevelopment, but rather of the long-delayed development that insecure and divided government entails. Such prolonged delay reveals not merely the impotence of government, but also the continued dependency of the community. Far from independence having been won, as the nationalist founding fathers proclaimed so proudly, the inner corruption and inauthenticity, the real lack of autonomy, of the community have become blatant and undeniable. And the more dependent upon others the community appears, the more likelihood of a radical Marxist nationalism taking over the reins of power. The more peripheral and divided and neglected the area, the more chance for a Marxist nationalism to take root.

Hence the optimal general conditions of a successful Marxist nationalism are: a sense of delayed modernisation; perception of the community or area as peripheral in wealth and power; weak and ineffective government after independence; and finally an external intrusion, economic or military, actual or threatened. In general, Marxist nationalisms tend to be 'second-wave' nationalisms, riding to power on the backs of earlier dissipated independence movements, much as Mao's communists displaced the Kuomintang, and Castro's guerillas met the challenge posed by the 1933 revolution, which had been so long postponed.[29] The key to their success lies in the growth of a sense of externally manipulated underdevelopment, marginality and powerlessness, all of which only a Marxist reliance on communal labour, centralised planning and heavy industrialisation can overcome. Hence Marxist nationalisms are invoked as much for their state-building potentialities as for their promise of social development.[30]

Two types of 'power dependency' are particularly pertinent to the rise of Marxist nationalisms. The first is the familiar case of long-delayed independence, of a colonialism that has clung to its possessions too long, as did the Portuguese in Africa, or which sought to return to territories it had been temporarily forced to abandon, as with the French in Indochina. Here delayed development only serves to inflame the sense of degrading dependency at the strategic level, at the very moment when neighbouring liberated territories appear to have begun their developmental programmes. The second type of dependence situation can be equally humiliating. Here the country is nominally independent, but economically, and sometimes militarily, dependent upon neighbouring or distant powers. Thus Cubans throughout the twentieth century have felt the presence of the United States as an economic menace; Ethiopia has till recently resented its military dependence upon the same great power; while China before Mao's triumph felt humiliated and dependent upon a number of western powers,

even before the Japanese invasion. Furthermore, where internal
ethnic conflict is superimposed upon external threats or outright
invasion, as in Ethiopia or Yugoslavia, they create intractable
problems for liberal or military nationalisms, and only a Marxist
centralised solution appears to offer an escape from the humiliations of prolonged dependency and internal divisions.

The situation, therefore, that evokes a Marxist nationalism
is as much political as economic, and involves recourse both
to the mobilising potential of the Party and to the countervailing
power of the State. In these circumstances the attractions of
the Soviet model are apparent. The Soviet Union, as has often
been noted, is seen not simply as a source of development recipes,
but as a model of military, political and social development;
an engine for generating vast resources of will and energy through
efficient élite organisation allied to popular commitment, resources
that have made it in fact, and not just nominally, independent
of any rival power constellation. Soviet Marxism is viewed as
a method not for overcoming human self-alienation through conscious revolutionary labour, but for escaping a degrading state
of political and military dependency and achieving genuine parity
with the West.[31]

Even the socialist nationalisms that have opposed the Soviet
brand of communism reveal their essentially political motivation.
In the Middle East, for example, some regimes adopted an 'Arab
socialism', which equates the national struggle with a global
form of anti-imperialist 'class conflict', and with the mobilisation
of resources for communal modernisation. In both tasks, the
State and Party played a crucial role. Thus under Nasser's regime,
the Egyptian press, radio and school system were subordinated
to state control, and the state-supervised army and bureaucracy
were greatly expanded. Large sectors of the economy, including
many banks, industries and insurance companies, were nationalised
and Egyptianised.[32] Conversely, since 1970 relaxation of state
and party control has proceeded apace with the diminished interest
in 'Arab socialism' and the Soviet model. In Syria and Iraq,
on the other hand, party dominance by wings of the Ba'ath
has continued to entail state control of much of the economy
and a persistent interest in the Soviet organisational model.[33]

In Africa, too, a strongly *étatiste* left-wing nationalism has taken
root in some of the new states, starting with Guinea and Mali.

Single-party regimes have attempted to build strong state institutions especially in countries whose weak strategic position and prolonged dependency have been aggravated by severe problems of delayed development. Yet here, too, only some aspects of European Marxism have been selected. Notably absent is the cardinal Marxist concept of class struggle which Sékou Touré, for example, found irrelevant to the African scene.[34] Similarly, the European constructs of 'feudalism' and the 'dictatorship of the proletariat' mean little in a continent that knew neither vassalage nor the fief, and that so far has hardly begun to develop a large-scale proletariat. In Africa, 'tribalism' and the mobilisation of the peasantry must take the place of the European concepts, and they in turn must gain their meaning and force from the real division and overriding conflict today – that between colonisers or 'neo-colonialists' and the colonised. Hence with a few exceptions like Somalia, even the Soviet Union's organisational model is viewed with suspicion; 'socialist' nationalisms in Senegal, Tanzania and Algeria look elsewhere for their recipes and inspiration.[35]

Marxist nationalisms, then, arise in situations of prolonged dependency or disunity and aim to liberate the affected population from this situation as a prelude to confronting the problems of delayed development. Such Marxist regimes should not be confused with their European counterparts. Their interest in Marxism is neither philosophical nor primarily economic; what concerns the left-nationalists is Marxism's, or rather Leninism's, *étatisme* and its party apparatus, which alone appears able to incorporate a mobilised population into a stable and effective institutional framework in a backward country.[36] For only with such a political machine can a community hope to extricate itself from a situation of power dependency and economic stagnation or decline, a situation especially irksome to intellectuals and professionals.

Populism and the intellectuals

In 1882 Engels wrote to Karl Kautsky apropos of the issue of Polish independence:

It is historically impossible for a large people to discuss seriously any internal questions as long as its national independence is lacking. . . . An international movement of the proletariat is in general only possible between independent nations. . . . To get rid of national oppression is the basic condition of all free and healthy development. . . .[37]

Engels's declaration accurately foreshadows the views of the leadership in today's developing countries. There can be no question of a 'healthy and free development' until real independence has been won; not just political sovereignty, which turns out so often to be merely nominal, but fundamental economic and military autarchy. The attack on neo-colonialism and 'neo-imperialism' of the northern powers provides the justification for the 'polycentrism' of nationalist Marxisms as well as for the Marxism of radical nationalisms. For the paths to a socialist nation and a national communism are naturally manifold and various; just as there are many kinds and sources of dependency, so there are many types of 'liberation'. And no one movement can determine the route for the others, and no one regime can provide a universal model. Each must find its own liberation route, before it can contribute to a global social development.[38]

The people who feel the humiliations of backwardness and of political dependence most acutely are the intelligentsia, military and civilian. Indeed, the origins and success of Marxist nationalisms owe a great deal to the relative strength, position and divisions of the intelligentsia. In communities where native bourgeoisies and proletariats are very small and weak, middle-class leadership, which sprang up everywhere in the wake of colonial and imperial intrusion, passes naturally to intellectuals and professionals, especially to lawyers, doctors, teachers, journalists and technicians of every sort. It is these strata who spearheaded the nationalist revolt against the colonial power in the first place, and who stand to gain most from its success. Even during the campaign for independence, however, differences began to appear in the ranks of the intelligentsia, not just over campaign tactics, but over ideals and goals. The revolutionaries who espoused more militant methods became increasingly attracted to more collectivist concepts of nationhood and envisaged greater state control and central planning, to achieve autarchy more swiftly. Western or Soviet communist parties, agents and example, certainly played a part in radicalising indigenous nationalisms; but equally important was the course of the independence struggle itself. Thus Castro's guerillas in the mountains of the Sierra Maestra became more committed to wholesale communist goals as the only solution to the many deficiencies of their society, which revealed themselves during the struggle; hence they came to renounce their earlier social democratic and populist platform for a more thoroughgoing Marxist nationalism.[39] Indeed, guerilla wars have often been a potent mechanism for both national mobilisation and Marxist incorporation of the mobilised.[40]

The origins of such a transition to Marxist nationalism have to be sought in the first place, however, in the position of the intelligentsia itself. Generally speaking, that position is one of intense isolation. In a few cases, it is true, there was a fairly smooth and quick transfer of power from traditional authorities to the nationalist intelligentsia, which permitted an accommodation with tradition and the old authorities. Such was the case in Japan. More usually, however, no such accommodation is reached. The transfer of power is delayed, the intelligentsia is spurned, and the independence struggle, its base broadened, turns militant and sometimes violent. It is just because their claims to leadership are disdained that the westernised intelligentsia attempt to break out of their isolation through an alliance with 'the people'. They develop a populistic platform, which combines elements of popular values and traditions with radical programmes of social modernisation. They extol the virtues of the simple life, of the countryside and its mores, and of the peasant and his customs. They do so, however, not simply to ease their westernising consciences or to strengthen their political position, but also because they sense that native values and local numbers, if properly organised and galvanised, can offset that communal dependency and backwardness that they so deplore. Regimes like U Nu's Buddhist Marxism or Nyerere's Christian socialism aimed (and aim) to mobilise the peasant masses for the tasks of 'nation-building' and of social development and autarchy, utilising their own moral strength and native resources as a counter to Western wealth and technology. This is still very much in line with the maxim of ambivalent westernisers who would reject the West: 'Western arts, Eastern morality'. Descended from the romantic *narodnik*, such latter-day populist nationalists reject the urban and industrial life-style as part of their programme of escape from dependence upon the industrial powers. Their populism is born of their frustrated nationalism, and goes beyond the latter only in its militancy and its appeal to the peasantry, which it identifies with the real 'nation'. Straddling the two worlds of westernism and native tradition, but belonging to neither, the radicalised intelligentsia feel the need to 'return to the people', to serve the peasant masses in a more personal and ethical manner than a bureaucratic welfare colonialism could ever hope to do, and thus to escape their isolation.[41]

Populism may thus be regarded as the immediate social and emotional matrix of Marxist nationalisms in those countries where it has not been an external imposition. Even where, as in Cuba, Soviet Russia has provided massive aid and an organisational model, the Marxist–nationalist movement came to power on a wave of indigenous populism stemming from the persistent exclusion of the nationalist intelligentsia by local dictatorial cliques or colonialisms. In other cases, the failure of liberal or military nationalisms to unite the population against colonialisms or foreign invasion gave the Marxist–nationalists an opportunity to supplant them; this was the case in China, Yugoslavia and Angola. In yet other cases, the external presence was more distant, though quite as powerful. Thus the military regime in Ethiopia, which ousted Haile Selassie, became ever more dependent upon arms from the United States as its internal divisions and problems mounted. Failure to end the war on several fronts precipitated a pro-Soviet Marxist coup within the Dergue. But from its reactions to Soviet proposals of territorial federalism or dismemberment, the nationalism of even the Marxist wing of the Dergue is self-evident; its refusal to treat with Eritrean Marxist separatists or Somali claims show how much the regime's Marxism is a function of its political and military humiliations.

Cuba's Marxism, too, sprang initially out of a sense of dependence upon United States economic interests coupled with corrupt local regimes. The nationalist intelligentsia was excluded after the 1933 revolution and the 1940 social democrat constitution was largely shelved even before Batista's assumption of personal power. At the beginning of his career, Castro's goals and attitudes were mainly social democratic and populist, as his trial defence speech after his abortive attack on the Moncada barracks in 1953 revealed. It was only during his guerilla campaign in the

Oriente province that his populism hardened into a Marxist nationalism, which saw in United States landholding and commercial interests the foundation of Cuba's longstanding political dependency and social stagnation.[42] It was the corruption and nationalist failure of the nominally independent local leadership that gave Castroism its opportunity.[43]

The link that populism furnishes between communism and nationalism is demonstrated with great clarity by the Chinese movement. Indeed, Mao laid down that 'In the final analysis, a national struggle is a question of class struggle'; but his understanding of the latter was distinctly non-European. Thus, after its failure in 1927, his party was quite ready to jettison its urban proletarian base in exchange for a far broader and deeper base among the xenophobic peasantry. To begin with, the Communists adopted a standard populist platform, and appealed for land reform in south and central China. But this still failed to unite all the peasants or prevent the encirclement of the reformed areas by Kuomintang forces. Only after 1934, and especially after the Japanese invasion of 1937, did the Communists find in the national issue a unifying force which would mobilise the peasants of the north-west and allow their incorporation within the communist organisational framework.[44] Since that time, a strong emphasis upon Chinese territorial integrity and Chinese identity has remained a powerful component of both Maoism and the Chinese Party.

The same sequence from populism to nationalism was to be found in other socialist and Marxist movements, such as Algeria and Vietnam, where a broad nationalist hatred of the exploiting alien overrode differences within the peasantry and between them and the urban strata. Even within Europe, populism has furnished a strong impetus towards communist nationalisms. This is well illustrated by the Yugoslav case, where, ever since its formation in 1919, the Communist Party had a particularly strong following in backward Montenegro and Macedonia, and among the non-Serb nationalities who resisted King Alexander's Serbian-dominated dictatorship.[45] However, it was not until the Nazi invasion in 1941 that Tito's Communists could find a unifying platform that could check the centrifugal tendencies of ethnic separatism. Tito appealed to workers and peasants of every ethnic group to work for a pan-Yugoslav 'federal' nation-state. Social and economic reforms after 1945, stemming in part from the partisan guerilla experience of the War, have gone hand in hand with a 'Yugoslavism' which respects the distinct character and territory of its seven constituent nationalities. Cement for this blend of state centralism with cultural federalism has been the strategic vulnerability of Yugoslavia and its ideological differences with the Soviet Union. As the Communists became more strongly identified with national resistance, first to German nazism, then to Russian communism, and as Tito adopted a foreign policy of positive national non-alignment, so again the early populism of the Communists has hardened into a Marxist pan-Yugoslav nationalism. For the latter is increasingly viewed as the only means of escaping political and military dependence resulting from internal separatist divisions and social stagnation.[46]

If populist–communist movements have profited from the weakness and inefficiencies of earlier nationalist regimes, they have also had to acknowledge the continuing force of nationalist sentiments. Indeed, it is possible to maintain that only when they have realised this need by waging a 'people's war', did they become a real force in the land. For the only way to defeat a numerically and technically superior invading power was through the political mobilisation of the xenophobic peasantry. The Marxist–Leninist emphasis upon the proletarian class struggle has given way, accordingly, to Mao's doctrine of the 'mass line', of 'integrating the efforts of the leadership and the masses', in a people's war conducted through guerilla tactics in the countryside and supported by peasants won over through the appeal to nationalism.[47] It is a strategy that not only Mao, but Tito, Ho Chi Minh and Castro have adopted, one in which even the social problems of the peasants themselves have been reinterpreted and subordinated to their sense of a national grievance against the exploiting alien.[48] The solution to the national ills proffered by communist nationalisms is the creation of a strong, centralised state based on adequate resources, including the active participation of enthusiastic 'broad masses' under party tutelage. In this way, communist nationalisms inevitably lose much of their original classical Marxist inspiration through their adoption of a populist nationalism which can unite the intelligentsia with its peasantry.

CURRENT RELATIONSHIPS

Attractions of Marxist 'self-realisation'

Although they appeal to members of other strata, both Marxism and nationalism are primarily ideologies of the intelligentsia. They address themselves, in the first place, to the crisis of identity and sense of isolation of westernised intellectuals, professionals and technicians, torn between an alien world of modernisation, repellant but fascinating, and the warm but stagnant traditions of their native communities. Since the intelligentsia furnishes most of the leadership in the new states, the communist version of nationalism must compete with earlier more romantic versions of nationalism and populism, as well as with other more religiously tinged ideologies. The argument so far is that its success is in proportion to the failure of competing ideologies, and to its own ability to appropriate the main themes and goals of rival nationalisms.

How far, then, has Marxist nationalism been able to pass itself off as the legitimate heir of orthodox liberal nationalisms, and wherein lie its specific attractions? To take the second question first, the key to Marxist success lies in its identification of the isolation and powerlessness of the intelligentsia with the political and economic humiliation of the community in a world of industrial giants. Its attraction for isolated and thwarted professionals lies in the clarity of its solution to this situation: rapid industrialisation through forced savings and investment, which will reverse the trend towards economic and hence political dependency, and towards alienation and impotence for the intelligentsia. The identity crisis of the latter will be overcome through communal regeneration, which in turn can be achieved only through accelerated industrial development by a heavily centralised and monolithic state. Marxists in developing countries regard the economic sector as the necessary instrument for attaining national ends, and they aim to cure a political and psychological malaise as much as any economic backwardness.[49]

It is important to realise that, in developing societies with a strong sense of inferiority and dependence among educated élites, massive industrialisation is regarded primarily, even by

Marxists, from an 'external standpoint'; that is to say, it is no longer seen as the internal pre-condition of that abundance which for Marx was to be the only basis for socialism. Rather, it becomes a pre-condition for political and military power in a more interdependent world system. Of course, some Marxist nationalists will still be genuinely interested in social development for its own sake. But the measure of that development is increasingly external; that is, either Western or Soviet. For the intelligentsia, the West remains its touchstone of the meaning of 'development', and therefore industrialisation and modernisation become increasingly a function of international prestige and external power. Marxism, if anything, abets this trend; as a radical Western offshoot with an international outlook, it is particularly attractive because it offers a total view of mankind's progress, a theory that is at once optimistic, 'scientific' and relevant to every intelligentsia and each community.[50]

Marxist nationalism holds other attractions for such intelligentsias. By emphasising state control of industry, it offers a ready-made niche to cadres of bureaucratic intellectuals whom it turns into planners and administrators. By its use of war and guerilla tactics to mobilise and indoctrinate the peasants, it creates outlets for the intelligentsia's technical expertise and its unfulfilled ambition to command. Even more important, Marxism's advocacy of the centralised party offers a close-knit social organisation of comrades at a moment when traditional kinship groups are becoming looser and more fragmented through mobility and secular education.

The party principle has given the Marxist nationalist a clear edge over his rivals. Many non-Marxist nationalist organisations are unwieldy and even inchoate; indeed, a given nationalist movement may in fact consist in a number of loosely related committees, parties and societies, each split into factions. Marxists, on the other hand, pride themselves on their tightly-knit organisation with its highly centralised command structure revolving around a small, but powerful, Politburo and a larger, more subservient Central Committee. Both in turn may be subordinated to a clique within the Politburo, or even to one leader.[51] Discussion and 'criticism' are allowed before decisions are taken, but not afterwards. Hence, party 'democratic centralism' combines, in the intelligentsia's eyes, two virtues: the harnessing of their ideas and talents for collective ends, and their translation into effective action, into instruments of power. This is Marxism's great advance over their earlier, easily dissipated, populism. It provides a framework, a clear 'line of march' for the intelligentsia in its search for community with the people. Not only does it bridge their isolation from other strata, it places them at the head of the advancing column. By submitting to Party authority and the educative state, the intelligentsia becomes the leading stratum of the new communist nation, and thereby restores to itself its shattered inner harmony and lost identity. Communism ultimately appears to solve the nationalist problems of roots and self-realisation by externalising their meaning, and by equating the individual's search for authentic identity with the community's quest for industrial power and autarchy.

Now, nationalism too is an ideology of social regeneration and individual self-realisation, and by incorporating and reinterpreting these nationalist motifs, Marxism in developing countries has to a large extent been able to assume the mantle of earlier liberal or populist nationalisms. Marxism, like nationalism, is an ideology of modernisation and self-renewal, and involves a social revolution. Both movements are profoundly activist. They rely on mass mobilisation and envisage a partnership between westernised élites and traditional peasant masses, although communist nationalisms have implemented this relationship in a much more radical manner. Both ideologies are also, in their consequences, *étatiste*. Whatever their declared intentions, their effect is to strengthen the State until it dominates society. Though it predicts the 'withering away' of the State under socialism, communism in practice has built up state institutions through its predilection for bureaucratic planning and central control. A similar paradox attends the relationship of both ideologies to the military, with communism's guerilla tactics and military industrialism undergirding the power of the military to an even greater extent than envisaged by nationalists. In general, though both nationalists and communists have preached the peaceful brotherhood of peoples, their practice has nearly always increased the incidence of warfare and the importance of militarism.

In all these respects, Marxism may legitimately claim to be carrying out nationalist ideals and programmes much more efficiently than the nationalists themselves. Since their goals have been incorporated into the Marxist programmes, the nationalist movements have allegedly become superfluous. Communism not only preserves the nation and its cultural boundaries; it actually strengthens the nation, levels internal ethnic and social differences, builds up its protective shell in the form of the bureaucratic state, and utilises the socially regenerated community to abolish the state of external dependency and to overcome the intelligentsia's sense of loneliness. Truly, it is the legitimate heir of nationalism in the developing countries.

An uneasy symbiosis

And yet, the mutual suspicions and antagonism between nationalists and communists continue unabated. To a nationalist, communism has incorporated his ideals and goals by perverting them. To a communist, the nationalists always seem to want something more than he offers, some insidious bourgeois deviation which will tempt the community off the communist route to self-realisation. For all their need of each other, nationalism and communism remain uneasy bedfellows, their symbiosis uncertain and fragile.

Historically, the roots of this antagonism go back to Marx's and Engels's ambivalence towards nationalism, as they encountered it in mid nineteenth century Europe. While they both envisaged the survival of nations and national cultures in a socialist era, they spurned the existing bourgeois nation-state and its chauvinism. Thus, on the one hand they declared of existing nation-states: 'The workingmen have no country. We cannot take from them what they have not got.' On the other hand, they claimed that

> Since the proletariat must first of all acquire political supremacy, must rise to be the leading class of the nation, must constitute itself *the* nation, it is, so far, itself national, though not in the bourgeois sense of the word.[52]

Again, Marx and Engels appear to disparage nationhood when they assert of the proletariat that it is 'the expression of the dissolution of all classes, nationalities, etc. within present society'.[53] In the same vein, *The Communist Manifesto* declares:

> The intellectual creations of individual nations become common

property. National one-sidedness and narrow-mindedness become more and more impossible, and from the numerous national and local literatures there arises a world literature.[54]

To insist upon nationality is, moreover, a strictly bourgeois phenomenon, specially dear to bourgeois writers;[55] however, peasants too, and even the proletariat, are not free of national sentiments. Thus in an article for the *New York Tribune* of 1855, Marx wrote: 'Both British and French proletarians are filled with an honourable national spirit, though they are more or less free from the antiquated national prejudices common in both countries to the peasantry.'[56] It is, of course, this 'antiquated prejudice' that has proved so invaluable for present-day Marxists in developing societies; and the attempt to distinguish it from an 'honourable national spirit' of the proletarian has proved difficult to sustain.[57] These stereotypes are more a product of theory than of fact, and of a theory that treats national phenomena, including national sentiment itself, in mainly instrumental terms. Fundamentally, Marx and Engels have no objection to either nations or nationalism, so long as they serve the historical process and its socialist culmination. Indeed, in a revealing passage, Marx appears to have placed national relationships alongside 'natural' ones, and to have considered them as 'human' relationships.[58] Engels, as we saw, regarded national liberation as a 'basic condition of all healthy and free development', and in *Po und Rhein* he went even further, advancing the Hegelian thesis of the incorporation of smaller ethnic groups by the large and viable European nations which he felt should be given 'their true national boundaries, which are determined by language and sympathies'.[59]

Nevertheless, though both he and Marx envisaged a world of nations after the withering away of the state under socialism, their attitude to the nation remained largely instrumental. The nation-state is treated as the proper arena for the proletarian struggle:

Though not in substance, yet in form, the struggle of the proletariat with the bourgeoisie is at first a national struggle. The proletariat of each country must, of course, first of all settle matters with its own bourgeoisie.[60]

The aim of this struggle is the abolition of class exploitation, and hence the reintegration of socialised humanity with itself. With the end of class exploitation, international exploitation will also be removed:

> In proportion as the exploitation of one individual by another is ended, is the exploitation of one nation by another ended too. . . . In proportion as the antagonism between classes within the nation vanishes, the hostility of one nation to another will come to an end.[61]

The emphasis falls always upon class conflicts and class abolition. National conflicts and their resolution are secondary and dependent phenomena; at best, they provide a formal framework for the class drama, at worst, a bourgeois tool and weapon to divert attention away from that drama. The possibility that this framework and weapon may possess a causal force independent of and equal to the class dimension is never seriously entertained by either Marx or Engels.[62]

For all its emotional ambivalence towards nationalism, Marxism's position on the national question has remained consistent with its founders' theoretical premises. Conversely, nationalist criticisms of Marxism have been based upon equally coherent and identifiable assumptions. The most fundamental issue concerns the definition of social interests. For Marx and Engels, and for most of their followers, those interests are *ultimately* defined in economic terms, however they are perceived by the participants in any situation. To a nationalist, such a definition is too circumscribed; questions of status, power and affinity enter into any full definition of 'interest'. Hence nationalists tend to accuse Marxism of ignoring or relegating cultural and spiritual dimensions. They point to Marx's insistence upon the 'material conditions' of life, which form the foundation for the ideological, political and legal 'superstructures', and which provide the key to explaining social change.[63] While Marx clearly recognised that man's consciousness and his cultural products can exert a counter-influence upon his economic conditions of production, there is no doubt that, in his theoretical statements, Marx sought to trace back every phenomenon, including that of the nation, to its economic roots and to man's material conditions. In this vein, too, Stalin in 1913 linked the growth of nations to early capitalist activity, even while he included other non-economic elements in his definition of the nation.[64]

It is just this tendency to restrict explanation, and definition, of national phenomena to preponderantly economic causes that nationalists reject. For them, material forces neither determine nor condition man's social life. On the contrary: material forces can be controlled by human will and purposes. Of course, Marx too recognised the creative power of human praxis in shaping circumstances, though always within definite limits set by those circumstances. Where the nationalist departs from Marxism is in his choice of explanatory categories, in his cultural theory of the formation of the collective will and human purposes.

At first glance it might seem that, for nationalists, human will and purposes are paramount, that they possess a unique status. Nations are willed into being by nationalism. The hero, through his foresight and willpower, can create by teaching and example a true national consciousness. All this is certainly part of the rhetoric of nationalism, from Rousseau and Fichte to Mazzini and Nkrumah. But behind the rhetoric lies a different theory. A hero cannot create the nation *ex nihilo*. He requires not just dedicated followers and an organisation, but also *latent* sympathies among the chosen population. His task is to 'awaken' those sympathies. Whence come those sympathies? From the bonds of religion, language, customs, common myths of origins, a shared history – in a word, from common ethnicity and common culture. The stronger the sense of belonging to a separate ethnic group with a unique culture, the stronger and more durable the collective will and purpose to emerge, given the right social conditions. In other words, the collective will is shaped by 'national character', which in turn is formed over many generations by the sense of common descent and by common memories and institutions. Political action may influence economic conditions, but it, in turn, is shaped by ethnic and cultural bonds.

From this essential difference in their explanations of social action spring all the specific contrasts between Marxist and nationalist concepts. In speaking of 'national interests', for example, a nationalist tends to place more emphasis upon the nation's 'dignity' or prestige than upon its position in the international division of labour and production. He tends also to explain the lack of dignity in political and cultural rather than social or economic terms. He regards the 'nation' not as an 'interest' category, but as a 'prestige' category, or in some cases as a 'power' category.[65] The enemy, too, is defined in quite different terms. For Marxists, the 'anti-class' are those whose material interests are necessarily opposed to those of the proletariat, i.e. the exploiting capitalists. For nationalists, the 'anti-nation' are those who corrupt and oppress the honour and freedom of the nation, i.e. the alien tyrant or indigestible minority, who impair the nation's cultural unity and authenticity.

Nationalism's emphasis upon culture and ethnic purity leads to further divergences from Marxism. Ideologically, they differ in their attitudes to time and to the past. Both have a linear view of history, and both are future-oriented. Their respective 'golden ages' lie ahead, waiting to be built by the nation or the proletariat. But, whereas communism merely accepts the past in order to transcend it, nationalism seeks inspiration from the communal past, in order to link past, present and future together. The past, for a nationalist, is a guide for today's builder, but it is also an essential 'link in the chain' of national identity. For this reason, nationalists tend to pay greater respect to traditions, and to seek greater continuity with the past for their national revolution.

Sociologically, too, nationalism's cultural interests and its lack of recognised founders or sacred texts has meant a greater flexibility and looseness in its organisations. In times of stress, nationalists have been able to forge highly centralised élite organisations, as did the Jacobins in 1793-4, during the war emergency. But nationalists have never been committed to Lenin's idea of the dedicated professional vanguard élite; nor have they sought inspiration or guidance from specific centres of doctrine or organisation, as communists look to Russia or China. On the contrary: nationalist movements look to native traditions and local virtues; they seek to incorporate rather than destroy existing institutions; they do not deny family attachments, only teach that even family loyalties must ultimately be subordinated to the nation's wellbeing, in the manner of antique heroes like Brutus or Cincinnatus.[66] Nor is a nationalist bound by doctrinal considerations such as those that inhibit, from time to time, a Marxist; nor does he have to look over his shoulder for guidance from any other national centre.

In one other respect, nationalism's flexibility allows considerable divergence from communist ideals. It is not committed, as a matter of theory, to heavy industrialisation, or to the introduction of any specific 'mode of production'. Ideologically, nationalism has, if anything, a penchant for agricultural self-sufficiency; and given the fact that agricultural development and problems are increasingly seen as the crucial ones for modernisation, nationalism is here at a distinct advantage. Not that ideological considerations have deterred nationalists from embracing industrialism when it suited their view of the 'national interest'. Since, however, the economic sector is regarded instrumentally by nationalists, as a means to achieving national dignity and identity, and not as an integral element of the historical process, such apparent inconsistency and flexibility is neither cynical nor opportunistic, but allows a more realistic view of local possibilities.

All in all, the picture that emerges of the relations between Marxism and nationalism in the developing societies is a very mixed one. On the one hand, there is considerable doctrinal and sociological overlap; on the other, deep suspicions and ambivalence. For Marxists, nationalism represents both a progressive and a reactionary force. Stalin saw its liberating and progressive aspect in the era of early capitalism; but he also saw how easily it could turn into a weapon of reactionary bourgeoisies once capitalism had reached the stage of maturity.[67] Therefore, the communist must learn how to ride the nationalist tiger, come to power on his back and then tame him through his own superior ideology and organisation, lest nationalism become a new opiate for the masses, a new form of bourgeois 'idealism' which diverts people away from recognising their true material interests and veils the class war in the cloudy rhetoric of national unity.

The nationalist, too, finds two faces in Marxism – the agent of popular mobilisation and the new tyranny that divides the community. Thus, on the one hand Marxism helps to activate and liberate the peasant and the worker, and makes them conscious of their political rights in the nation; on the other it divides them from other groups in the community and imposes on all a new totalitarian form of oppression. The middle strata become subordinated or decimated, and the Party seeks to exercise a tight control over every organisation and sphere of activity. Hence, nationalists today suspect the communists of subverting the national unity and national rights they ostensibly support, by means of populist dictatorships which camouflage deep-seated communist goals. In the process, the cultural nation loses its freedom and is converted into a mere economic category without spiritual identity or heritage.

The nationalisation of Marxism

In theory, nationalists are perhaps justified in their suspicions of ultimate Marxist aims. In practice, however, the 'Marxism' of communist cadres in the developing states today has undergone so much transformation that it now bears only a tenuous relationship to the Marxism of Marx or that of the present Soviet leadership. Besides, orthodox nationalism itself remains a powerful magnet for many strata in these states, both within communist ranks and outside – often strong enough to offset or even neutralise the more Marxist elements within the left–nationalist regimes, and to outlast the communist movement. As a result, though as a doctrine Marxism is often hostile to nationalism (and vice versa), communist practice outside the Soviet bloc has become increasingly permeated with nationalist sentiments and ideals.

This conclusion requires some elaboration. Its claim is supported by two arguments. The first of these contends that Marxist nationalisms in the developing states have increasingly nationalised and thereby denatured the elements of classical Marxism as they developed in the West. For, as we saw, the basic conditions of non-western societies today, their delayed development and relative power dependency, have forced through a deep revision of Marxist concepts and categories. Each of Marxism's traditional categories have been reinterpreted and modified. Some of the ensuing changes can be briefly summarised.

(1) For the traditional primacy of the urban proletariat in the class war, today's communist nationalists have substituted the peasantry, or a coalition of workers, soldiers and peasants.[68]

(2) Today's communist nationalists have generally replaced the bourgeoisie as the traditional class enemy with the alien 'imperialists' or 'neo-colonialists' who stand outside the

nation.

(3) 'Class warfare' has become the 'people's war of liberation', and the 'class' has been equated with the whole 'people' against another people-class of alien oppressors.

(4) Evolutionary certainties and dogmas have been overshadowed by the revolutionary political activism of a national élite and by the 'dynamism' of 'heroic' national elements.

(5) Political and even cultural factors have become increasingly common elements in the explanation of historical movements and events, while purely economic explanations have been discarded.

(6) Even the Marxist ideal of overcoming the division of labour has yielded ground to the nationalist belief in self-sacrifice and service for the community.

(7) Despite Bandung and 'positive non-alignment', the older socialist internationalism has given way to a new interest in national roots and ethnic self-assertion.

What then remains of Marxism in today's communist nationalisms? The main contribution of Marxism today is organisational and tactical. It consists in the use of guerilla warfare (rather than urban insurrection), in the commitment to rapid industrialisation, in its party organisation, above all in its totalitarian centralisation of bureaucratic state power. Such behavioural and tactical components, however, can be adopted by non-communists, in so far as their inflexibilities do not prove a greater handicap than a benefit for the ruling intelligentsia; and both aspects of this challenge are being weighed by the nationalists. Meanwhile, the doctrinal character of Marxism has been thoroughly transformed and denatured during the course of its quest for power.

The second argument is even more important. For, even if the Marxism in developing states had retained its doctrinal purity, nationalism would still prove more attractive, because it is at once more flexible and more immediately relevant for different groups in the population. The very ambiguity and haziness of nationalist concepts and sentiments constitute its greatest assets. Its interpretation can be varied with greater subtlety and its many facets can unite quite disparate outlooks and interests in a common pursuit. Where there is so much heterogeneity of sentiments and goals in a community, a 'chameleon' ideology like nationalism is at a considerable advantage over a highly intellectualised and rigid doctrine like Marxism, which has first to be denatured to make it serviceable in such a social environment. On the other side, nationalism's simplicity gives it a more direct impact and greater relevance, especially for the crisis of identity among the intelligentsia. Nationalism's resolution of this crisis is clear and effective. Man can regain his identity only through solidarity with his community. He must recognise within himself the deep roots and affinities of his 'national' nature. He must accept these, if he would regain his inner harmony. Only then can he find his true identity and purpose, and raise his head again among his fellow men. There is nothing matching the clarity and immediacy of this conception in Marxism. True, current communist nationalisms have placed the intelligentsia at the head of the 'line of march'. But this has occurred at the expense of Marxist doctrine, and its effectiveness is dependent upon the adoption of the nationalist cure by the communists.

Moreover, nationalisms possess much greater emotive content and individual relevance for members of specific communities. Despite Marx's own early humanism, many Marxist formulations appear as so many lifeless abstractions and collective categories linked by abstruse reasonings. Theoretical consistency has been achieved, but Marxism too often fails to touch the status situation, or stir the emotional temper, of the individual or his group. But it is exactly at these points that nationalism's romanticism excels. Its rich images and palpable visions – the land of milk and honey, the love of soil and hearth, the purity of language, the brotherhood of true patriots, self-determination and the rest – are embodied in vivid symbols and slogans, which Marxism can rarely match. *Its* slogans are attractive only when they proclaim the revolution and the overthrow of a capitalist exploitation which can be identified with imperialism. Once independence is won, and the revolution accomplished, Marxism's utopia becomes remote, its golden age pale and abstract, besides the joy and warmth of fraternity with one's own people in the resurrected nation.

Besides, the very internationalism of our era strengthens the appeals of nationalism. For as nation-states become more interdependent, their élites tend to look outwards for standards of behaviour and policy. The very idea of what constitutes 'national dignity' becomes external and internationalised; emulating some nations, dissociating themselves from others, the identity and self-assertion of these élites is continually reinforced by external pressures and events. Unlike Marxism, nationalism as a doctrine embodies the basic assumption that the world is divided 'naturally' and rightly into nations, locked in competition; and whereas for Marxism its 'proletarian internationalism' (which, incidentally, should not be mistaken for a non-national cosmopolitanism) is a rather tepid and secondary matter, the nationalist bases his whole outlook and *raison d'être* on the existence and sanctity of the international framework and of a 'world of nations'.[69]

Finally, nationalism's flexibility allows it to pose simultaneously as a revolutionary doctrine and as the true heir of religious tradition. Since the peasantry and many of the urban lower classes are still deeply attached to these traditions, the attitude of modern ideologies to such traditions can be decisive. Now, unlike Marxism, for whom such traditions represent a pre-industrial opiate to be abolished or privatised once socialism has been achieved, nationalism seeks to utilise for its own secular ends the emotions and bonds that these historic traditions embody. Its attitude to tradition, therefore, is both respectful and manipulative. It has to respect the people's traditions since they form a 'link in the chain' of their history and generations, even while it tries to canalise the emotions evoked by them into new, national channels. Hence it will try to keep alive traditions that still have resonance and can, through reinterpretation and a change of emphasis, serve its own secular goals. In this way, nationalism reassures the people that rapid change will not sweep away all their cherished emotional landmarks, and that the national revolution seeks to build upon ancient and revered foundations. In the battle for popular loyalties, this is one of nationalism's most potent weapons.[70]

These are some of the grounds for claiming that nationalism today possesses greater vitality and staying-power than its most serious rival, and that it remains a compelling force in developing societies, both within the Marxist camp and in its own right. Greater international interdependence and a halting modernisation can only strengthen the appeal of radical and populistic nationalisms, at the expense of other ideologies, including the Western or Soviet varieties of Marxism.

CHAPTER 6

Ethnic Resurgence in the West[*]

In much of the literature on political ideologies, nationalism is classified as a conservative, right-wing movement, an example of authoritarian collectivism. Many commentators, indeed, regard it as a milder form of fascism. They claim that the right wing in politics, though it adheres to an economic individualism, to free market competition, firmly places the interests of the group, be it the State, the Nation or the Race, above those of the individual. Conservatives and nationalists, the argument runs, are inherently intolerant, militarist and anti-intellectual. Conversely, left-wingers and liberals tend to be political individualists, although they may admit state intervention in the economic sector. They also include more committed intellectuals, more idealists and doctrinaire philosophers, for whom national loyalties must appear narrow and merely tribal.[1]

MINORITIES AND 'MASS SOCIETY'

A liberal version of this argument achieved particular prominence in the 1950s. A number of writers, in Europe and America, claimed that extreme right- and left-wing ideologies could emerge and appeal widely only in a 'mass society', where large numbers of people living in vast, impersonal cities felt atomised and insecure. With their traditional bonds and roles destroyed, unemployed or underemployed workers and intellectuals lost all sense of purpose and identity, and became easy victims of demagogues who promised

* This chapter is based upon the Fourth Harold Walsby Memorial Lecture given on 2 May 1977, and I should like to record my thanks to the Harold Walsby Society for their invitation.

150

to sweep away a corrupt society and replace it with an organic and 'natural' community which would restore to each individual his true identity. These writers traced this anti-democratic development to the pressures of large-scale, complex industrial societies, in which traditional élites were vulnerable and the masses exposed. They also accepted many of the formulations of 'crowd psychology' advanced by Le Bon, McDougall and the later Freud: the fear of non-conformity, of exposure outside the group, had intensified in the large, anonymous city.[2]

The popularity of 'mass society' analyses owed much to the fear of communist advances during the Cold War era, but even more to the traumatic experiences of the fall of the Weimar Republic, the Spanish Civil War and the Second World War itself. Both this sociological thesis and the political analysis to which it was attached were undoubtedly relevant to the circumstances of that era, despite the many criticisms that were raised even then.

There are, however, certain difficulties with this approach, which make it less applicable for current ideological developments in the West. Two of these are germane to my theme, the role of nationalism today. The first is the classic problem that every democracy faces, that of dealing with the demands of minorities or out-groups. A majority government must face a crucial problem of social cohesion wherever there are minorities who do not share the main assumptions and values underlying the political system. Second, there is the current resurgence of nationalism in the West itself, a nationalism that is often social-democrat in flavour and which attracts much support from the intelligentsia. This nationalism is a minority movement. It represents a protest against the *status quo*, against the majority's institutions, in the name of freedom and the right to differ. Hence it does not easily fit into the Left–Right spectrum of 'mass society' theory.

In fact, the two difficulties may be connected. I want to argue that the present resurgence of nationalism in the West should be seen as a protest by ethnic minorities against the failure on the part of old established states, many of them democratic and liberal, to recognise their identity and their rights. Theirs is a protest against delayed democracy, sham democracy and failed democracy. They express the hope of the French Revolution that greater ethnic democratic participation can regenerate a society and a state visibly in decay and decline; and in this fundamental respect they hark back to the earliest nationalisms, even though the political style and particular arguments advanced by today's movements are quite different. In this sense also, current nationalisms of minorities are individualistic and democratic in relation to an established majority system, while at the same time they equate individual rights and dignity with the autonomy and individuality of the unique ethnic community.

THE RESURGENCE OF NATIONALISM

Without doubt, nationalism has experienced a profound renewal today, in its western homelands. It is no longer held to be *passé* or discredited. The link in the public mind between fascism and nationalism, so strong just after the last War, has faded, and a 'healthy' state nationalism is espoused.[3] Economic bargaining between Common Market countries has, in some ways, fuelled this latent national sentiment; while the Common Market association itself may well involve a new nationalism on a broader inter-state level, a pan-Europeanism dreamed of by more than one protagonist of the European movement.[4]

Such developments have surprised many who predicted the early demise of nationalism. It was widely assumed that, with full industrialisation, democracy and mass education, petty allegiances to an outmoded nation-state would wither, to be replaced by continental or even global loyalties. The world was becoming too interdependent to accommodate mere tribal chauvinisms.[5]

But it must now be clear that the so-called 'demise of nationalism' in mid-century Europe has been more apparent than real. True, for a time nationalists were outstripped, in rhetoric and action, by the fascists, and they suffered a kind of guilt by association after fascism's collapse.[6] But recent events have demonstrated both the institutional stability of the nation-state and the strength and endurance of national loyalties. Indeed, in many ways we are witnessing the proliferation of nationalisms.

Globally we can distinguish four main types of nationalism today. The first, the anti-colonial '*war of liberation*' is still to be found in southern Africa, and in economic form in Africa and Latin America. A more common form of Third World nationalism today, however, is the '*integration*' regime of newly established states. Here the State tries to mould its often culturally diverse populations into a single 'nation' on the European model. The old established states of the West exhibit a third type of nationalism, that of state '*renewal*'. Gaullism, for example, aimed not merely to preserve an existing sovereign state, but also to revitalise it by enhancing its popular authority and rapport. And finally, standing opposed to both integration and renewal nationalisms, there are the many examples of ethnic '*separatisms*' of minorities, which concern us here.[7]

Ethnic separatisms are to be found in every part of the globe, but Europe has witnessed an extraordinary ethnic renaissance in the last two decades. Quite apart from Scotland, Wales and Ulster, Britain alone has seen ethnic stirrings in Cornwall, the Isle of Man, and Shetland and Orkneys. In France, Bretons have been emulated by Corsicans, Occitanians and Alsatians. Spain has its Basque, Catalan, Galician and Andalusian movements, not to mention the Canaries. In Holland, Frisian agitation has spread to Groeningen and Gelderland. Belgium remains agitated by the Flemish-Walloon linguistic problem, and Switzerland has its Jurassiens, and foreign workers there have produced a backlash. Italy must reckon with a murmuring Sicilian separatism and Tyrolean agitation, and in North America a wealthy Canada is faced with a major challenge in Quebecois separatism. Even a regionally devolved Germany must placate Strauss's Bavaria.[8]

The aims and specific context of each of these movements naturally varies as much as their scope and intensity. But they do have this in common: these autonomist movements have arisen this century in their political form, in well established, often ancient states, with clear and recognised national boundaries, and with a relatively prosperous economy. While not minimising considerable differences of degree, all these states are fairly industrialised, and much of the population is literate and even quite well educated. And yet, despite all these advantages, which led theorists to postulate the early demise of nationalism, the ethnic minorities seem more discontented than before, and some even wish to go it alone.

AUTONOMISTS AND SEPARATISTS

To grasp the reasons for this paradoxical state of affairs, we must ask ourselves three questions. First, what exactly do these minority nationalists want, and what is the meaning of their ethnic revival? Second, who are the nationalists, both leaders and followers, and what is the social basis of their movements? Finally, why have their nationalisms emerged now, and in these western states? How do we explain the timing and incidence of these movements?

In one sense, the goals and meaning of today's ethnic nationalisms are perfectly clear and consistent. On a general level, they desire only what nationalists of all ages and climes have demanded: group autonomy, group cohesion and group identity. They want, first, to be free and self-governing citizens with equal rights and duties, following their own laws and customs without external regulation or interference. Second, they desire unity, to be and feel a solid, compact and integrated body of men and women, bound to a recognised homeland and rooted in their ancestral soil, which through toil and enthusiasm can be made to nurture and sustain them, body and soul, as a fraternal unit. And finally, they want to be recognised as distinctive and unique; to have and be seen to have their own individuality, to stand out from the majority and be different, to follow their own way, think their own thoughts, draw on their own memories, and build their own destiny. They are searching for their hidden inner self in the communal past, so that each man can be reborn and regenerated.

At first glance, these rather general ideals seem far removed from the immediate goals of today's separatists. Their arguments are usually couched in administrative or economic terms. But closer inspection will reveal that they are really only applying the general ideals to local conditions. And even where economics takes precedence over language or vice versa, as in Quebec or Flanders, this is only because social cohesion and its economic dimension appears to be a more pressing current issue, or because a threatened language symbolises and expresses a sense of cultural erosion or undermined identity. We should not be misled by differences in emphasis and phasing between current separatisms into a denial of their essential logical coherence.[9]

Present-day Western separatists advance really three main arguments for a change in the *status quo*. Economically, they claim that central government favours the more prosperous, central regions at the expense of poorer, outlying areas, or drains the resources of more prosperous, outlying regions to feed and support a poorer, more stagnant central area. Thus a Plaid Cymru manifesto declares:

> Nothing displays the callousness of the Labour Party as much as its lack of concern for the coal and slate areas of Wales. It is on the backs of miners and quarrymen that the Labour Party came to power. Once in power, the welfare of these areas had no place in its governing priorities.[10]

And a Scottish National Party (SNP) economist links this economic argument to the premise of autonomy when he writes that

> Self-government is good, not just because it may lead to greater efficiency in running the Scottish economy: self-government is good as an end in itself because it means that people are learning by doing. This means that, if we take the responsibility for running our own affairs, then as producers we are likely to benefit from this responsibility, because in exercising it we make ourselves more efficient and become better able to do the job. . . .
> For a long time now we have had inflicted on us various policies such as taxation of employment in services, and periodic restrictions on bank lending which, however appropriate they may have been for the south-east of England, have certainly never been appropriate for the Scottish economy. They have simply accelerated the trends in emigration and unemployment.[11]

Similarly, Bretons claim that their depressed economy was the result of decades of neglect by French planners; and Corsicans protest against tourist and strategic exploitation, against sea pollution and colons operating large landholdings and the wine trade.[12] In Spain, on the other hand, the Basques and Catalans allege that their more industrialised and advanced economies underpin, to their own disadvantage, the poorer, more stagnant economies of Castile and Leon.[13]

Second, there is the political argument against over-centralisation. Separatists claim that the modern state has become too rationalised, too bureaucratic, to meet man's social and political needs. Only the small-scale living community can cope today. As John Osmond wrote,

The road of the Corporate State leads to a dead end. . . . The
only rational alternative is a view of life that gives precedence
to the concept of community. . . . The first requirement of a
community is that it be given a human scale in which people
can reasonably seek a sense of purpose, responsibility and identity.[14]

And in his recent massive study of Celtic ethnic groups in Britain,
Michael Hechter reached a similar conclusion: 'The most recent
crystallisation of Celtic nationalism may ultimately be understood
as a trenchant critique of the principle of bureaucratic centralism.'[15]

Finally, there is the cultural attack on assimilation. This usually
takes the form of clinging to an ancient or revived language.
But sometimes religion becomes the focus of identity, as in Ulster
or the Jura. Or it may be a series of distinctive institutions, like
the legal, educational and ecclesiastical systems of Scotland. All
these foci can serve as symbols for articulating a sense of common
history which embodies a unique communal experience and personality; and it is this personality or identity that is felt to be
under threat from larger external entities intruding into a sacred
realm. This is why smallness as such becomes a cultural and political
virtue, and individuality becomes equated with freedom.

There are, however, a few differences that mark off recent separatisms from earlier nationalisms, at least to some extent. Nineteenth-
century nationalists wanted their own sovereign states, whereas
many of today's ethnic movements prefer a federal or autonomist
status within a larger unit. In Spain, for example, the Catalan
and Basque mainstream is still largely 'autonomist', desiring maxi-
mum 'home rule' within a federal Spain, as in the 1930s.[16] Despite
some calls for a Groot-Nederland or closer links with Francophones
in other European states, the main body of Flemish and Walloon
sentiment remains firmly within the limits of a Belgian patriotism.
The continuing language conflict, particularly in the Brussels area,
has the character of a struggle for hegemony within an existing
state, even though cultural guidance is sought from the Hague
or Paris. In Switzerland, Romansch-speakers and Jurassiens
demanded cultural recognition as a linguistic or cantonal entity,
while Frisians and Groeningers want Dutch government support
of their language and educational institutions.[17] Even in Brittany,
Wales and Scotland, despite the existence of outright separatist

parties, mainstream sentiment seems to be autonomist and federalist so far.

A second difference between today's autonomist movements and earlier nationalisms is the former's tendency towards economic planning. Many current ethnic movements have a strong social democrat or socialist element, with an emphasis upon economic self-sufficiency which harks back to the theses of List, the German economist of the 1840s.[18] Nationalism has always stressed the need for control over one's own resources, ever since Rousseau's idealisation of Corsican natural simplicity and agricultural virtue.[19] But it is really only in the twentieth century that the social basis for this aspect of nationalist doctrine has emerged, giving it a prominence it never enjoyed in the nineteenth century. In this respect, later twentieth century nationalisms looked back to the earliest nationalist movements in the later eighteenth century rather than the often more conservative ones of the last century.

Finally, as previously mentioned, current autonomist movements differ from previous nationalisms in their context. They are no longer protests against dynastic or imperial tyrannies, but against old established democratic states, which are felt to have perverted or ossified their democratic ideals. In this respect, Spain stands somewhat apart, though there too the drive for ethnic recognition goes hand in hand with a protest against a long-delayed democratisation. In general, however, the new autonomisms have arisen in industrialised and liberal nation-states, among enfranchised citizens.

Nevertheless, despite these differences, the latterday autonomist movements conform to the basic pattern of nationalism. Whether the argument concerns oil or tourism, university locations or language rights, migration or regional powers, the ultimate premises are never in doubt. It is always collective autonomy, collective solidarity and collective identity which is being sought and found, in the hope of ethnic regeneration and fraternity which is embodied in the concept of 'nationhood'.

THE NEW TECHNICAL INTELLIGENTSIA

If we turn to the question of the social basis of the new autonomism, we find considerable variation in detail, but also a general pattern familiar from earlier nationalisms. Typically, nationalism attracts many of the intelligentsia – the intellectual and professional strata, who apply and disseminate ideas and techniques, who achieve recognition through their diplomas. Other 'middle-class' groups – officers, bureaucrats, lower clergy and entrepreneurs – may then be won over to the cause. If the movement and the struggle continues for a long time and becomes intense, other strata may be drawn in. But on the whole, the peasants and urban workers are much less nationalistic.[20]

Nationalism originates usually among more literary and romantic circles of the intelligentsia – among poets, novelists, artists and academics. In this stage, nationalism is largely a cultural movement. To become a political force, it must also attract members of the liberal professions – doctors, lawyers, journalists, schoolteachers. The new nationalisms have their share of the literary and professional intelligentsias, men whom one would define as true intellectuals as well as those with an encyclopedic, broad intelligence. For example, in the cultural foundation of Breton or Scots nationalisms in the last century, or of Welsh or Flemish nationalisms in this century, historians, poets, philosophers and writers have played an important role. Catalan nationalism has continuously built upon the work of Catalan artists and intellectuals for two centuries, and the various linguistic movements – Romansch, Frisian, Gaelic – owe a great debt to the efforts of scholars. Besides, the ideology of nationalism itself was originally formulated by leading intellectuals in the later eighteenth century, by Rousseau, Montesquieu, Burke, Herder and Fichte, non-conformists who challenged prevailing cosmopolitan assumptions in the name of new ideas of authenticity and civic virtue.[21]

There is, however, one important difference in the social composition of present-day nationalisms, at least of the more developed ones. There is a greater technical element among the intelligentsia today. Technicians, planners and social engineers, ranging from social workers to town planners and agronomists, have rallied to the nationalist cause; and they have given the movement a more practical and vocational bias. Hence also the trend towards welfare socialism. The movements' leaders must cater to their need for better outlets for their underutilised talents, by planning a more 'rational', that is locally appropriate, economy and society. Whether Breton farmers want rural subsidies or Welsh dons seek institutional recognition; whether Scots businessmen are looking for commercial outlets or Basque industrialists are irked by central government restrictions, their discontent is attached by the liberal and technical intelligentsia to a radical solution for their thwarted mobility and lack of status. Lacking a high status or strategic location in the wider society, the new autonomist nationalisms, whether of Quebec or Scotland, are becoming increasingly technocratic and socialist as they attract more middle-class technicians and professionals into their ranks. And conversely, the smaller the numbers of this technical and professional element, the more culturally romantic becomes the ethnic movement, as was the case in Wales, Flanders and Brittany.[22]

A greater economic collectivism, therefore, is a hallmark of the more developed among the recent movements for autonomy. For it is only in this century that a strong technical intelligentsia has superseded the more literary early groups and their allies among the bourgeois strata. Later twentieth-century nationalism is, accordingly, a much more practical and hard-headed drive for mobility and economic self-sufficiency. The nationalists hope that, by creating their own bureaucratic and professional institutions, separate from those of the wider society, they can satisfy the frustrated ambitions and unused talents of their members.

UNDERDEVELOPMENT AND HISTORICITY

Our third question, why these autonomist movements have arisen when and where they have, has attracted a number of explanations. In many ways these theories echo nationalist arguments and overemphasise the novelty of the ethnic movements. It is well to remember that most of the recent movements were active before the last War, and some reach back into the last century.[23]

The occurrence of these ethnic autonomisms is often put down to over-centralisation. Thus, recently Patricia Mayo has claimed that the Breton, Basque and Welsh movements must be viewed as protests against a political malaise induced by the bureaucratic apparatus and control in the modern Jacobin state. Peripheral areas, in particular, are bound to be neglected or ill-used by a remote but omnipotent bureaucracy. It is not quite clear whether it is neglect or intrusion that is most feared; but the real difficulty with this line of argument is its failure to explain why such feelings of individual anomie and malaise should attach themselves to the ethnic community or nation. In one sense, we all feel powerless in the face of a vast, impersonal bureaucracy. Yet autonomist sentiments are confined to members of specific ethnic groups, and often to minorities of those groups. Besides, can we term societies like Canada, Belgium or Switzerland over-centralised, Jacobin states like France? Bureaucratism is an important motif in any explanation, but is inadequate as an account on its own.[24]

Differences in regional economic development are also cited as grounds for the rise of recent autonomism. As we saw, some areas are under- or over-developed in relation to others and the centre: Catalonia or the Basque region in relation to Castile, or Ulster to Ireland, exemplify overdevelopment; while north Wales, Occitania, Friesland, Brittany or the Jura and Corsica were underdeveloped rural areas exploited for tourism or for food resources.[25] There is a good deal in this view, as far as it goes. If a region already has a strong sense of cultural distinctiveness, and it also happens to be more under- or over-developed than the centre of the state, then the chances of radical separatism emerging there are much greater. But this explanation is at best partial. It does not, of course, account for the original sense of distinctiveness, or for the fact that other under- or over-developed regions, like the north-east of England or the south of Italy, have failed to evolve an ethnic, let alone separatist, sentiment, despite their many grievances. Moreover, some 'regions' like Scotland, with its oil potential, have recently passed from a state of relative underdevelopment *vis-à-vis* the centre to one of parity, and their national sentiment has actually intensified rather than declined, as this theory would lead one to expect.

While bureaucracy and underdevelopment may heighten an existing feeling of ethnic distinctiveness, that feeling itself must stem from some objective cultural differences in the population. Religion, customs, institutions, language or history must have acted for some generations as barriers marking off people within a larger state. Particularly important is the subjective feeling of separate ethnic origins and history that these cultural differences symbolise. It is just this ethnic sense that gives these ancient cultural cleavages in the old established states their sting. In one degree or another, each of the autonomist movements builds upon a belief in distinctive ethnic roots. No doubt, some of these ethnic 'sub-nations' are more 'historic' than others. Scotland and Catalonia can point to centuries of historic existence as independent states, whereas Wales, Brittany and Friesland have fewer memories of an independent state existence. No doubt this difference helps us to explain some of the characteristics of their varied ethnic movements. What it does not, and cannot, tell us is why these movements have become more intense recently and why they have proliferated. We should remember that it was only in the last century that poets and scholars began to notice these ancient and historic cleavages in the old states. Till then nobody had really bothered to unearth primordial legends or revive poetic languages. Today, however, all these sub-nations feel themselves to be ethnically separate and culturally distinct, whether they are 'historic' nations or not. So we cannot invoke these cultural cleavages to explain the resurgence of nationalism in the West today.[26]

IMPERIAL DEMISE AND DEMOCRATIC FAILURE

To explain this recent resurgence of nationalism, we must look at the changing position of ethnic minorities in regard to broader, international transformations in culture and politics.

Let me take culture first. Since the end of the eighteenth century, the West has witnessed two main cultural changes, one technical, the other substantive. Technically, there has been a vast acceleration in communications. By the mid twentieth century, even the most remote rural hinterland in Europe was drawn into this dense network. Quebec, Flanders, north Wales, Brittany, the Jura – areas that had remained outside this modernising stream – have now all been engulfed by a general Western culture, in varying degrees. And what is the content of this continental culture? Broadly speaking, it is a secular, rationalist, scientific culture, which erodes religious beliefs and traditions. In the metropolitan centres the secularising process started two centuries ago, but distant and economically depressed regions managed yet to retain their rural heritage. Now, with the decline of the Church's hold even there, these 'late-seculariser' regions have followed the lead of the main urban centres, producing their own scientific and professional élites, who have often been educated abroad.

The secular culture that these élites have absorbed is innovatory, experimental and anti-traditional. It is also humanist and egalitarian. It is closely bound up with the democratic movement, which it underpins and promotes. This is one source of recent ethnic radicalism, a general one.

For more specific causes of recent ethnic radicalism, we must turn to international political developments and their social consequences. One of the main developments of postWar politics has been the demise of imperialism in the West. All the old established European states have had their imperial role divested from them, and have been reduced to a second-rank status well below that of the superpowers. In England, France, Belgium, Holland and Spain, the ensuing contraction is not merely physical and economic; it is even more political and psychological. Europe and Canada have been dwarfed by continental superpowers on either side, and have not yet succeeded in adopting an alternative Atlantic, or European, identity. The result has been a mixture of self-doubt and spurts of affirmation. But the disillusion remains. The recent sudden global shift in wealth and power has made many Europeans today feel a sense of decay and decline, especially in the oldest states.[27]

One important social consequence of this vast geopolitical shift has been a contraction of outlets for native ambition and talent. Before, Scots and Corsicans could administer and police an empire; now, in the shrunken arenas of Britain and France, more often than not they cannot find posts with an equivalent status and matching their qualifications or aspirations.[28] The number of professionally and technically educated people has grown, but the area in which their talents can be utilised, and the wealth to support it, has been whittled away to its heartlands. As the ambitious flock to Brussels, Paris or the south-east of England out of the depressed areas, they inevitably encounter a shortage of facilities and openings to satisfy their demands.

Here we have the makings of a 'crisis of identity' among the new professional élites coming from the outlying areas. Tardy secularisation has eroded their religious beliefs. They can no longer wholeheartedly identify with their rural traditions. They no longer see themselves as villagers or simply as Christians, or as Catholics,

Methodists, Presbyterians and so on. At the same time, this problem of who they are and where they belong becomes more important to them, as they compete alongside others with different accents, religions, dress, colour and customs, in the great urban centres. As Karl Kautsky once remarked, 'The railways are the greatest breeder of national hatreds.'[29] In the large city ethnic differences become more obvious, and ethnic antagonisms, long dormant, perhaps, are often rekindled. Besides, when there is a scarcity of jobs and resources, it is so easy to exclude people on ethnic grounds, and much more comforting to explain rejection in the same way.

But there is more to present ethnic discontent than urban discrimination and competition. The man from a culturally distinct region, whose traditional beliefs have been undermined and whose career is blocked, finds he cannot identify with the existing nation-state in the same way as his neighbour from the centre. Disadvantaged in the social competition, he cannot feel a first loyalty to a decaying and declining state, which, because of its social composition, must always favour the cultural majority. Here two quite separate modern trends collide; the belated secularisation of distant regions, and the sudden and recent collapse of empire, with its social contraction. The result of this collision can be dramatic: it may produce large-scale emigration, or ethnic radicalism.[30]

Quite a few do, in fact, emigrate, and not only from the ethnic minorities. But many more, for one reason or another, cannot. They remain behind, frustrated and disgruntled, unable to find a suitable niche at the centre and feeling estranged. They stand uneasily between unviable native traditions and the unfulfilled promise of a rationalist modernity. In this crisis of identity and purpose, some turn away from assimilation into the dominant society. Instead, they try to discover their own roots and thereby to raise the prestige and position of their own ethnic community. They return to their native histories, but from a modern standpoint. In this history they find a new identity, and one that can provide the foundation for a new society and a new state, in which they will no longer be disadvantaged and no longer estranged.

The fact that more and more members of the regional ethnic groups are opting for a return to their historic roots points to a fundamental failure of the older democracies. In many cases, democratic leaders have realised this too late. The 'devolution' they belatedly offer only whets the separatist appetite. The fact is that ethnic autonomists feel that the democratic systems have nothing to offer them, are irrelevant to their needs, and of necessity cannot identify with an ethnic minority. The party system has been built up on the basis of class alignments, and the conflict among the majorities between a liberal–democratic centre and so-called extremists of the Right and Left is of little relevance to the ethnic minority. The problems of inflation and industrial conflict that beset the older democracies only encourage radical autonomists to tread their own path. For them, it has become a case of democratic sclerosis, a situation in which apparently democratic institutions are so rigid that they cannot respond to changes and to the needs of the new élites.[31]

At the same time, these new élites have imbibed to the full the secular, rationalist culture of the majority, with its democratic and egalitarian aspirations. They have also, as we saw in Quebec, Catalonia and Scotland, moved towards a mild form of economic collectivism, with an emphasis upon welfare and planning. Their demand for greater participation is now fused with an aspiration for a new status and dignity based on a return to their roots. The ethnic revival has been joined to the call for a more real and meaningful democracy, in which new institutions will be created which are, by definition, responsive to local needs. There is a logic in this movement; for the old nation-state democracy to admit the justice of ethnic claims would be to imperil even further its viability and prestige and to admit that it had, after so many centuries, failed to bind all its citizens together into a compact body sharing a common 'civil theology' and common sentiments of identity.[32]

CONCLUSION

Democracy's test today is a crisis of social cohesion. As long as empire and global position buttressed democracy, this ordeal could be postponed. As long as secularisation had not penetrated into the rural hinterlands, there were no provincial intelligentsias to raise the democratic banner against an ossified democracy. With the demise of empire and the growth of communications, all that has changed. New professional élites from outlying regions are challenging the ascendancy of older metropolitan ones, just as the latter are going through a crisis of confidence. The new élites have found that existing democratic institutions cannot cater to their needs or to those of their regions, with which they now increasingly identify against the majority and its nation-state. Sometimes, as in Flanders, where the Flemish constitute an actual majority, they have managed to attain a sort of parity and achieve some of their goals within the Belgian state. Sometimes, as in Switzerland, the democratic system is flexible and decentralised enough to accommodate new regional–ethnic demands. In other cases, where the state is more centralised, the struggle for ethnic recognition continues. And in Spain, the ethnic struggle is also a battle for a long-delayed democratisation.

Everywhere, however, it has proved impossible to ignore the ethnic minorities. And the more democratic the regime, the more intense become their demands, and the more seriously they have to be taken.

CHAPTER 7

The Bureaucratic Cycle

From the late eighteenth century until today, the national ideal has expanded and proliferated into the most powerful yet elusive of all modern ideologies. It started life as a middle-class quest for social emancipation and community against the arbitrary rule of despots. It soon became a weapon in defence of privilege, and later a justification for state expansion and overseas imperialism. At the same time, it was taken up by intelligentsias of ethnic minorities, who sought in the goal of national self-determination to secede from vast empires and unify all those who shared their culture in a single state. In the later nineteenth century nationalism also united with populism, to preach the need for roots in the small town and countryside to a newly urbanised and uprooted population.

In our own century, the national ideal has been used for various purposes and has appeared in different guises. There is first the familiar anti-colonial drive for modernisation associated with the westernising intelligentsias of underdeveloped countries in Asia, Africa and Latin America, which started in a protest for liberation and has now turned into a quest for homogeneity and integration in the new states. There is also, and often in league with anti-colonial integration, the populist ideal, which seeks to re-identify intelligent-sias with their peasantries in these new states, and through a 'national communism' to promote their industrial modernisation. In Europe we have witnessed a revival of the same national ideal in a spate of ethnic 'neo-nationalisms', which hark back to the earlier ethnic secessionism but add new motifs and reflect a different phase of the political and economic cycle.[1] And finally, there are the colour and 'pan' nationalisms, still a vital force in some parts of the world, which may be seen as mechanisms for reversing racial or cultural exploitation and rediscovering a lost dignity and identity.

The appeals of the national ideal are as varied today as they were in the last century; but the ideal itself, though it has expanded in scope and deepened and changed in part, contains certain fixed *leitmotivs*: the quest for autonomy and self-government, for solidarity in a 'homeland' and for an identity discoverable through a unique history and culture. The questions that naturally arise are: how is it that this ideal remains so strong and persistent, and what are the common roots of its appeal in such diverse settings, over and above any specific and local sources? Is there a common denominator in the appeals of nationalism today?

Two Senses of 'Nation'

Part of the answer lies in the distinction between the 'nation' as a 'natural' unit in history and the 'nation' as a historically specific and political goal or ideal.

Behind the 'national ideal' of nationalist ideologies there stands the very old and quasi-organic formation of the nation as a cultural and ethnic organisation. In *this* sense, the distinction between an ethnic group or people and a 'nation' is only a matter of degree, and of our tendency, often political in intent, to reserve the term 'nation' for the larger, more developed ethnic groups. Historically and etymologically, the term *'natio'* often referred to distant and barbarian tribes, who were recognised as separate ethnic and cultural units possessing unique origins and an identifiable territory. In this sense, the nation looks back to its etymological association with nature and birthplace, and combines what Debray calls the two 'sacred' founding processes of all large-scale human association: an assignation of origins in time, and a delimitation of community in an enclosed space.[2] Indeed, the development of the terms *'natio'* and 'nation' illustrates the fluidity of man's understanding of his cultural organisation; for these terms have changed their referents from the far to the near, from smaller to larger, from simpler to more complex associations, in accord with the growth in political importance of these associations. In the classical past, *'natio'* could refer to a constellation of clans; the term was often interchangeable with the *'gens'*.[3] Today, the term 'nation' is reserved only for the most important and largest kinds of cultural association, and we tend to argue whether smaller (and more distant) cultural groups are 'really' nations.

The ethnic nation is essentially an ancient historical and cultural entity, often religious in its origins, and always closely tied up with the rhythms of 'nature'. It often evokes a collective sentiment of ethnocentrism, in which the peasant's rootedness in his ethnic–tribal community, itself tied to the soil, is taken for granted and accepted without question. Origins and descent on the one hand, and a close link with soil and territory on the other define the oldest and most basic forms of human association. They have persisted in the modern world as cultural and historical data which continue to evoke mass emotion and to constitute an often unshakeable barrier against the inroads of both modern technologies and modern non-national ideologies.

But there is another sense of 'nation', to mean the sole basis for politics and government, and the true historical route to social justice and progress. This is a modern, revolutionary and specifically nationalist concept, a political ideal peculiar to an era of massive change. In this conception, nationalism becomes rather more than a mass emotion based on ethnocentrism, more than 'national sentiment' or 'national consciousness'; it becomes an ideology itself, a rival to other political ideologies, yet distinguishable by its firm base in the 'natural' mass emotion that always accompanies ethnic association. By contrast, there is something strained and artificial about the 'class', 'state' and 'race' bases of communism, fascism and racism; the latter are more strictly products of peculiarly modern, even industrial, conditions, and they lack nationalism's ability to harness older conceptions and emotions. Nationalism is the natural heir of an unbroken tradition, which it seeks to use and channel for its own political ends. Even racism must invent broad and novel categories like 'Caucasian' or 'Alpine', or batten on to more ancient religious or ethnic hatreds, to gain its own ends. We may go further: as we saw, most of the victories of communism and populism were achieved through an alliance with nationalism, with nationalism the dominant partner, and fascism's success in interWar Europe was partly due to nationalism's temporary eclipse after 1918. Conversely, the failures of communism or fascism have been partly the result of their attacks on national emotions and nationalism. Even in Bolshevik Russia, the one great example of an international communist revolution, patriotism and nationalism re-emerged as a vital force in the defensive struggles of 1919–22, and under Stalin.

In this second sense, then, 'nations' are not just repositories of everything sacred and 'natural', or all that is truly 'rooted'. They become now vehicles of self-sacrifice, instruments of social mobilisation and arenas for revolution. Nationalism politicises the nation. It turns culture into the basis and criterion of politics, and provides the chief political framework for social development in our era. It transforms the nation into the 'nation-state'. The nation now is a specifically modern ideal, and to it are attached all those peculiarly modern strivings for authenticity, self-realisation, autonomy, participation and belonging that only seem to arise when the conditions for their attainment are lacking. The ideology of nationalism makes its appearance at that moment when modern conditions have disrupted, but not destroyed, the ancient cultural tradition and emotion of the ethnic nation.[4]

BUREAUCRATIC NATIONALISM

The existence of an ethnic tradition and mass emotion on which nationalists could draw goes part of the way towards explaining the breadth and depth of nationalism's appeal in the modern world. But it does not explain the success and popularity of nationalism as a modern political ideology of the nation-state and of national liberation. To understand its continuing appeal, indeed its resurgence today, we must look at a peculiarly modern cycle of processes whose effect is to enhance the status and appeal of the ethnic nation among the population.

We are often told that we live in a post-romantic age. We no longer share the exaggerated emotions and individualism of the romantic artist or poet, or his naive hopes and infinite yearnings. Ours is a practical, even pragmatic, epoch. Its dominant values are utilitarian, rationalistic and acquisitive. Efficiency and material wellbeing are sought as ends in themselves rather than means to the spiritual exaltation and self-absorption in nature that the romantics strove to attain. An ethic of competition and a dedication to method have replaced the earlier cult of individual genius and creative imagination; sentiment and innocence are distrusted or lamented; and advances in technology and psychology have eroded individual privacy and threatened man's autonomy.

These familiar antitheses rest on certain assumptions about the nature of twentieth-century society. We are, it is claimed, living in a 'mass society', in which communications, urban sprawl and the demographic explosion have generated anxieties and insecurities with which our welfare agencies are unable to cope and which our constitutional parties cannot harness to constructive ends. Rapid democratisation and industrialisation have destroyed traditions, thrown large numbers of disoriented individuals into vast urban melting pots and undermined the authority and prestige of old ruling élites.[5] At the same time, our societies are not shapeless masses or chaotic juxtapositions of purposeless individuals and institutions. They are dominated by vast bureaucratic organisations which regulate and control the lives, not only of their members, but also of large numbers of outsiders. Of these organisations, the most characteristic is the huge corporation, today often multinational, with its immense resources, skilled personnel and giant planning apparatus. But the same features can be found in government-dominated organisations like the armies of the superpowers or the great nationalised or state enterprises of mixed or socialist economies. The most inclusive organisation of all, the State, exhibits similar bureaucratic traits to a high degree. It organises responsibilities on the basis of clearly defined offices; it requires an hierarchical discipline, adheres to fixed routines and procedures, encourages large-scale planning and is judged according to a norm of efficiency, which is sought for its own sake.

Like other large organisations, the bureaucratic state is necessarily impersonal and rationalist. It deals in statistical categories and strata, and its *raison d'état* is indifferent to the fate of individuals. The individual is relevant only as a test case or precedent; for the bureaucrat he must become a depersonalised unit. The growing dependence of bureaucracy upon scientific and technical expertise abets this depersonalising trend. The drive towards cost effectiveness requires continual streamlining of methods and organisation, and a ceaseless incorporation of the latest knowledge and techniques in the field. Of course, this is the ideal to which bureaucracy strives. In practice, many administrations fall far short of the target and become hermetic networks of regulations and procedures which bear little relation to any official or external goals, as was the case with a number of preWar east European bureaucracies.[6] Alternatively, they may become riddled with corruption, as in some underdeveloped countries today; the organisation has become too cumbersome to effect anything without operating a system of connections and bribery. But in more advanced economies, inter-state and corporation competition must increasingly resort to the sort of marginal advantages that scientific expertise can alone confer and which technological resources can alone effect. Despite much internal resistance by some bureaucrats, the trend towards scientific rationalisation continues to accelerate.

State bureaucracies also differ from other large organisations in some important respects. Their range, of course, is much more comprehensive. In theory, no matter, however trivial, lies outside their domain. It is to the State that every citizen must look for his children's education, for his health and insurance services, for defence, taxation, justice, communications, for most of his information and much of his recreational facilities. Second, state bureaucracies have jurisdiction throughout a clearly delimited territory. It is this territorial definition and authority that has helped state bureaucracies to play so vital a part in creating a compact body of 'citizens', men and women who possess equal rights and duties before the State and are free to move where they like within the boundaries of the State. In doing so, state bureaucracies inevitably set their citizenry in potential opposition to the members of analogous state units. Through the use of devices like passports, frontier customs and currency controls, they screen the citizens of different territorial units off from each other, and so over time instil in them a sense of distinctiveness.[7] Third, the bureaucratic state finds it much more necessary than other large organisations to integrate its members into a homogeneous and even uniform body. Despite a political awareness of the uses of cultural pluralism, the trend of bureaucratisation within the State runs in the opposite direction. Laws and regulations have to be uniform and clearly understood by all; welfare services must be equitably provided; information universally disseminated and political rights and offices open to all on the basis of merit. The State must operate according to agreed or enforced rules covering every citizen on the basis of shared values. For this purpose a common language is helpful, or at least a common 'administrative language'; or there must be special arrangements for multilingual communities such as

Canada and Switzerland.[8] Hence the growth of a 'political culture', in which shared historic experiences are mirrored in the formation of common values and institutions which help to integrate different cultural and social groups.[9]

The growth of a political culture may soon foster a bureaucratic nationalism, whose chief attraction is to promise order and stability in periods of rapid change. The State is regarded as both a bulwark against too much or too swift change, and as an instrument for executing desired changes. Similarly, the State organises the nation's defence and excludes intruders, while simultaneously developing the internal resources and wellbeing of the community. In other words, the bureaucratic state fulfils for the nation its two primordial needs of stemming the uncontrollable march of time and enclosing a clearly delimited space. To accomplish these and other tasks, the nation today, in a world of nation-states, requires the political might and scientific expertise of the bureaucratic state. When a scientific state has taken 'root' and is regarded by its members as their true defence against external hostility and internal disintegration, when it becomes closely identified with the national history and territory, then it turns into a 'nation-state', and *étatisme* gives place to bureaucratic nationalism, as we find it in England and France over the centuries.[10]

Homelessness and Anarchy

For all the popularity of state or bureaucratic nationalisms in the modern era, they account for roughly only half of current nationalisms, and for only part of the appeal of nationalism as a modern political ideology. Nationalism today, as before, is also a movement of national liberation and ethnic revival. It not only serves ancient and well preserved ethnic nations; it also unites and revives scattered or disintegrated ethnic groups and even co-alesces several ethnic groups into a single political nation. Here its action is revolutionary rather than stabilising. It mobilises groups and welds them together, originating new nations and defining new ethnic territories, particularly in sub-Saharan Africa.[11] In Western Europe, on the other hand, the movement of ethnic revival and autonomy aims in some cases to separate distinctive parts of existing nation-states from the larger body and to create mini-states for those *ethnie*. In both the anti-colonial liberation struggles and the ethnic separatisms, the movement has been aimed primarily against the existing state and its bureaucratic apparatus; and by no stretch of the imagination can we call these movements bureaucratic nationalisms – if anything, they are a throwback to the older romantic nationalisms.

Anti-bureaucratic nationalisms are often treated as reactions to and imitations of state nationalisms. The very success of a bureaucratic nationalism of the majority induces a reaction by the less privileged minority which takes the form of wanting to imitate its success. In other words, minority nationalisms are simply 'second-wave' movements, which find a new cultural base for their political claims.[12] The success of the Belgian experiment induced an imitative reaction among the disprivileged Flemish; and in Pakistan the neglected Bengalis found in language a new base from which to promote their minority revolt. It is the 'demonstration effect' of a successful bid for independence that by itself spreads the desire for autonomy to any group with enough cultural self-consciousness, and which feels itself locked into an inferior position within a larger nation-state.

There is little doubt that the spectacle of a successful independence bid can serve as spur and example to incorporated minorities. But we still have to explain why they come, at this point in time, to feel neglected or disprivileged, and why they attribute this to their incorporation into an existing political unit. What is it that promotes their new cultural self-awareness and their political resentment?

A large part of the answer must lie in the social and cultural effects of excessive bureaucratic control and regimentation. Three aspects of this control, especially, encourage protest and resistance on the part of individuals and groups. The most obvious of these is the impersonality of the bureaucratic machine. Several experiments in large industrial plants revealed how small informal groups of friends and colleagues were formed as a reaction to the monolithic impersonality and uniformity of the large formal organisation. These small friendship groups counteract feelings of insignificance and insecurity often created by depersonalised organisations. The new experience of becoming part of a giant machine governed by universal procedures and purely instrumental ties produces in many a nostalgia for smaller, traditional groups and a new awareness of the importance of 'belonging'. It is not difficult for men to feel atomised in such large organisations, divorced from their processes and purposes, cynical about their leaders, and apathetic towards their symbols and rationales. Increasingly unable to identify with bureaucratic goals, they search for communities in which personal relationships and emotional ties replace rules and procedures as the binding force in society. At the highest and most inclusive level of the bureaucratic state, it is the nation that appears to many to fulfil the promise of truly fraternal ties and emotional solidarity.

While impersonality and its counterpart, a 'desire to belong', are important general consequences of bureaucratisation, they do not as yet explain why bureaucracies tend to generate such anarchic protests or how they promote a new romanticism and nationalism. To understand this, we must consider two other aspects of bureaucracy: its technological rationalism, and its centralised planning, both of which are highly developed in the State. Ever since the eighteenth century, enlightened despots and administrations have utilised scientific methods and techniques, but never to such a high degree and on such a scale as in our century. Owing to the late nineteenth-century technological–scientific revolution based on electricity and chemicals, which altered everyday life in an unprecedented manner, bureaucratic corporations and organisations can penetrate into every sector of the economy and society, reach every social class and region, and bring technical solutions to bear on every social problem.[13] The new technology of industrial and governmental bureaucracies, the marriage between scientific technology and the State, has transformed many a formerly personal affair into a social problem with a technical and collective solution. As it developed, the bureaucratic and scientific state has based its appeal and rationale increasingly upon this ability to call on tools and expertise beyond the reach of individuals or smaller groups. It must therefore keep pace with modernisation, with the applications of scientific method and techniques to social life. Today, for example, it relies on the use of computer technology and electronics for many of its operations, and utilises systems analysis for the solution of many problems.

But, in so far as the machine of the bureaucratic state is necessarily powered by the engine of modernisation, its operations, and even more its approach to problems, must be heavily mechanistic and technical. The operators of the bureaucratic state machine increasingly identify reason and understanding with technique, procedure and system. Confronted by large-scale problems with variant solutions, bureaucratic operators tend to think in terms of statistical categories and input–output models, which in turn allow small scope for individual vagaries or historical differences and intensities. Indeed, the understanding of continuities and changes over generations, or of the effect of traumatic events, both of which are so important for historical analysis, lies generally outside the purview of a highly mechanised and rationalised bureaucratic organisation like the modern state. The scientific state is largely ahistorical in character; it can have little sense of the historic compromises between classes, regions and ethnic groups that have played so large a role in the formation of today's nation-states.

Today, however, we are witnessing a strong reaction in several spheres to 'modernisation'. This is true whether we understand by 'modernisation' self-sustaining economic growth, or, more generally, the increasing social utilisation of scientific methods and machine-powered technology.[14] It is no accident that ecological movements have sprung up at the same time as the ethnic revival, women's liberation and neo-Marxism. For what they all share is a rejection of the bureaucratic approach with its heavily mechanistic emphasis and its systemic model. In contrast, the 'minority' movements have all stressed the need for more open, subjective approaches, identifying understanding with immediate experience or even intuition. They have rejected the dogmas of economic development and social engineering, i.e. much of what passes for modernisation, in order to find authentic personal experience, a richer participation in social life, and a more individual self-expression. In rejecting the mechanistic rationalism underlying the bureaucratic state, they have also called into question the need for the State itself, and have opened the door to anarchic solutions and terroristic protests.

If technological rationalism induces a subjective flight from reason, the highly centralised planning characteristic of state bureaucracies only aggravates the problem. However sensitive individual planners may be to local issues, the systemic model and demands for uniformity and homogeneity required by external and internal pressures make it exceedingly difficult to cater to regional and historical needs of the different sections of the population. The modernising drive of the bureaucratic machine has already destroyed the delicate balance of forces that resulted from the historic compromises on which the State was built, compromises like the union of Scotland and England, or the incorporation of Brittany, or the compromise between Galla, Tigre and Amharic tribes which formed the basis of the Ethiopian state.[15] Planned centralism erodes traditional regional, tribal–ethnic or linguistic groups which till recently managed to shield individuals from the severest effects of bureaucratic intrusion. Inevitably, with its lack of historical understanding and its relegation of the local for the state-wide problem, the bureaucratic machine neglects or misconstrues the special problems of specific groups, with their very different resources, stages of development, cultural features and social institutions. Worse, when it starts to 'develop' these areas and impinge on these groups, it must inflame and magnify existing differences, making the disparities more visible and public. For all its concern with 'special needs' of local areas, a highly centralised state authority inevitably removes still further to the centre all important decisions that form an essential part of its overall development plan.

Little wonder, then, that minority reaction to what is seen as an insensitive and exploitative juggernaut may spill over into a wholesale rejection of any social order so dependent upon modernisation and planning. Small wonder also that the slogan of 'small is beautiful' sounds so alluring, when the brute fact of size appears to be at the root of both neglect and centralised development alike. In these circumstances, the sense of 'homelessness' and the rejection of state authority go hand in hand, and lead to futile anarchic terrorism – or to nationalism.

THE NEW ROMANTICISM

Anarchism and nationalism may, of course, be closely intertwined, especially during a terroristic phase, but in the long run a choice has to be made between the chiliastic cult of revolution and disorder, and the sober commitment to founding a new social and cultural order or 'nation'. It is a choice between an abstract universal ideal implying a nomadic global existence, and a more practical and limited vision rooted in historical differences in a fixed area. In forsaking anarchic and utopian protest for ethnic nationalism, the new romantic detaches himself from a revolutionary but largely élitist intellectual and cosmopolitan ideal and immerses himself in the vision and reality of a mass cultural entity into which he invests his revolutionary fervour. In this respect, the cultural and psychological unit of the 'nation' is much superior to the purely economic category of 'class' or the excessively ideological 'sect' of professional revolutionaries. The nation offers much greater opportunities for both irrationalism and mass mobilisation.

We have recently become familiar with the more direct forms of anarchic protest against modernising bureaucracy. But repeated onslaughts on governments and corporations, and the kidnapping and murder of their representatives, constitute a small fraction, albeit in extreme and vivid form, of the new anarchic romanticism. Equally important are the various campaigns on behalf of minorities – homosexuals, Blacks, women – and for the protection of the environment. Perhaps even more influential have been the indirect protests against positivist and rationalistic modes of thought, ranging from the cult of the extrasensory and occult to various brands of idealistic neo-Marxism, which emphasise Marx's humanism in his early writings.[16] In their different ways, such movements bear witness to the current popularity of the flight from reason. They are equally vehement in their rejection of positivism, of economic explanations and of technical expertise, all of which play such a vital role in the running of the bureaucratic machine. Instead, they emphasise the importance of authenticity, of discovering one's true self and holding fast to it, and of self-expression; of experiencing life for oneself and allowing those experiences unhindered play. To authenticity and self-expression they add the value of autonomy, of the need for man to act as his own guide in life and to obey his own inner dictates without advice or compulsion from outside. The new romantics are thoroughgoing subjectivists. For them, every conception and position is ideological and value-laden. They fight against the dominant technological and acquisitive values of society, which, they claim, are reifications imposed on the individual from without and which strangle his capacity for true experience and self-expression.

In this context, the revival of a romantic type of ethnic nationalism becomes more intelligible. Like other forms of romanticism, the new nationalism is directed against the technological and bureaucratic state and the 'false' bureaucratic nationalism that it generates. The ethnic nation becomes the new bearer of self-liberation, because it appears to embody mass emotion unalloyed by the ratiocinations of élites committed to utilising the State's bureaucratic machine to maintain their own position and modernise their societies. Even more important, the ethnic nation provides the stratum most exposed to bureaucratic ravages, the intelligentsia, with a mode of re-identification with other strata from which it had been cut adrift by its secular education and commitment to rational modernisation. Closer and longer contact with the impersonality, mechanistic rationalism and centralised planning of bureaucratic regimentation has turned many professionals and intellectuals into estranged and disillusioned anti-rationalists ripe for the new subjective romanticism. The latter promises to restore an identity shattered and fragmented by bureaucratic modernisation. It matters little whether such an identity really existed before the onset of modernisation. It becomes now an object of intense yearning as the scientific state advances in space and depth. The search for new identities based preferably upon primordial roots helps not only to restore a threatened continuity with the past, but also to control and channel the drives of scientific modernisation. In the ethnic nation, the intelligentsia discerns an instrument for subjugating and harnessing the modernising energies of the scientific state and its bureaucratic apparatus.[17] Hence its appeal for the new romantic. Through the nation he can mobilise and summon up a source of energy superior to that of the scientific state, for the nation's roots draw on factors far older and more profound than even the most powerful system or technique utilised by the State. The nation is, as we saw, rooted in the primal need for location against chaos in time and space, the need for origins and the need for territorial enclosure. But such needs are liberating as much as they are stabilising, for they are products not of reason and technique but of more fluid, 'natural' rhythms, formed by man's relations with his natural environment. It is, of course, to 'nature' that neo-romantics, like their predecessors, make their appeal; and here again we find an easy affinity between the new romanticism and ethnic neo-nationalisms in Europe or populist nationalisms outside. Neo-romantic nationalists can once again juxtapose the 'natural' cultural entity of the nation to the harsh and artificial 'iron grid' of the scientific state: everything that is life-giving and authentic, which the bureaucratic state threatens to crush and deprive us of, the earth-rooted nation will restore and replenish.

THE FASCIST ALTERNATIVE

Quite clearly, we do not inhabit a post-romantic world; rather, one in which romantic ideas and activities, like the sightseeing tour, come to us well-packaged and trivialised. The romantic experience has not vanished, nor has it lost its meaning for many people. But it is no longer easily accessible, except in an attenuated form. Commercialism and bureaucracy have denatured romantic experiences, and science has attempted to explain them away. Yet, despite these pressures, romantic tendencies persist and find new supporters among younger generations.

But the very vagueness and emotionalism of the new romanticism poses a threat to nationalism. The search for new identities can take more radical forms under the aegis of an ethnic revival. Thus neo-fascist organisations may utilise the romantic groundswell to evoke racial feelings which are identified with national loyalties. Nationalist racisms, as we found, utilise national sentiment on behalf of the race. For their adherents, the nation is subordinate to the race, and cultural differences are explained in biological terms, as the result of a particular 'stock' or 'blood'. But such nationalist racisms depend for their efficacy upon the seizure and utilisation of an effective state machine, in which parliaments and parties may be proscribed and the nation organised along military lines in preparation for the possibility of war. Not all nationalistic racisms turn fascist and embrace an ethic of violence for its own sake, a Darwinian conception of the world struggle for mastery, and a cult of the Leader and the State. But the probability remains. The very radicalism of racial thought, the exclusiveness and superiority that it breeds, encourages a resort to violence and war, and a belief in the infallibility of the State and the Leader who alone knows the secrets of the race.

The dangers of racial fascism to nationalism are enhanced by nationalism's emotional proclivities. Although in itself the national ideal is largely unrelated to fascist themes, it can, in certain circumstances, be subverted by racism or fascism or both. Ascertaining those conditions constitutes an important task for future research.

Clearly, some versions of nationalism possess a greater affinity for racial motifs or state violence than others; but this is only the first step in any social analysis. Economic crises may well breed more radical solutions to an identity crisis, but it is in the political institutions as they interact with cultural traditions that we must seek the roots of the transformation of nationalism into fascism. How far these institutions can cope with crises of purpose and identity; how far a nation's cultural traditions enable it to meet external challenges to its identity, are questions that may throw more light on the crucial turn towards fascism.

THE BUREAUCRATIC CYCLE

The need for nationalism to tap popular emotions renders it susceptible not only to racism and fascism, but also to a populist anarchism. In other circumstances, again, we find popular national sentiment reinforcing the bureaucratic state and social order. In fact, the ideal of the nation oscillates in popular feeling between an impulse to liberation and romantic protest and a bastion of public order and stability. A direct external threat will generally swing the popular mood behind the State; but the more long-term and invisible competition of foreign powers coupled with internal divisions or decay can foster a romantic anti-state nationalism, appealing to a mystic notion of the ethnic nation above the heads of existing authority.

As an ideology, too, nationalism normally veers between the two poles of anarchism and *étatisme*. Starting as a romantic protest against excessive bureaucracy and rationalism, it aspires to liberate the true cultural nation from the toils of a bureaucratic machine run by an unrepresentative élite along centralised and modernising lines. At this juncture, nationalism aims to secure autonomy and authenticity for the cultural entity that it has singled out on historical grounds. By doing so, it hopes to be able to restore the 'people' of the nation to their true identity and rightful 'home'. By securing international recognition of the homeland as a territorial unit, it hopes to end the inner feeling of estrangement and homelessness among the 'people'.

In the next stage of the cycle, the nationalists have secured this recognition and are embarked upon the tasks of 'nation-building'. They are constructing out of the ethnic and cultural materials to hand the 'true' nation of their ideals. An essential part of this building process is the provision of an adequate central authority with sufficient powers and skills to serve the social and cultural needs of the whole population. In other words, extending the scope and efficiency of the bureaucratic machine and its systematic approach becomes the lynch-pin of 'nation-building'. This in turn means that the original liberating impulse of nationalism must be curbed. The quest for authenticity and autonomy must not be allowed to interfere with the integrating and moulding tasks of the bureaucratic machine. Romantic nationalism must give way to a more predictable and routinised bureaucratic nationalism. Besides, if the nation is to survive in a world of highly competitive nation-states, the State's authority and efficiency, and its ability to modernise and develop the country's resources, must be strengthened and supported in every way. The impact and urgency of the international situation allows little scope for the free expression of unbridled romantic impulses in the context of the nation-state. Romantic energies have to be harnessed and regulated in well-planned and centrally executed projects of state-building if a new kind of colonialism is to be staved off.

This leads to the third stage. The nation is identified with the State, with established and routine authority. National loyalty threatens to turn into acceptance of bureaucratic *diktat* and expertise, with representative institutions finding their powers eroded and trivialised. In the absence of an immediate external threat like war, the original nationalist vision is destroyed and the emotions that inspired it become ossified. They do not die, however. As the State increasingly depersonalises society, as bureaucratic control becomes ever more mechanistic and centralised, the majority of people become apathetic and alienated, and the intelligentsia disillusioned and resentful. The bureaucratic state is creating just those social needs and unfulfilled longings for a true identity and home, and just that revolt against scientific modernisation, that prompted the original national ideal.

And so we arrive back at the first stage in the cycle, where part of the intelligentsia decide to forsake anarchic protests and abstract intellectual ideals in order to attach themselves to a limited but historic mass entity, the nation. Given a world of separate and competing states, the bureaucratic cycle appears to be self-reproducing. Moreover, where a nation-state contains more than one ethnic group, there is a ready-made focus for romantic protests against bureaucracy. Nor does there seem to be any prospect of an end to the cycle when the current ethnic nationalisms are satisfied. What one may call the 'Shetland effect', where a smaller ethnic entity within a larger ethnic nationalism stakes out its own claims, as with the Shetland Isles in Scotland, appears to be widespread and likely to proliferate.[18]

A large part of the appeal of nationalism today derives then from the bureaucratic cycle, with its built-in tendency to generate new movements of liberation. In their flight from excessive rationalism and bureaucracy, the intelligentsia's neo-romanticism is largely in tune with the ethnic tradition and popular emotions of the nation which nationalists aim to exploit. But in choosing to attach his romantic and subjective outlook to the nation, the protester, whether he appreciates it or not, has taken a decisive step back on to the road of modernisation. By immersing his own liberation in his ethnic community's regeneration, by seeking his own identity and self-expression through his nation's recreation, the romantic and irrationalist protester begins to engage in tasks of collective mobilisation and development which require rational techniques and scientific procedures, as well as the organisation furnished by the State. He must therefore exchange his world of impulse and spontaneity for one in which rational control, logic and calculation become paramount, for a world increasingly dominated by a hitherto despised technology. And so nationalism becomes, unintentionally, an agent of modernisation, despite its current predominantly anti-modernising sources.

THE NATION AS BUFFER

I have suggested two reasons for the present resurgence of nationalism. The first is general: the existence of a strong ethnic tradition and deep, if muted, popular sentiments of nationality on which nationalists can draw. The second is historically specific; the operations of the bureaucratic cycle, which throw up two kinds of nationalism today, a state-oriented nationalism and, by way of reaction, a romantic ethnic nationalism. Both kinds of nationalism, of course, gain immeasurably from the division of the globe, over the last two centuries, into an increasing number of sovereign nation-states, and by the demonstrable successes of nationalist movements.

Sentiments of nationality are often cloudy and unstable. Yet there has been something constant in the invocation of the 'nation' as touchstone of culture and politics. The nation appears to combine and balance out conflicting social needs, and to act as a buffer between the Scylla of a mechanistic bureaucracy and the Charybdis of utopian and anarchic irrationalism. Though the ideology of nationalism may at times waver between these poles, the nation itself seems to be able to reconcile antagonistic needs for order and mastery and for autonomy and self-expression. Its persistence as the foremost social category owes a good deal to this capacity for absorbing and reconciling opposites. As long as bureaucratism and irrationalism are accounted dangers to the social fabric, the nation is likely to continue as refuge and court of appeal. And with every turn in the bureaucratic cycle, nationalism's hold must extend and grow.

The national ideal draws on emotions and ties that stretch back into antiquity, but it flourishes best in the modern conditions of rationalism, bureaucracy and the world state system; for they produce just those needs and aspirations for home and identity that nationalism was created to satisfy and that it must periodically reaffirm.

CHAPTER 8

Internationalism

The apparent paradox that nationalism flourishes in an era of internationalism compels us to reassess the chances of transcending or abolishing nationalism in the future. If the impact of the bureaucratic cycle remains the chief 'internal' obstacle to such a transcendence, the internationalisation of nationalism is increasingly becoming the main 'external' impediment, and conversely the very foundation for a consolidation and resurgence of nationalism.

'SATISFIED' NATIONALISMS?

For at least a century, liberal cosmopolitans have dreamed of an interdependent world with a single broad civilisation and unimpeded mobility across continents. In our century this ideal was reinforced by aspirations for a world government, which first the League of Nations, and then the United Nations, were supposed to embody. As a first step, cosmopolitans hoped to transcend 'narrow nationalism' by regional–continental unions, such as the pan-European Common Market, the Arab League and the Organisation of African Unity. For the rest, it was expected that increasing mass tourism, the diffusion of news and opinions through the mass media and, above all, multilateral trade would render nationalism, if not nation-states, otiose. Echoing the Marxist prediction that from the many local cultures, capitalism and socialism would produce a 'world literature' which would erode national one-sidedness and 'narrow-mindedness', our latter-day cosmopolitans have seen in cultural and student exchanges, in education in current affairs and in the growth of new *linguae francae* the basis for a new world culture which will dissolve men's allegiances to narrow national units.[1]

There is no need to dwell on the *naïveté* of such hopes in the present, but it is instructive to inquire into the reasons for their disappointment. To begin with, they were entertained either by educated liberals in the old Western states, or by the upwardly mobile in the two new superpowers which controlled, directly or economically, the destinies of several smaller nations. As Seton-Watson points out, both America and the Soviet Union have had to deal with troublesome nationalisms within and outside their domains; and we may add that the old Western states are experiencing similar difficulties.[2] In both cases, the optimistic forecasts of liberals that urbanisation, industrialisation and mass education would diminish the appeals of nationalism, have proved erroneous. For, in the second place, modernisation itself appears to feed national sentiments and hatreds, rather than assuaging them. This is, of course, partly due to the uneven course of industrial and social development, which at different times will favour one area at the expense of others, so creating resentments and rivalries.[3] This unevenness, claims Gellner, is disruptive: it produces mobility, 'and mobility *in conjunction* with even relative poverty does breed discontent, where much greater poverty in stable conditions does not' (italics in original).[4] But modernisation is not only uneven; it involves group competition for scarce urban facilities.[5] Hence, it not only throws together hitherto relatively isolated ethnic groups, but it also sets them against each other. Their economic and cultural roles are no longer complementary, but competitive; they duplicate each other's activities well in excess of given levels of need.[6] Third, and by a similar token, the cultural exchange across national frontiers that modernisation encourages may well produce demands for national cultural rejuvenation. Fears of cultural imperialism today usually take the form of rejecting 'Western', 'Yankee' or 'Soviet' hegemony and tutelage (and within the 'West', of superpower influence and fashions). Just as mobility to cities within one's national unit often fuels ethnic rivalries by making ethnic groups that much more visible and 'threatening', so international mobility can, and does, sometimes promote a return to local springs of creativity and a new concern for historic and cultural identity.

If modernisation itself, contrary to liberal expectations, actually feeds national sentiment, can nationalism ever be satisfied? Surely, once nationalism's own demands for independence and unification are met, and the painful transition to full industrialism and modernity is over, nationalism will wither away of its own accord? For its tasks will be accomplished, its aspirations fulfilled.[7] This argument can also be found in a functionalist form. According to this version, nationalism is one of several ideologies that initially promote rationalisation and social development; but then their very success renders them superfluous or even an obstacle to further progress; i.e., rationalisation.[8] They must therefore gradually be superseded by other ideologies, or become 'de-ideologised', purely pragmatic and technical or, as Weber would say, routinised.

Oddly enough, this kind of 'routinisation' or 'normalisation' is just what many nationalisms aspire to, but never quite attain. At the simplest level, nationalists want world recognition of their movement and their nation; they want a vote in the United Nations. At a deeper level, they want a balanced division of labour, a full complement of social strata and cultural skills of the kind featured in the advanced Western nation-states. They also want the full organisational apparatus of the modern state and, above all, the sense of solidarity and uniqueness which, they feel, can alone sustain the national structure. Inverting the 'base–superstructure' metaphor of the Marxists, the nationalists require a cultural base of history, identity and language, on which to build and nurture the 'corresponding' forms of economic, class and bureaucratic superstructures. All this is 'normality' to a nationalist.

The trouble is that, as we can see, normality is continually coming up against the cult of the unique and different, against authenticity; and authenticity tends to be so unpredictable, so unroutinised. In other words, nationalism's sole means to its ends are in perennial tension with those ends. To become 'normal' you have to be unique; but you can never know in advance where the quest for uniqueness will lead, or when its stirrings and promptings will occur.

It is therefore not just the persistence of mass ethnic sentiments, or the bureaucratic cycle, that nurture national sentiment. There is something arbitrary and unpredictable built into the whole movement. Nationalism becomes self-reproducing in a world of nation-states. For once the world has defined 'normality' as national solidarity and national statehood, every nation must be vigilant against signs of cultural assimilation and must produce nationalists whose self-appointed task is to strengthen national identity and uniqueness in order to increase social cohesion and solidarity. In a world of nation-states, nationalism can never be ultimately satisfied. Perhaps full industrialisation and mass education may diminish national aggressiveness; Gellner cites the case of Switzerland as a 'traditional society which has weathered modernisation' and so can tolerate linguistic pluralism.[9] But even here there are linguistic difficulties in the Jura; and very special factors, like their heavily armed neutrality and geopolitical situation, operate to consolidate their profound sense of a distinct Swiss solidarity, which is often exclusive and inward-looking.[10] As Gellner later acknowledged, full industrialism and the satisfaction of most of the nationalist goals did not diminish national violence and aggression in Japan and Germany, a violence that fascism was able to exploit.[11] But these are only extreme cases of a far wider phenomenon. The real point is that the persistence of nationalism, even after its initial political demands have been met and even after modernisation is attained, is a function of the international system itself. Nationalism may initially have helped to create that system; now it is in turn maintained by that system, much as the industrial machine now maintains the capitalism that did so much to promote industrialism.[12] The conditions of the persistence of nationalism have shifted from those that originally promoted it, giving greater prominence to the new external factors that nationalism itself helped to generate.

In a World of Nation-States

Although the nature and degree of the new 'world state system' are subject to dispute, there is little doubt that many states today are linked in a series of near-global transactions and dependencies. Very few states are regionally isolated, and a good many states have important linkages with other states far from their cultural area. This makes traditional considerations like the 'balance of power', which played so important a role in the eighteenth-century European crucible of nationalism, even more important today. True, that balance is no longer exclusively between nation-states acting sovereignly and independently, as in nineteenth-century Europe. It is as much between regional blocs (Nato, Warsaw Pact, OAU, etc.) as between nations. Yet in practice, the blocs are rarely activated as such, but only in relation to national disputes, such as those between India and Pakistan, Algeria and Morocco or Ethiopia and Somalia. Even in the most dramatic example of an intra-regional conflict, that between Arabs and Israelis, it is not Nato or the Warsaw Pact as such that are involved, but Russia and America as national superpowers supporting local client-nations. Hence, nationalism's diffusion has simply globalised the traditional European 'balance of power' concepts and relationships, and these in turn are now reinforcing nationalisms. For the fact that there is such a balance of power, or of terror, allows much greater scope for nationalist aggressions and hatreds, and greater hope for national secessionists.

Indeed, the more closely one looks at the record, the more one is struck by the 'pincer' pattern of successful nationalist revolts. One arm of the pincer is internal: the native guerilla movement or the local party organisation demanding independence or secession. The other is external, in the form of support from one or more of the great powers which sees in the native movement a chance to weaken its rivals. Great power support may be abetted by a diaspora movement, which lends its local brethren material and moral resources, and influences the great power. Very rarely can a native movement succeed without this external support, as the Greek rebels learnt in 1827, and the Armenians and Kurds to their bitter cost in our century.[13] The particular geopolitical constellation must allow sufficient room for manoeuvre, and find one of the powers committed to the support of a movement, if that movement is to have any chance against determined opposition. Even where the imperial or colonial power wants to divest itself of its irksome possessions, the geopolitical balance must be favourable; it was so for Britain in 1947, in so far as America could ensure the necessary stability and balance, which an otherwise hasty retreat might have upset.

Native nationalisms have quickly learnt to internationalise their image and networks. They are already well versed in the arts of propaganda and make full use of the mass media to reach a large public in countries whose governments can tip the balance in their direction. International terrorism is another nationalist weapon; by acquiring the language and contacts of the international revolutionary sects, nationalist guerillas of submerged and neglected ethnic groups can bring their cause to public notice and put some pressure on unfriendly governments to make concessions. There are signs, however, that this particular tactic can misfire; and besides, it again requires at least one favourable great power to have anything more than nuisance value.[14]

Apart from global balances of power blocs, several other aspects of the world state system help to consolidate and entrench nationalist ideals and national fervour. In one of its aspects, the world system entails a competition for global prestige between national élites. It is hardly surprising that a 'system of locks', into which nationalism has divided the world, should generate deep feelings of inferiority and dishonour among national élites.[15] Under colonialism, these élites were frequently thrown together in the dominant metropolis, where they acquired many Western values and realised their own powerlessness and the indignity and decline of their communities. The urge to reach parity or equivalence with the West was a natural consequence of their atimic perceptions and feelings. In the nature of the situation, these feelings are not likely to be easily assuaged. Short of centralised planning by a world authority, social and economic modernisation will continue to proceed both unevenly and nationally, and to favour those already ahead in the race. Besides, mineral and other resources being unevenly distributed across the globe, some latecomers are likely to outstrip others, exacerbating tensions in local regions between national élites. This is of particular importance where ethnic groups already have a history of mutual antagonism, and where perhaps one of them enjoys the favour and protection of a great power. Both the economic and the political aspects of an international system of client-states must therefore sharpen nationalist tensions in the southern and poorer hemisphere, despite their professed non-alignment.

Closely allied to this élite competition is the transformation of the leadership of the new states. In the later days of colonialism, nationalist leaders tended to balance their local concerns with a strong commitment to more universal ideals. In this, they approached those cosmopolitan intellectuals who, from the time of the Enlightenment, have looked forward to a single global civilisation and regarded themselves as citizens of the world. Few of these intellectuals who arrived in Europe or America desiring such a total assimilation were idealistic enough to transcend the frankly nationalist realities of their new environment. Most of these intellectuals returned disillusioned with the West and resentful of its double standards. Yet many still retained an intellectual substructure in their outlook to support their specific local aspirations, and they tended to seek the first opportunity to tie in their local nationalisms with a wider continental ideal such as pan-Africanism.

Today, this intellectual leadership is being gradually replaced by local intelligentsias whose acquaintance with Western ways and thought is more superficial and short-lived. As nationalism penetrates the local social structure, it tends to bring most of the intelligentsia into its orbit, men and women whose whole *raison d'être* and life-chances depend upon diplomas which today are increasingly conferred by native bodies according to local requirements and standards. There is, of course, still a considerable Western influence in many countries in the form of borrowed academics and technicians, at least in the non-socialist states. But even there, that influence is being mediated by the local intelligentsia, which is succeeding a more cosmopolitan generation of intellectuals, and whose vision is correspondingly more circumscribed and inward-looking.

For this intelligentsia the primary concern becomes the provision of suitable posts and niches for the 'career open to talent', and hence the promotion of enough social and economic development to accommodate their growing number. Their interest is naturally focused upon the governmental and local bureaucracies and the professions, which form the structural core of a modern self-supporting and viable state. Hence their interest in replicating bureaucracies to provide an area of closed competition for status. Both the territorial and structural aspects of the nation-state answer ideally to their status needs, providing ladders of ascent for ambitious, qualified professionals. A sense of international equivalence can be partially satisfied by these means: even if one cannot catch up with the West, one can develop a local status system and apparatus superior perhaps to those of one's neighbours.

This is also one source of another familiar demand of today's nationalists: economic autarchy. To maintain the bureaucratic apparatus necessary for a local status system suited to the new educated strata, there must be sufficient sustained economic growth and enough local control of resources and wealth. Otherwise, corruption will devalue the new status hierarchy and imperil its efficacy; or the new élites and their institutions will become dependent again on one or other of the great powers. Since both outcomes are not infrequent, nationalist intelligentsias are particularly concerned to maximise production and diversify their economies, in the face of world price fluctuations and adverse trade balances.

In this, they are abetted by international advisers from the United Nations and other world bodies, who emphasise the virtues of self-help and self-sufficiency.[16] Once again, the national élites' reactions to an interdependent world state system strengthens their commitment to nationalist goals and their desire to mobilise national sentiment among their populations.

The nationalism of local élites is, somewhat paradoxically, fortified by the prescriptions of international élites. These latter are particularly prominent in various international agencies like the United Nations and its agencies, the World Bank, IMF, OECD and the like. The international corps of advisers – technocrats, economists, agronomists, educationists, health and welfare experts – are often selected on a national and regional basis, and tend to be called in to advise national governments on development plans which again are necessarily national in scope. Their statistics, too, are collected on a national basis; and not merely the data, but also the assumptions behind such information-gathering operations, are bound up with a nationalist framework which views 'societies' as 'naturally' determined by the boundaries and properties of nation-states.[17] Perhaps it is not after all so surprising that international advisers, drawn as they are from national catchments, should conceptualise world development in terms of an aggregate of 'nation-building' operations, as the sum of national development programmes. But we should also remember that even the metropolitan and superpower élite advisers in these international organisations are wedded to an interpretation of development that is autarchic, if not outright protectionist; in other words, 'development' is 'self-development' using native resources and indigenous skills.[18]

These 'national' interpretations of progress and change extend equally into the sphere of theory. The study of 'society' today is, almost without question, equated with the analysis of nation-states; the principle of 'methodological nationalism' operates at every level in the sociology, politics, economics and history of mankind in the modern era.[19] There are very good practical reasons for proceeding in this way, but the theoretical underpinning derives much of its force from acceptance of nationalist conceptions, and goes a long way to reinforce those conceptions. In this way, the world nation-state system has become an enduring and stable component of our whole cognitive outlook, quite apart from the psychological satisfactions it confers.

CONSEQUENCES OF INTERNATIONAL DISRUPTIONS

The upshot of our argument so far has been to demonstrate the mechanisms through which an emergent international system today actually reinforces the nationalism that helped to produce it. Through the 'globalisation' of the balance of power between states, and through the competitive economic and status concerns of nationalist intelligentsias, the world state system sharpens nationalist tensions, while turning national sentiment and nationalist ideals into 'normal' and 'natural' properties of that system. Internationalism legitimates nationalism. If it has not so far tamed nationalism, it has made it respectable. Even the theories and activities of internationalist élites buttress national assumptions and nationalist activities.

This means, of course, that we can no longer oppose, as is still often done, 'internationalism' to nationalism. Cosmopolitanism is the real enemy of nationalism; internationalism is simply the mutual recognition and legitimation of other people's nationalisms, institutionalised in a global framework.

But beyond this, 'internationalism' tends to support only certain kinds of nationalism, the nationalism of nation-states duly constituted and broadly recognised. It cannot legitimate the aspirations of ethnic groups or nationalist movements who challenge an existing nation-state constituent of the international order. Internationalism therefore exists in a state of perennial tension with aspirant and secessionist nationalisms. Abhorring separatism, it must treat such movements as instances of international disruption. Similarly, supporters of the international order of nation-states must view with suspicion attempts to unify states by 'pan' movements, operating on the basis of criteria far removed from the state-based principles that govern acceptance into the international system. Not only do 'pan' unification movements pose a threat to existing balances of power, global and regional; they also undermine the historical and legal framework of the international order. The international order as such, therefore, always appears as a bulwark of the nationalism of nation-states against those of units outside the state.

Many nation-states, however, are threatened today with either absorption into larger units, or balkanisation into smaller ones. As we have seen, the principle of self-determination can be invoked by groups and units of every size and type; there is no universally agreed set of criteria for constituting a 'nation', no consensus on the scale of nations. The non-Western world has simply not followed the West in this respect. It has thrown overboard the principle of a 'medium scale' (between sprawling empires and self-sufficient villages or cities) in order to safeguard other more central precepts of nationalism, treating the former as 'appearance', the latter as 'substance'. The scale of England and France, albeit convenient, was after all accidental; there is no good *a priori* reason why smaller, or larger, groups cannot have autonomy, solidarity and identity.[20]

The more therefore the international order backs up the claims of existing nation-states, the more it treats other claims as 'disruptive', the more it fans the flames of ethnic and 'pan' nationalisms; and the greater becomes the temptation for separatist movements, in particular, to seek the aid of a great power to upset the balance of power temporarily, in order to gain admission to the club of nation-states hallowed by internationalism. Here too, then, internationalism indirectly feeds nationalisms by backing some national units at the expense of others, and so tempting one or other of its national constituents to break ranks so as to support aspirant nationalisms.

Ethnic and 'pan' movements in turn bolster and rejuvenate the nationalism of existing nation-states. 'Integration' and 'homogenisation' become pressing needs, not just remote ideals, for the often fragile new states in reaction to the threat of balkanisation or absorption. In Africa, especially, the chances of 'tribal' secession lend a new force and urgency to the bureaucratic nationalisms of the sub-Saharan states.[21] Even in Europe, the neo-nationalist separatist movements are beginning to reinforce the national sentiments of the majority ethnic group in old states like Britain and France, themselves involved in regional and international competition for markets and prestige.

Consequently, nationalism and internationalism are involved in a vicious circle of mutual reinforcement, operating through frequent local disruptions of the international order, as well as élite competition and power balances. Each local disruption of that order strengthens it; every international legitimation of existing states helps to provoke local attacks on that order and upset the balance of power that it upholds. And finally, every disruption of the international system sharpens national conflicts both at the local and international levels, raising the threshold of national consciousness among the affected populations.

SUPRANATIONALISM

If nationalism and internationalism are really two sides of the same coin, perhaps cosmopolitan hopes of submerging nationalism can be better served by the trend towards supranationalism in some areas? This is a question posed particularly by the development of the European Economic Community and its apparent challenge to existing state nationalisms.

The 'European' ideal and its translation into the EEC institutions are products of a partnership between pan-European idealists and national European technocrats. The result is an uneasy compromise between a *confederation des patries* centring on the Council of Ministers and the European union envisaged by the idealists and focused on the European Commission and the European Parliament. If the technocrats and national élites find in Europe a convenient extension and hinterland for national prestige and national products, the pan-European idealists have from the inception of their movement in The Hague in 1948 sought a genuine political union and an authentic European identity to replace existing national identities.[22]

From the standpoint of cosmopolitan dreams, the latter kind of pan-Europeanism is apt to be disappointing. It bears too close a resemblance to the nationalism of existing nation-states. There is a similar incentive, the fear of external enemies, this time rival superpower blocs to the east and west. There is a similar set of goals, a shared desire for political unification and autonomy, and a similar concern with an identity based on a common Christian–medieval past. There are the same nationalist drives for world prestige and economic self-sufficiency and self-development. Nor need the multilingual nature of the Community prove an insuperable obstacle; does not Switzerland manage perfectly well with four languages? Common political institutions will, over time, create a common political culture and a shared purpose and will.[23]

Supranationalism, therefore, may decrease the number of competing nationalisms in an area, but only at the cost of creating a new 'supernationalism' of a far more potent and all-embracing kind. This is also the case with such shadowy unions as the Arab League, the pan-African OAU and the Latin American organisations. They remain 'shadowy' as yet, because the claims of the existing national states have deprived them of that cohesive force that would allow them to act in the same manner as existing national units. Were unification to proceed, however, to a much greater degree, the likelihood is that such superstates or supernations would act in a manner analogous to that of present nation-states and possess similar goals and ideals. The main evidence for this claim is, of course, to be found in the 'pan' nationalist basis of such incipient political unions; the African or Arab 'nations' would be created on the foundations of nationalist assumptions and categories, and would compete once again in a world of continental nations. The scale would have changed, but not the mechanics of élite competition or power balances; and we could foresee similar local disruptions to the new continental order, as can be witnessed today. There is also the evidence to be gleaned from the foreign policy practices of the EEC to date, practices that differ only in the degree of caution (so far) from those of individual states.

There is also the possibility that the trend to supranationalism fosters the growth of 'sub-national' and indeed national movements by way of a reaction to the increasing remoteness of bureaucratic control. We cannot be certain, but the 'devolution' desired by peripheral ethnic groups and their nationalisms may appear more viable in the context of an overall federation of states on a continental scale. There is, however, an equal chance of a reactive nationalism on the part of existing nation-states and their ethnic majorities caught between what seem to be the 'pincers' of local ethnic separatism and continental bureaucratic absorption.

What does seem fairly certain is that the greater fluidity introduced into the situation by both supranationalism and separatism provides more opportunities for different kinds of competing nationalisms, and greater chances for national conflicts to harden and erupt. The fact that men can have more than one national allegiance, provided that the circles of loyalty are concentric, does not alter the need to select one of these as the dominant circle in times of crisis or decision-making. The new fluidity and range of choice means that individuals will be pulled in different directions, and increases the chances of nationalist conflict and the level of national sentiments.[24]

CONCLUSION

Neither internationalism nor supranationalism, therefore, offers much hope for that dissolution of nationalism for which cosmopolitan utopians have prayed so fervently. Nationalism, which is so firmly entrenched in the social and political landscape of modernity, is supported both at the local 'internal' and international 'external' levels by a variety of mechanisms. At the local level, the operations of the bureaucratic cycle feeding on pre-existing ethnic traditions among the mass of the population continually revive the fortunes of nationalism after it has become ossified in the bureaucratic machine. At the external international level, world interdependence has diffused balance of power considerations and transformed them into a balance of terror, under whose umbrella both superpowers and other nation-states seek local advantages. Internationalism has also sharpened the rivalry between national élites, who increasingly consist of the local intelligentsia bent on securing their status aspirations within local bureaucracies on the basis of local self-sufficiency. International organisations and their international corps of advisers actually reinforce these nationalist aims through their theory and practice, while the international order itself, by backing the claims of existing nation-states, whets the appetites of both separatist ethnic nationalisms and 'pan' unification movements. Finally, even the supranationalist ventures turn out to parallel, step by step, the goals and activities of the nationalisms they set out to rival and overthrow, and to replicate at a continental level the existing state system.

We must therefore conclude that the very attempt to eradicate nationalism actually helps to entrench it further, and to provoke its periodic resurgence, and it would appear more sensible and appropriate to try to live with it, taming its excesses through mutual recognitions and legitimations, in so far as these seem practicable in given areas. More importantly, nationalism's persistence and appeal must be derived from the conjunction of the three sets of forces that shaped it originally: longstanding ethnic traditions, the birth of new secular ideals, and the peculiar characteristics of modernisation and its social concomitants. It is at these three levels that research needs to be focused if we are to grasp nationalism's manifold and continuing appeals; their conjunctions and interplay can alone reveal why this particular ideal and movement should have gained the immense hold that it has achieved over the minds and hearts of modern generations. The specific conditions that foster given nationalist movements naturally vary with successive historical periods and in different milieux; yet the ubiquitous nature of its basic ideals suggests that we should search for the common threads in the pattern of nationalism.

Notes

CHAPTER I

1. This is the message of one of the first nationalist manifestos, the Abbé Sieyès's *Qu'est-ce que le Tiers Etat?* written in early 1789. It also appears in the Declaration of Rights of 26 August 1789: 'The source of all sovereignty resides essentially in the nation.'

2. These ideas fill many pages of the *cahiers* and pamphlets of 1788–9; cf. B. Hyslop, *French Nationalism in 1789 According to the General Cahiers*, Columbia University Press, New York 1934.

3. H. Kohn, *Prelude to Nation-States: The French and German Experience, 1789–1815*, Van Nostrand, Princeton 1967, emphasises both the revolutionary drive for social unity and the patriot belief in linguistic and cultural identity, especially their love of the French language and arts, and their emphasis on national education.

4. Danton's call for France to reach her 'natural frontiers' in 1792 echoed ideas of some Frenchmen under Louis XIV; cf. K. Minogue, *Nationalism*, Batsford, London 1967, p. 43. Even the Italian sense of the Alps as a natural frontier has left some problems unresolved. The Tyrol furnishes an instructive parallel to the issues raised by the Revolutionary acquisition of Alsace; cf. E. Kedourie, *Nationalism*, Hutchinson, London 1969, pp. 16–17, and L. Doob, *Patriotism and Nationalism*, Yale University Press, New Haven 1964.

5. On these debates, cf. P. Gay, *The Enlightenment: an Interpretation*, Wildwood House, London 1973, Part I, Bk I, ch. 2, and Bk II, ch. 5.

6. cf. M. Laclotte, 'J-L. David, Reform and Revolution', in Arts Council, *The Age of Neo-Classicism*, Shenval Press, London 1972, pp. lxvi–lxxi.

7. On the cult of early Rome, cf. R. Herbert, *David, Voltaire, Brutus and the French Revolution*, Allen Lane, London 1972. There was also an admiration for the ancient Jews whom Moses had 'encumbered' with rites and customs to make them distinctive, a theme that appears in Rousseau's advice to the Poles (1772).

8. R. Anchor, *The Enlightenment Tradition*, Harper & Row, New York 1967; and H. Honour, *Neo-Classicism*, Penguin, Harmondsworth 1968.

9. F. Barnard: *Herder's Social and Political Thought: From Enlightenment to Nationalism*, Clarendon Press, Oxford 1965, ch. 1; and H. Kohn, *The Idea of Nationalism*, Macmillan, New York 1967, ch. 7.

10. cf. P. Sugar and I. Lederer (eds), *Nationalism in Eastern Europe*, Far Eastern and Russian Institute, University of Washington, Seattle 1969: essays by Barany and Brock.

11. J. K. Campbell and P. Sherrard, *Modern Greece*, Benn, London 1968, chs 1–3; and L. Stavrianos, 'Antecedents of the Balkan Revolutions of the 19th Century', *Journal of Modern History* 29, 1957, 333–48.
12. A. P. Whitaker, *Nationalism in Latin America, Past and Present*, University of Florida Press, Gainesville 1962.
13. This is the thesis of Kohn, op. cit., and his *Nationalism: Its Meaning and History*, Van Nostrand, Princeton 1955.
14. As shown in R. W. Harris, *Romanticism and the Social Order, 1780–1830*, Blandford Press, London 1969; and D. Irwin, *English Neo-Classical Art*, Faber & Faber, London 1966.
15. cf. A. Cohler, *Rousseau and Nationalism*, Basic Books, New York 1970, and I. Berlin, 'Herder and the Enlightenment', in E. A. Wasserman (ed.), *Aspects of the Eighteenth Century*, Johns Hopkins University Press, Baltimore 1965.
16. For arguments showing the affinity between neoclassical and early or 'pre'-Romantic nationalisms, cf. M. Florisoone, 'The Romantic and Neo-Classical Conflict' in Arts Council, *The Romantic Movement*, London 1959, pp. 21–6; and A. D. Smith, 'Neo-Classicist and Romantic Elements in the Emergence of Nationalist Conceptions', in A. D. Smith (ed.), *Nationalist Movements*, Macmillan, London 1976, pp. 74–87.
17. On the early Latin American movements of San Martin and Bolivar in 1810, cf. the essays of R. A. Humphreys and J. Lynch (eds), *The Origins of the Latin American Revolutions, 1808–26*, Knopf, New York 1965.
18. cf. Mickiewicz's *Books of the Polish Nation and its Pilgrimage* (1831): 'And they martyred the Polish people and laid it in the grave, and its soul descended into darkness.

    But on the third day the soul shall return to the body and the nation shall rise from the dead and free all the peoples of Europe from slavery.' Cited in K. Pruszynski, *Adam Mickiewicz, 1798–1855*, Polish Cultural Institute, London 1955, pp. 35–6.
19. There is a vivid account of the clergy's role in the Greek war of independence in C. A. Frazee, *The Orthodox Church and Independent Greece, 1821–52*, Cambridge University Press, Cambridge 1969. For later Serbian intellectual developments, cf. T. Stoianovitch, 'The Pattern of Serbian Intellectual Evolution', *Comparative Studies in Society and History* 1, 1958, 242–72.
20. cf. F. Heer, *Europe, Mother of Revolutions*, Weidenfeld & Nicolson, London 1971, ch. 3, pp. 47–57.
21. D. Beales, *The Risorgimento and the Unification of Italy*, Allen & Unwin, London 1971, for Gioberti and d'Azeglio; on Karamzin, see L. Shapiro, *Rationalism and Nationalism in Russian 19th Century Political Thought*, Yale University Press, New Haven and London 1967.
22. cf. E. E. Hales, *Mazzini and the Secret Societies: The Making of a Myth*, Kennedy, New York 1956. For a résumé of the respective ideals of Rousseau and Mazzini, cf. S. Baron, *Modern Nationalism and Religion*, Meridian Books, New York 1960, ch. 2.
23. On Michelet's nationalism, cf. H. Kohn, *Prophets and Peoples*, Macmillan, New York 1961.
24. J. Droz: *Europe between Revolutions, 1815–1848*, Collins, London and Glasgow 1967, pp. 147–8, 152–3.
25. On Treitschke, cf. I. Weiss, *Conservatism in Europe, 1770–1945*, Thames & Hudson, London 1977, pp. 84–9; and on Lagarde, cf. G. Mosse, *The Crisis of German Ideology*, Grosset & Dunlap, New York 1964, ch. 2.
26. This point is well made by B. Akzin, *State and Nation*, Hutchinson, London 1964, pp. 55 *et seq.*

27. F. Znaniecki, *Modern Nationalities*, University of Illinois Press, Urbana 1952; and K. Symmons-Symonolewicz, *Nationalist Movements: A Comparative View*, Maplewood Press, Meadville, Pa. 1970.
28. M. Crowder, *West Africa under Colonial Rule*, Hutchinson, London 1968.
29. R. Pierce, *Russian Central Asia, 1867–1917: A Study in Colonial Rule*, University of California Press, Berkeley 1960; and R. Szporluk, 'Nationalities and the Russian Problem in the USSR: An Historical Outline', *Journal of International Affairs* 27, 1973, 22–40.
30. P. Curtin, *The Image of Africa*, University of Wisconsin Press, Madison 1964.
31. cf. the essays by A. Walicki and R. Hofstadter in E. Gellner and G. Ionescu (eds), *Populism, its Meanings and National Characteristics*, Weidenfeld & Nicolson, London 1970.
32. See below, ch. 3, and G. Mosse, op. cit., *passim*.
33. On these phases, cf. A. R. Desai, *The Social Background of Indian Nationalism*, Bombay Publishing Company, Bombay 1954.
34. M. Kilson, 'Nationalism and Social Classes in British West Africa' *Journal of Politics* 20, 1958, 268–87; and more generally P. C. Lloyd, *Africa in Social Change*, Penguin, Harmondsworth 1967, chs 5, 8–9.
35. But cf. B. B. Misra, *The Indian Middle Classes: Their Growth in Modern Times*, Oxford University Press, London 1961, for the Indian case.
36. M. Maruyama, *Thought and Behaviour in Modern Japanese Politics*, ed. Ivan Morris, Oxford University Press, London 1960; M. C. Wright, *The Last Stand of Chinese Conservatism*, Stanford University Press, Stanford, Ca. 1957.
37. On early manifestations of Arab nationalism, cf. C. E. Dawn, 'From Ottomanism to Arabism: the origins of an ideology', *Review of Politics* 23, 1961, 379–400.
38. On this stratum, cf. J. H. Kautsky (ed.), *Political Change in Underdeveloped Countries*, John Wiley, New York 1962, Introduction and the essays by Benda, Coleman and Matossian; and E. Shils, 'Intellectuals in the Political Development of New States', *World Politics* 12, 1960, 329–68.
39. The German 'organic' version of nationalism elaborated by the early nineteenth-century Romantics is often treated as the classic or true doctrine. For a critique of this view, cf. A. D. Smith, *Theories of Nationalism*, Duckworth, London 1971, ch. 1.
40. C. J. H. Hayes, *The Historical Evolution of Modern Nationalism*, Smith, New York 1931.
41. For a useful account of different versions of nationalism, cf. F. Hertz, *Nationalism in History and Politics*, Routledge & Kegan Paul, London 1944.

CHAPTER 2

1. The biblical text most often cited comes from Revelations 20: 4–6:

> And I saw thrones, and they sat upon them, and judgment was given unto them; and I saw the souls of them that were beheaded for the witness of Jesus, and the word of God, and which had not worshipped the beast, neither his image, neither had received his mark upon their foreheads, or in their hands; and they lived and reigned with Christ a thousand years.
>
> But the rest of the dead lived not again until the thousand years were finished. This is the first resurrection.

Blessed and holy is he that hath part in the first resurrection: on such the second death hath no power, but they shall be priests of God and of Christ, and shall reign with him a thousand years.

On the medieval millennarisms, cf. N. Cohn, 'Medieval Millennarism: Its Bearings on the Comparative Study of Millennarian Movements', in S. Thrupp (ed.), *Millennial Dreams in Action*, Nijhoff, The Hague 1962.

2. For a general survey, cf. B. Wilson, 'Millennialism in Comparative Perspective', *Comparative Studies in Society and History* 6, 1964, 93–114.

3. Y. Talmon, 'The Pursuit of the Millennium – the Relation Between Religious and Social Change', *European Journal of Sociology* 3, 1962, 125–48.

4. Indeed, a number of writers on early African and Asian nationalisms, – among them Hodgkin, Balandier, Coleman, Rotberg, von der Mehden, Bennigsen, Sarkisyanz – accept an 'evolutionary' framework of successive cognitive stages and social movements.

5. E. Kedourie, *Nationalism*, Hutchinson, London 1960; and even more, his later *Nationalism in Asia and Africa*, Weidenfeld & Nicolson, London 1971, Introduction.

6. E. Hobsbawm, *Primitive Rebels*, Manchester University Press, Manchester 1959; P. Worsley, *The Third World*, Weidenfeld & Nicolson, London 1964.

7. Kedourie: *Nationalism in Asia and Africa*, op. cit., Introduction, and Hobsbawm, op. cit., ch. 4. Kedourie draws a good deal on the description of such millennial movements as the Münster Anabaptists, given by N. Cohn, *The Pursuit of the Millennium*, Secker & Warburg, London 1957.

8. G. Balandier, *Sociologie actuelle de l'Afrique Noire*, Presses Universitaires de France, Paris 1955.

9. P. Worsley, *The Trumpet Shall Sound*, 2nd ed., MacGibbon & Kee, London 1968, p. 16.

10. cf. A. Wallace, 'Revitalisation Movements', *American Anthropologist* 58/2, 1956, 264–81.

11. cf. Cohn, op. cit., *passim*, and Kedourie, *Nationalism in Asia and Africa*, op. cit., Introduction.

12. G. Balandier, 'Messianismes et nationalismes en Afrique Noire', *Cahiers Internationaux de Sociologie* 14, 1953, 41–65.

13. G. Shepperson and T. Price, *Independent African; John Chilembwe and the Origins, Setting and Significance of the Nyasaland Native Rising of 1915*, Edinburgh University Press, Edinburgh 1958.

14. T. Hodgkin, *Nationalism in Colonial Africa*, Muller, London 1956, pp. 104, 109.

15. ibid., pp. 112–13, citing A. Le Grip, 'Le Mahdisme en Afrique Noire', *L'Afrique et L'Asie* 18, 1952.

16. E. Sarkisyanz, *Buddhist Backgrounds of the Burmese Revolution*, Nijhoff, The Hague 1965; and H. Tinker, 'Politics of Burma', in S. Rose (ed.): *Politics in Southern Asia*, Macmillan, London 1963.

17. Kedourie, *Nationalism in Asia and Africa*, Introduction; pp. 99–103.

18. W. Kolarz, *Peoples of the Soviet Far East*, Philip, London 1954, ch. 6. By contrast, Yakut and Buryat (pan-Mongol) nationalisms of the early twentieth century were not preceded by millennial outbursts (ibid., chs 4–5.).

19. On these, cf. Worsley, *The Trumpet Shall Sound*, op. cit., and I. C. Jarvie: *The Revolution in Anthropology*, Routledge & Kegan Paul, London 1964.

20. For the Tuka movement in Fiji, cf. K. Burridge, *New Heaven, New Earth*, Basil Blackwell, Oxford 1969, pp. 49–53.

21. J. Marcus (ed.), *The Jew in the Medieval World*, Harper & Row, New York 1965, pp. 261–9; and R. J. Werblowsky, 'Messianism in Jewish History', in H. H. Ben-Sasson and S. Ettinger, *Jewish Society through the Ages*, Valentine, Mitchell, London 1971.

22. H. Kohn, 'The Origins of English Nationalism', *Journal of the History of Ideas* 1, 1940, 69–94; L. Stone, 'The English Revolution', in R. Forster and J. P. Greene (eds), *Preconditions of Revolution in Early Modern Europe*, Johns Hopkins University Press, Baltimore and London 1972; and Cohn, op. cit., Appendix, on the Ranters.

23. V. Lanternari, *The Religions of the Oppressed*, Mentor Books, New York 1965.

24. P. Mayo, *The Roots of Identity*, Allen Lane, London 1974, and see chapter 6 (below).

25. R. Bastide, 'Messianisme et developpement economique et sociale', *Cahiers Internationaux de Sociologie* 31, 1961, 3–14.

26. On the Jewish background of Christian messianism, cf. S. G. F. Brandon, *Jesus and the Zealots*, Manchester University Press, Manchester 1967, and H. Maccoby, *Revolution in Judaea*, Ocean Books, London 1974.

27. On Joachim and his successors, cf. Cohn, op. cit., *passim*.

28. Kedourie, *Nationalism in Asia and Africa*, Introduction, pp. 92ff.

29. On both, cf. Cohn, op. cit., pp. 102–3, and ch. 12; the Taborites *were* more nationalistic, ibid., ch. 10.

30. Worsley, *The Trumpet Shall Sound*, op. cit., p. xlvii cites the Lumpa as a case of the evolutionary displacement of millennialism 'as the vehicle of a vigorous mass nationalism'. For other anti-nationalist millennialist sects, the Tijannya in Turkey and the Neturei Karta in Israel, cf. E. Marmorstein, 'Religious Opposition to Nationalism in the Middle East', *International Affairs* 28, 1952, 344–59.

31. On national sentiment in late medieval Europe, cf. C. L. Tipton (ed.), *Nationalism in the Middle Ages*, Holt, Rinehart & Winston, New York 1972.

32. On Mau Mau, cf. C. G. Rosberg and J. Nottingham, *The Myth of Mau Mau: Nationalism in Kenya*, Praeger, New York 1966.

33. cf. H. Kohn, *The Idea of Nationalism*, Macmillan, New York 1967, ch. 4.

34. For a critique of Kedourie's earlier thesis, cf. A. D. Smith, *Theories of Nationalism*, Duckworth, London 1971, chs 1–2.

35. On the social composition of nationalism, cf. A. D. Smith (ed.): *Nationalist Movements*, Macmillan, London 1976, chapters by Argyle, Warburton and Kiernan; also A. D. Smith, *Theories of Nationalism*, op. cit., ch. 6.

36. For Worsley's 'élite–mass' distinction, cf. his *The Third World*, Weidenfeld & Nicolson, London 1964; and the critique in A. D. Smith, 'Nationalism, A Trend Report and Bibliography', *Current Sociology* 21/3, Mouton, The Hague, 1973, section V. On millennialism's social composition, cf. B. Wilson, *Sects and Society*, Oxford University Press, Oxford 1961, and the works by Lanternari, Cohn, Balandier and Worsley.

37. For the role of education, commerce and the professions in the make-up of nationalist movements, cf. D. Kimble, *A Political History of Ghana: The Rise of Gold Coast Nationalism, 1850–1928*, Clarendon Press, Oxford 1963; I. Wallerstein, 'Elites in French-Speaking West Africa', *Journal of Modern African Studies* 3, 1965, 1–33; L. S. Stavrianos, *The Balkans Since 1453*, Holt, New York 1961; H. Carrère d'Encausse, *Réforme et Révolution chez les Musulmans de l'Empire Russe, Bukhara 1867–1924*, Armand Colin, Paris 1966; B. T. McCulley, *English Education and the Origins of Indian Nationalism*, Smith, Gloucester, Mass. 1966; A. L. Tibawi, 'The American Missionaries in Beirut and Butrus al-Bustani', *St Antony's Papers* 16, 1963, 137–82.

38. K. Mannheim, *Ideology and Utopia*, Routledge & Kegan Paul, London 1936.
39. This aspect was pioneered by Herder, cf. F. M. Barnard, 'Culture and Political Development: Herder's Suggestive Insights', *American Political Science Review* 62, 1969, 379–97. For an original explanation of the specific role of linguistic education in creating modern nations, cf. E. Gellner, *Thought and Change*, Weidenfeld & Nicolson, London 1964, ch. 7.
40. For example, the reconstructions of Cheikh Anta Diop; cf. I. Geiss, *The Pan-African Movement*, Methuen, London 1974, p. 123.
41. J. Talmon: *Political Messianism: The Romantic Phase*, London 1960. On Polish 'messianism', cf. H. Kohn: *PanSlavism*, Vintage Books, New York 1960, ch. 2.
42. cf. K. Deutsch and W. Foltz, *Nation-Building*, Atherton, New York 1963, and R. Bendix, *Nation-Building and Citizenship*, Wiley, New York 1964, for two accounts of 'nationalism' or rather the 'growth of nations', in terms of this nationalist ideological concept which seemed so well suited to an optimistic, expansive sociology and political science.
43. E. Hobsbawm, op. cit., p. 84. Everything of the here and now of an evil world had to be destroyed.
44. Worsley, *The Trumpet Shall Sound*, op. cit., pp. xlii, xliv.
45. For typical nationalist arguments and demands, cf. L. Snyder (ed.), *The Dynamics of Nationalism*, Van Nostrand, New York 1964.
46. Thus the picture of nationalism given by Kedourie, *Nationalism*, op. cit., pp. 85–9, really applies to the millennial movements only.
47. Report in *New York Times*, 9 December 1948; cited in M. Halpern, *The Politics of Social Change in the Middle East and North Africa*, Princeton University Press, Princeton 1963, p. 150, n. 32.
48. C. P. Harris, *Nationalism and Revolution in Egypt: The Role of the Muslim Brotherhood*, Mouton, The Hague 1964.
49. Halpern: op. cit., pp. 136, 143, 146–7n.; 150–2 on Pakistan and Iran.
50. On al-Afghani, cf. E. Kedourie: *Afghani and Abduh*, Cass, London and New York 1966.
51. H. Brechert, 'Buddhism and Mass Politics in Burma and Ceylon', in D. E. Smith (ed.), *Religion and Political Modernisation*, Yale University Press, New Haven and London 1974, esp. pp. 152–4.
52. D. E. Smith, *Religion and Politics in Burma*, Princeton University Press, Princeton 1965.
53. Sarkisyanz, op. cit.; and on the Khilafat movement cf. E. Rosenthal, *Islam in the Modern National State*, Cambridge University Press, Cambridge 1965.
54. Kedourie, *Nationalism in Asia and Africa*, op. cit., Introduction, pp. 70–1.
55. ibid., pp. 71 *et seq.*, and R. I. Crane, 'Problems of Divergent Developments within Indian Nationalism, 1895–1905', in R. K. Sakai (ed.): *Studies on Asia*, University of Nebraska Press, Lincoln 1961.
56. R. Bellah (ed.), *Religion and Progress in Modern Asia*, Free Press, Glencoe, Ill. 1965, Epilogue; and D. C. Holtom, *Modern Japan and Shinto Nationalism*, University of Chicago Press, Chicago 1943.
57. cf. L. Binder, *The Ideological Revolution in the Middle East*, John Wiley, New York 1964; and G. E. von Grunebaum, Problems of Muslim Nationalism, in R. N. Frye (ed.): *Islam and the West*, Mouton, The Hague 1957.
58. cf. J. Gusfield, 'Tradition and Modernity: Misplaced Polarities in the Study of Social Change', *American Journal of Sociology* 72, 1967, 351–62, with special reference to the process of 'Sanskritisation' of the lower castes in India today.
59. On religious reform movements in general, cf. W. Wertheim, 'Religious Reform Movements in South and South-East Asia', *Archives de Sociologie des Religions*

12, 1961, 53–62. His emphasis falls upon the waves of capitalist intrusion in the area: mine tends to stress the impact of bureaucracy and science, cf. A. D. Smith, 'Nationalism and Religion: The Role of Religious Reform in the Genesis of Arab and Jewish Nationalism', *Archives de Sociologie des Religions* 35, 1973, 23–43.

60. W. D. Robson-Scott, *The Literary Background of the Gothic Revival in Germany*, London 1965; H. S. Reiss (ed.), *The Political Thought of the German Romantics, 1973–1815*, Blackwell, Oxford 1955, and F. Heer, *Europe, Mother of Revolutions*, Weidenfeld & Nicolson, London 1971, ch. 3.

61. G. Mosse, *The Crisis of German Ideology: Intellectual Origins of the Third Reich*, Grosset & Dunlap, New York 1964, especially ch. 2.

62. L. Shapiro, *Rationalism and Nationalism in Russian 19th Century Political Thought*, Yale University Press, New Haven and London 1967; and M. B. Petrovich, *The Emergence of Russian PanSlavism, 1856–70*, Columbia University Press, New York 1956.

63. E. C. Thaden, *Conservative Nationalism in 19th Century Russia*, University of Washington Press, Seattle 1964, chs 3, 6, 7.

64. cf. the excellent study of H. A. R. Gibb, *Modern Trends in Islam*, Chicago University Press, Chicago 1947. Abduh's reformism was more radical, and contributed to liberal Egyptian nationalism; cf. N. Safran, *Egypt in Search of Political Community*, Harvard University Press, Cambridge, Mass. 1961. cf. also L. C. Brown, 'The Islamic Reformist Movement in North Africa', *Journal of Modern African Studies* 2, 1964, 55–63.

65. G. Shepperson, 'Ethiopianism and African Nationalism', *Phylon* 14, 1953, 9–18.

66. A theme underlying the reader of R. Rotberg and A. Mazrui (eds), *Protest and Power in Black Africa*, Oxford University Press, New York 1970.

67. C. Heimsath, *Indian Nationalism and Hindu Social Reform*, Princeton University Press, Princeton 1964.

68. D. Pocock, 'Notes on the Interaction of English and Indian Thought in the 19th Century', *Journal of World History* 4, 1958, 833–48; and A. R. Desai, *The Social Background of Indian Nationalism*, Bombay Publishing Company, Bombay 1954, chs 13, 17.

69. M. A. Meyer, *The Origins of the Modern Jew: Jewish Identity and European Culture in Germany, 1749–1824*, Wayne State University Press, Detroit 1967; and J. Katz, 'Jews and Judaism in the 19th Century', *Journal of World History* 4, 1958, 881–900.

70. Katz, op. cit.; J. L. Blau, *Modern Varieties of Judaism*, Columbia University Press, New York 1966, especially chs 2, 5.

71. S. A. Zenkovsky, *Pan-Turkism and Islam in Russia*, Harvard University Press, Cambridge, Mass. 1960; and 'A Century of Tatar Revival', *Slavic Review* 12, 1953, 303–18.

72. On the concept of 'reform', cf. G. Ladner, *The Idea of Reform*, Harvard University Press, Cambridge, Mass. 1959.

73. An interplay epitomised by the career of Chinese reformers like Li'ang Ch'i Ch'ao, cf. J. R. Levenson, *Li'ang Ch'i Ch'ao and the Mind of Modern China*, University of California Press, Berkeley and Los Angeles 1959.

74. On the Pochvenniki, cf. Thaden, op. cit., ch. 5.; on the Burmese YMBA cf. Sarkisyanz, op. cit., pp. 114 *et seq.*

75. cf. A. D. Smith, 'Nationalism, A Trend Report', op. cit., section 5.

76. On reformist denominations, cf. D. Martin: *Pacifism*, Routledge & Kegan Paul, London 1965.

77. As can be seen in the Malayan case, cf. W. Roff, *The Origins of Malay Nationalism*, Yale University Press, New Haven 1967. The reformist-nationalist élites were

far removed from the mainly rural groups who supported the nineteenth-century millennial Padri movement with its pan-Islamic overtones; cf. A. Reid, 'Nine-teenth-century pan-Islam in Indonesia and Malaysia', *Journal of Asian Studies* 26, 1967, 267–83.

78. cf. E. Gellner, 'Scale and Nation', *Philosophy of the Social Sciences* 3, 1973, 1–17, on the role of education and mobility.
79. On this, cf. Gibb, op. cit., and A. D. Smith, 'Nationalism and Religion . . .', op. cit.
80. K. Minogue, 'Nationalism and the Patriotism of City-states', in A. D. Smith (ed.), *Nationalist Movements*, Macmillan, London 1976.
81. W. Bruford, *Germany in the Eighteenth Century*, Cambridge University Press, Cambridge 1965.
82. On the 'national' and 'international' aspects of neoclassicism, cf. H. Honour, *Neo-Classicism*, Penguin, Harmondsworth 1968.
83. J. Lively (ed.), *The Enlightenment*, Longman, London 1966, pp. 51, 56–9, 154–62, especially on Voltaire's reaction.
84. On the 'stoic' cult of antiquity and virtue, cf. R. Rosenblum, *Transformations in Late 18th-Century Art*, Princeton University Press, Princeton 1967, ch. 2.
85. Kedourie, *Nationalism in Asia and Africa*, op. cit., pp. 77–92, gives some examples, and stresses the bitterness caused.
86. cf. R. L. Herbert, *David, Voltaire, Brutus and French Revolution*, Allen Lane, London 1972; and Honour, op. cit.
87. D. G. McCrae, *Ideology and Society*, Heinemann, London 1961, ch. 16.
88. Isaiah 65:17.
89. Amos 9:14.
90. Isaiah 35:10.

CHAPTER 3

1. The evolutionary view is held by R. Butler, *The Roots of National Socialism*, Faber & Faber, London 1941, and E. Vermeil, 'The Origin, Nature and Development of German Nationalist Ideology in the 19th and 20th Centuries', in *The Third Reich*, a study published under the auspices of the International Council for Philosophy and Humanistic Studies, with the assistance of Unesco; Praeger, New York 1955. For the 'totalitarian' view as applied to Germany, cf. G. Ritter, 'The Historical Foundations of the Rise of National Socialism', in *The Third Reich*, op. cit.
2. K. Popper, *The Open Society and its Enemies*, 4th ed., Routledge & Kegan Paul, London 1962, vol. II, ch. 12, pp. 51, 49.
3. E. Kedourie, *Nationalism*, Hutchinson, London 1960, p. 72.
4. For the classic Marxist view of nazism as a phenomenon of the era of 'monopoly capitalism' cf. F. Neumann, *Behemoth, the Structure and Practise of National Socialism 1933–44*, Oxford University Press, New York 1944.
5. H. Seton-Watson, *Nationalism, Old and New*, Sydney University Press, Sydney 1965, p. 21.
6. W. Kornhauser, *The Politics of Mass Societies*, Routledge & Kegan Paul, London 1959.
7. K. Bracher, *The German Dictatorship: The Origins, Structure and Effects of National Socialism*, Penguin, Harmondsworth 1973, p. 88.
8. cf. W. McDougall, *The Group Mind*, Methuen, Cambridge 1920; and G. Le Bon, *The Crowd*, Unwin, London 1896. For Freud's belief that the masses

require an authority figure, cf. his *Moses and Monotheism* (trans. K. Jones), Hogarth Press, London 1939, p. 185.

9. J. Kaplow (ed.), *New Perspectives on the French Revolution*, John Wiley, New York 1965.

10. H. M. Pachter, 'Nazi and Fascist Propaganda for Power', in *The Third Reich*, op. cit.

11. Z. Barbu, 'Nationalism as a Source of Aggression', in Ciba Foundation, *Conflict*, London 1966.

12. K. Appel, 'Nationalism and Sovereignty: A Psychiatric View', *Journal of Abnormal and Social Psychology* 40, 1945, 355–63; cf. also T. Parsons, 'Sources and Patterns of Aggression', in P. Mullahy (ed.), *A Study of Interpersonal Relations: New Contributions to Psychiatry*, Hermitage Press, New York 1949, for a social psychological view.

13. cf. N. J. Smelser, *A Theory of Collective Behaviour*, Routledge & Kegan Paul, London 1962, for a general approach to social movements and mass outbursts.

14. For mass reactions to modernisation cf. S. N. Eisenstadt, 'Social Change and Development', in S. N. Eisenstadt (ed.), *Readings in Social Evolution and Development*, Pergamon Press, Oxford and London 1970.

15. For nationalism and fascism as secularised millennial opiates, cf. E. Kedourie (ed.), *Nationalism in Asia and Africa*, Weidenfeld & Nicolson, London 1971.

16. cf. the study of the size and constituency of nationalist movements in the Habsburg empire by W. J. Argyle: 'Size and Scale as Factors in the Development of Nationalist Movements', in A. D. Smith (ed.), *Nationalist Movements*, Macmillan, London 1976.

17. On the relations between nationalism and industrialisation and economic growth, cf. H. G. Johnson, 'A Theoretical Model of Economic Nationalism in New and Developing Countries', *Political Science Quarterly* 80, 1965, 169–85; A. Pepelassis, 'The Image of the Past and Economic Backwardness', *Human Organisation* 17, 1958, 19–27; and A. D. Smith, *Theories of Nationalism*, Duckworth, London 1971, ch. 6.

18. Indeed, Sieyès's definition of the nation is contractual and political: 'What is a nation?' he asked. 'A body of associates living under one common law and represented by the same legislature.' The treatise, *Qu'est-ce que le Tiers Etat?*, Paris 1789, also defined the 'nation' in class and ethnic terms, harking back to and reversing Boulainvilliers's distinction between the conquering Franks and the subjugated Gauls; cf. J. Barzun: *The French Race*, Columbia University Press, New York 1932.

19. J. H. Füssli, *Catechetische Anleitung zu dem politischen Pflichten* (Catechism of Political Duties), cited in H. Kohn, *The Idea of Nationalism*, Collier-Macmillan, New York 1967, p. 385.

20. T. Jefferson, letter to Mr Weightman, 24 June 1826, (in Jefferson's *Writings*, ed. A. A. Lipscomb, vol. IV pp. 380 *et seq.*), cited in Kohn, op. cit., p. 311, and n. 130, p. 678.

21. On this international cultural movement, cf. H. Honour, *Neo-Classicism*, Penguin, Harmondsworth 1968; and A. D. Smith, 'Neoclassicist and Romantic elements in the Emergence of Nationalist Conceptions', in A. D. Smith (ed.), *Nationalist Movements*, Macmillan, London 1976.

22. N. Webster, *Sketches of American Policy*, ed. H. R. Warfel, New York, cited in Kohn, op. cit., p. 287.

23. In fact, the Jacobins inherited the absolutist centralism of the monarchs they had helped to dethrone; cf. A. Cobban, 'The Enlightenment and the French Revolution', in *Aspects of the French Revolution*, Paladin, London 1968.

24. The letter appeared in Smolenskin's journal *HaShaar X*, pp. 244–5, and is

reprinted in A. Hertzberg (ed.), *The Zionist Idea*, Meridian Books, New York 1960, pp. 160–5.

25. For the ethnic–linguistic dimension of French nationalism during the Revolution, cf. H. Kohn, *Prelude to Nation-States: the French and German Experience, 1789–1815*, Van Nostrand, Princeton 1967, chs. 12–14; also J-Y. Lartichaux, 'Linguistic Politics during the French Revolution', *Diogenes* 97, 1977, 65–84.

26. cf. F. Antal, *Classicism and Romanticism, with other Studies in Art History*, Routledge & Kegan Paul, London 1966, for the concept of 'pre-Romanticism'.

27. The importance of history in the eighteenth century, and the primacy of historical writing in spurring cultural interests towards ethnic revival and nationalism, is documented in P. Walch, 'Charles Rollin and early Neoclassicism', *Art Bulletin* 49, 1967, 123–7, and in R. Rosenblum, *Transformations in Late 18th Century Art*, Princeton University Press, Princeton 1967.

28. F. Schlegel, *Philosophical Lectures in the Years 1804 to 1806*. This and the preceding quotation are cited in H. Kohn, *The Mind of Germany; the Education of a Nation*, Macmillan, London 1965, pp. 59–60, where it is pointed out that for Schlegel, the Christian nation under its old monarchy (the Habsburgs) must be united both by blood and by language as a single ethnic family, and this would ensure loyalty to traditions and customs that were authentically German.

29. Cited by Kohn, *The Mind of Germany* op cit., p. 76. Here we find, too, the beginnings of the dual enemy of German purity and unity, French trumpery and Jewish cosmopolitanism, which dominated German nationalism later.

30. A. P. Whitaker and D. C. Jordan, *Nationalism in Contemporary Latin America*, Free Press, New York 1966; and J. Johnson, 'The New Latin American Nationalism', *The Yale Review* 54, 1965, 187–204. On economic nationalism generally, cf. H. G. Johnson (ed.), *Economic Nationalism in Old and New States*, Allen and Unwin, London 1968.

31. For fuller discussions of the problem of defining nationalism, cf. A. D. Smith, *Theories of Nationalism*, Duckworth, London 1971, ch. 7; and 'Nationalism, a Trend Report and Bibliography', *Current Sociology* 21, 1973, section 2, where more emphasis is laid on self-government.

32. B. Mussolini, *The Political and Social Doctrine of Fascism*, Hogarth Press, London 1936.

33. B. Mussolini, 'Fascismo', *Enciclopedia Italiana*, vol. 14, 848a, cited in E. Nolte, *Three Faces of Fascism* (trans. L. Vennewitz), New York and Toronto 1969, p. 314.

34. The statute of 12 October 1926, cited in Nolte, op. cit., pp. 338–9.

35. *Opera Omnia di Benito Mussolini*, 30, 154, Florence 1951f., cited in Nolte, op. cit., p. 346; cf. also his statement in Nolte, p. 346; 'You know me for a eulogist of the party. The party is in truth the soul, the motor of the nation.'

36. Nolte, op. cit., pp. 315, 333, cites two of Mussolini's formulations of this fascist 'style':

> this antipacifist spirit is transported by fascism into the lives of individuals as well. The proud squadrist motto, 'I don't give a damn' is an act of philosophy which is more than stoical, the epitome of a doctrine which is more than political: inherent in it are the discipline to fight, the acceptance of dangers: it is a new style of Italian life. [*Enciclopedia Italiana*, XIV, 849a]
> Democracy has deprived the life of the people of 'style', that is, a line of conduct, the color, the strength, the picturesque, the unexpected, the mystical; in sum, all that counts in the soul of the masses. We play the

lyre on all its strings: from violence to religion, from art to politics. [*Opera Omnia*, op. cit., XVIII, 438]

37. Cited in G. Mosse, 'The Genesis of Fascism', *Journal of Contemporary History* 1/1, 1966, 14.

38. R. J. Soucy, 'The Nature of Fascism in France', *Journal of Contemporary History*, 1/1, 1966, 50 *et seq*. But it is as part of an élite team that he becomes a 'hero'; that way, wrote Drieu, the 'paralysis' of individualism is overcome, and men relearn '*la vie de groupe*'.

39. ibid., p. 48, and Mosse, op. cit., p. 38.

40. Horia Sima, *Destinee du Nationalisme*, Paris, n.d., p. 19, cited by Mosse, op. cit., p. 39. But 'spiritual' here must be understood as 'instinctual' and primitivist, demanding a spartan attitude and life, disciplined, virile and aggressive, in which only the strong survive.

41. Mosse, op. cit., p. 23.

42. Not that every nationalism has abjured expansion and self-aggrandisement! But it is of fascism's essence to be warlike and aim to dominate other states, whereas, once irredentist claims have been satisfied, nationalism must rest, in the belief that national frontiers are sacred and 'natural'. For the impetus to Italian fascism given by late 19th century Italian nationalism, and the conservative, traditionalist influence which the latter exercised, cf. Alexander J. de Grand: *The Italian Nationalist Association and the Rise of Fascism in Italy*, University of Nebraska Press, Lincoln and London 1978.

43. For such 'polycentric' nationalist developments within communism cf. R. Lowenthal, 'Communism versus Nationalism', *Problems of Communism* 11, 1962, 37–44. On American 'liberal nationalism', cf. R. B. Nye, *The Cultural Life of the New Nation, 1776–1830*, Hamish Hamilton, London 1960.

44. Rousseau's influence in France, Switzerland, Germany and America (through Jefferson) was particularly important in this respect, and has been carried overseas to Africa in particular: cf. H. Kohn, *Nationalism and Liberty*, Macmillan, London 1956, for this agricultural dimension in Switzerland; and T. Hodgkin, 'A Note on the Language of African Nationalism', *St Antony's Papers* 10, 1961, 22–40, for such Rousseau influences in Africa.

45. P. M. Hayes, 'Quisling's Political Ideas', *Journal of Contemporary History* 1/1, 1966, 149; and Nolte, op. cit., p. 495.

46. cf. W. Friedlander, *David to Delacroix*, Schocken Books, New York 1968.

47. Mosse, op. cit., p. 16.

48. The distinction is vital; cf. P. van den Berghe, *Race and Racism*, John Wiley, New York 1967, pp. 9–10.

49. A. Hertzberg, *The French Enlightenment and the Jews*, Schocken Books, New York 1968, p. 360.

50. Early intimations of this transition appeared even within the French Enlightenment, in Voltaire; and his political 'pupil', the Jacobin deputy for Alsace – Rewbell – opposed Jewish emancipation; Hertzberg, op. cit., pp. 354 *et seq*. For French anti-Semitism in the Dreyfus Affair cf. R. Kedward, *The Dreyfus Affair*, Longman, London 1965.

51. cf. Mosse, op. cit., pp. 23–4. For Mussolini's incipient anti-Semitism, cf. Nolte, op. cit., pp. 295–7, 575.

52. Soucy, op. cit., pp. 42–3.

53. cf. L. Poliakov, *Harvest of Hate*, Syracuse University Press, New York 1954. Seton-Watson singles out Poles, Ukrainians, Slovaks and Rumanians as being especially anti-Semitic, largely owing to the very large concentrations of Jews in the Pale; in Germany and Austria it was rather their economic and cultural competition that attracted German enmity; cf. H. Seton-Watson, 'Fascism,

Right and Left', *Journal of Contemporary History* 1/1, 1966, 189–91.

54. Poliakov, op. cit., pp. 5–8, 310; and H. Arendt, *The Origins of Totalitarianism*, Harcourt, Brace, New York 1951.
55. For example, Drieu de la Rochelle: cf. Soucy, op. cit., pp. 37–42.
56. E. Weber, 'The Men of the Archangel', *Journal of Contemporary History* 1/1, 1966, 101–26.
57. For example, the Muslim Brotherhood or Sukarno's and Nkrumah's charismatic regimes. On the Muslim Brotherhood cf. C. Harris, *Nationalism and Revolution in Egypt: The Role of the Muslim Brotherhood*, Mouton, The Hague 1964.
58. On nationalism's social composition, cf. A. D. Smith, *Theories of Nationalism*, Duckworth, London 1971, ch. 6, and 'The Formation of Nationalist Movements', in A. D. Smith (ed.), *Nationalist Movements*, Macmillan, London 1976.
59. cf. Weber, op. cit., p. 107; and R. Rogowski, 'The Gauleiter and the Social Origins of Fascism', *Comparative Studies in Society and History* 19, 1977, 399–430.
60. cf. table (I) in H. Gerth, 'The Nazi Party: Its Leadership and Composition', *The American Journal of Sociology* 45, 1940, 517–41. It is based upon official Nazi Party statistics for 1935, showing the occupational composition of the party before 1933 and in 1935. Gerth underlines the under-representation of manual workers, and the over-representation of the 'middle classes', especially white-collar workers. The 30 per cent manual worker members of the Nazi Party represent, of course, a minority of the German working class as a whole.
61. cf. Weber, op. cit., p. 120, n. 11.
62. L. Jedlicka, 'The Austrian Heimwehr', *Journal of Contemporary History* 1/1, 1966, 128–9, 130–1, 134. Still more fascist was Colonel Hiltl's Frontkämpfer Association in Vienna, founded at the same time (1919), with its élite concept of the 'iron kernel' as the 'soul of the organisation – a soul imbued with the spirit and will of the leader' (cited in Jedlicka, op. cit., p. 132). Nevertheless, first the Frontkämpfer and then the Heimwehr lost ground to, or were absorbed by, the growing Austrian Nazi Party after 1932.
63. Mosse, op. cit., p. 21.
64. S. M. Lipset, *Political Man*, William Heinemann, London 1960, ch. 5. For a critique of the class approach, which emphasises the role of the politically apathetic and of new voters, cf. R. Bendix, 'Social Stratification and Political Power', in R. Bendix and S. M. Lipset (eds), *Class, Status and Power*, Free Press, Glencoe, Ill. 1956, and Lipset's comments in *Political Man*, op. cit., pp. 149–52; cf. Rogowski, op. cit., for the role of upward mobility in the army, in education and in white-collar sectors.
65. Lipset, op. cit., pp. 157–66. Poujadism was essentially a populism of the peasants, artisans and shopkeepers, especially in the South; although it contained fascist elements (anti-capitalism, anti-Semitism, anti-Marxism), it adhered to the 1789 Republican tradition against the 'politicians', on behalf of the 'people', and did not preach a Darwinian doctrine; cf. S. Hoffman, *Le Mouvement Poujade*, Armand Colin, Paris 1956.
66. As Seton-Watson, op. cit., and Weber, op. cit., pp. 188, 193-4 and 122-6 argue. The idealist motivation and agrarian and youth basis of Rumanian fascism before Antonescu is also brought out by S. Fischer-Galati, 'Rumanian Nationalism', in P. F. Sugar and I. J. Lederer (eds), *Nationalism in Eastern Europe*, University of Washington Press, Seattle and London 1969, pp. 392–3. The fullest account of the Iron Guard is E. Weber, 'Romania', in H. Rogger and E. Weber (eds), *The European Right: A Historical Profile*, University of California Press, Berkeley, Ca. 1965, pp. 501–74.
67. H. Thomas, 'The Hero in the Empty Room: Jose Antonio and Spanish Fascism',

Journal of Contemporary History 1/1, 1966, 174–82.
68. Kedourie, op. cit., p. 101.
69. For the differences between scholar–propagandists, agitator–activists and independence leaders of the nationalist movement, cf. A. D. Smith, 'Nationalism, A Trend Report and Bibliography', *Current Sociology* 21, 1973, 99–100.
70. On relations among the Nazi leadership, cf. Gerth, op. cit., and J. C. Fest, *The Face of the Third Reich* (trans. M. Bullock), Weidenfeld & Nicolson, London 1970. Both stress the rivalry of the henchmen and inner circle for the Leader's confidence, which is the sole criterion of power.
71. In India, Tilak succeeded in calling out the Bombay textile workers in 1908 in support of nationalist demands; cf. A. R. Desai, *The Social Background of Indian Nationalism*, Bombay Publishing Company, Bombay 1954. But the Congress generally were loth to stir up working-class discontent. Similarly with African nationalists, although in a few countries – Sudan, Ghana, Kenya, Tunisia, Algeria, Guinea, Mali and Ivory Coast, and to some extent Nigeria – trade unions did ally themselves with nationalist parties before independence, despite the small size of the working class at the time; cf. I. Davies, *African Trade Unions*, Penguin, Harmondsworth 1966, p. 96. In Poland, around 1905 Pilsudski did manage to harness a considerable proportion of the workers to his brand of nationalism; cf. O. Halecki, *A History of Poland*, rev. ed., J. M. Dent, London 1955, ch. 23.
72. On this, cf. A. D. Smith, ''Ideas' and 'Structure' in the formation of Independence Ideals', *Philosophy of the Social Sciences* 3, 1973, 19–39.
73. On the relationship between industrialisation and downward mobility, cf. M. Olson, 'Rapid Growth as a Destabilising Force', *Journal of Economic History* 23, 1963, 519–52. But cf. Rogowski, op. cit., on the role of upward mobility among the Gauleiters.
74. Nationalist sentiment grew in England and France throughout the eighteenth century, and in Poland, Corsica and America after 1760. In Corsica the 1734 revolt against Genoa assumed nationalist form under Paoli only around 1760; cf. P. Thrasher, *Pasquale Paoli*, Constable, London 1970, pp. 23–5; and in Switzerland the Helvetic Society was founded in 1761; cf. Kohn, *Nationalism and Liberty*, op. cit., p. 27.
75. For nationalism in medieval Europe, cf. C. L. Tipton (ed.), *Nationalism in the Middle Ages*, Holt, Rinehart & Winston, New York 1972, and J. Strayer, 'The Historical Experience of Nation-building in Europe', in K. Deutsch and W. Foltz (eds), *Nation-Building*, Atherton, New York 1963.
76. On ethnocentrism in antiquity, cf. M. Handelsman, 'Le rôle de la nationalité dans l'histoire de l'antiquité', *Bulletin of the International Committee of Historical Science* 2, 1929, 305–20; and A. D. Smith, 'Ethnocentrism, Nationalism and Social Change', *International Journal of Comparative Sociology* 13, 1972, 1–20.
77. For this Jacobin republican nationalism, cf. R. L. Herbert, *David, Voltaire, Brutus and the French Revolution*, Allen Lane, London 1972; also B. C. Shafer, 'Bourgeois Nationalism in the Pamphlets on the Eve of the French Revolution', *Journal of Modern History* 10, 1938, 31–50.
78. H. Rogger, 'Nationalism and the State: a Russian Dilemma', *Comparative Studies in Society and History* 4, 1962, 253–64. On Italy, cf. D. Beales, *The Risorgimento and the Unification of Italy*, Allen & Unwin, London 1971.
79. cf. Kedward, op. cit., ch. 2; also J. Weiss, *Conservatism in Europe 1770–1945*, Thames & Hudson, London 1977.
80. The formula is Seton-Watson's, op. cit., pp. 184–7, 191.
81. On this crucial development, cf. G. Barraclough, *An Introduction to Contemporary History*, Penguin, Harmondsworth 1967.

82. J. Plamenatz, 'Two Types of Nationalism', in E. Kamenka (ed.), *Nationalism: The Nature and Evolution of an Idea*, Australian National Press, Canberra 1973.
83. G. Mosse, *The Crisis of German Ideology*, Grosset and Dunlap, New York 1964, pp. 4 *et seq.*
84. *Von Deutscher Art und Kunst*, Hamburg 1773; ed. Philipp Reclam, Stuttgart.
85. These and other examples of German 'Gothic' medievalism are given in W. D. Robson-Scott, *The Literary Background of the Gothic Revival in Germany*, Clarendon Press, Oxford 1965.
86. The quotation is Fichte's, cited in K. D. Bracher, op. cit., p. 40. For Novalis, Schlegel and the Romantics, cf. Kohn, *The Mind of Germany*, op. cit., pp. 52–7.
87. Bracher, op. cit., p. 38.
88. cf. the excellent analysis in E. C. Thaden, *Conservative Nationalism in 19th Century Russia*, University of Washington Press, Seattle 1964.
89. Themes passionately enunciated by Shatov in Dostoevskii's *The Possessed*, Part II, especially 1/7.
90. On Aurobindo, cf. K. Singh, *Prophet of Indian Nationalism*, Allen & Unwin, London 1963. More generally, C. Heimsath, *Indian Nationalism and Hindu Social Reform*, Princeton University Press, Princeton 1964, and D. Pocock, 'Notes on the Interaction of English and Indian Thought in the 19th Century', *Journal of World History* 4, 1958, 833–48.
91. F. Jahn, *Das Deutsche Volkstum*, Lübeck 1810; cf. the translated extract in L. Snyder (ed.), *The Dynamics of Nationalism*, Van Nostrand, New York 1964, and the account in Kohn, *The Mind of Germany*, op. cit., pp. 88 *et seq.*
92. On Menzel, cf. Kohn, *The Mind of Germany*, op. cit., pp. 94 *et seq.*
93. J. G. Fichte, *Addresses to the German Nation* (1807–8), (trans. R. F. Jones and G. H. Turnbull), Open Court Publishing Co., Chicago 1922. Fichte's egalitarian Jacobinism is evident in his *The Characteristics of the Present Age* (1806), as in his earlier works. Müller's *étatisme* is more conservative, his backward-looking organic belief in the nation-state owing more to Bonald than to Burke; cf. Kohn, *The Mind of Germany*, op. cit., pp. 64–8.
94. On Wagner's conflation of *Edda*, *Nibelungenlied* and *Hohenstaufen*, his identification of Siegfried and Christ, and of the *Nibelungen* Hoard with the *Hohenstaufen's* Reich and Barbarossa's Holy Grail, cf. Kohn, *The Mind of Germany*, op. cit., ch. 9, especially pp. 194 *et seq.*
95. *Die Walküre*, Act II, Scene 2. On Wagner's anti-Semitism, cf. his essay *World Jewry in Music* (1869) and Bracher, op. cit., pp. 47–8.
96. For Wagner, this nihilism and heroic élitism are derived from his reading of Schopenhauer, despite the latter's disapproval.
97. cf. M. Banton, *Race Relations*, Tavistock Publications, London 1967, pp. 28–30. 32–3, 38–9. On Vacher de Lapouge and Chamberlain, cf. Nolte, op. cit., pp. 357–63. On Lagarde, Langbehn, Riehl and the whole *völkisch* outlook, cf. G. Mosse: *The Crisis of German Ideology*, op. cit., chs 1–7.
98. As Kohn, *The Mind of Germany*, op. cit., points out, Langbehn's outright racism went far beyond Lagarde's Germanic imperialism. His highly popular book, *Rembrandt as Educator, by a German* (1890), became even more influential after 1918. cf. also G. Mosse, 'The Mystical Origins of National Socialism', *Journal of the History of Ideas* 22, 1961, 81–96, on List, Schuler and Tarnhari.
99. On the growth of racial anti-Semitism at this time, cf. P. Pulzer, *The Rise of Political Anti-Semitism in Germany and Austria*, John Wiley, New York 1964, especially chs 10–12. Also Bracher, op. cit., pp. 55–63.
100. cf. Bracher, op. cit., pp. 63–66, 72–80; Pulzer, op. cit., chs 17–18.
101. The Germanen- und Wälsungsorder (Order of Teutons and Volsungs) was

one of a number of racialist organisations with a lodge-like structure, secret rites and symbolism approximating (though bitterly opposing) Freemasonry. The most anti-Semitic was Lange's Deutschbund, founded as early as 1894; cf. Pulzer, op. cit., pp. 230–1, and Bracher, op. cit., pp. 65, 109–112, 117, 119–20, 125. On the German Bünde, cf. G. Mosse, *The Crisis of German Ideology*, op. cit., ch. 12.

102. On Lanz, cf. Bracher, op. cit., p. 86; Pulzer, op. cit., pp. 315–17, and Mosse, op. cit., mention other mystical, cosmic and racialist pseudo-philosophies, particularly the runic and sun-worship ideas of Guido von List and Eugen Diederichs, who influenced the popular, neo-romantic escapism of the Youth Movement.

103. A. Hitler, *Mein Kampf*, p. 728, cited in Nolte, op. cit., p. 514.

104. In fact, Germany itself was composed of varied racial elements, of which the 'natural' ruler was the NSDAP itself, because it embodied the Aryan race nucleus of the German people; cf. Hitler, *Mein Kampf*, p. 433, in Nolte, op. cit., p. 518. The racial outlook emerged clearly after the 1935 Nuremberg laws.

105. The bacteriological analogy fits well with the whole Nazi biological Darwinist philosophy, as well as with Hitler's medical–sexual envy and preoccupations, and with the farmer Himmler's approach to agricultural disease; cf. Bracher, op. cit., p. 531, Pulzer, op. cit., pp. 60, 317.

106. On Hitler's mostly non-German models, cf. Nolte, op. cit., pp. 522–4. This is a suggestive counterpart of Hitler's rejection and destruction of much German (let alone European) culture, as in the burning of the books. Of course, other Nazi leaders were less imbued with the racial outlook than Hitler and the SS leaders, and some combined Nazi racialism with older nationalist pan-German motifs.

107. The element of land-cultivator derived from the rural ideology of the Youth Movement and of the Artamanen, which included Himmler, Hoess and Walther Darré, Hitler's minister of agriculture; cf. Mosse, op. cit., ch. 6, for the *völkisch* rural utopias of Theodor Fritsch and Willibald Hentschel.

108. Hitler, *Mein Kampf*, p. 358. For Dietrich Eckart's influence on the early Hitler, and for Eckart's own *Der Bolschewismus von Moses bis Lenin. Zwiegespräch zwischen Adolf Hitler und mir* (Munich 1924), with its crucial Jewish–Bolshevik interpretation of world history, cf. Nolte, op. cit., pp. 415–22, 511–13.

109. The conclusion of Himmler's speech in Goslau in 1935, 'The SS as an anti-Bolshevik combat organisation', is discussed in Nolte, op. cit., pp. 494–5. Eckart's nihilistic image of the 'dragon from hell' comes from his Nazi 'Storm Song'.

110. *Adolf Hitler in Franken – Reden aus der Kampfzeit* (Nuremberg 1939) p. 144, cited in Nolte, op. cit., p. 528. This, of course, is Hitler's 'law of nature', which Jewish intellect and spirit try to undermine and 'sap'.

111. On the Nazi perversion of Nietzsche's *Übermensch* concept, and on their debasement of his non-national asceticism and tough individualism, cf. Kohn, *The Mind of Germany*, op. cit., pp 212–21.

112. On the euthanasia programme for 'useless mouths' of Germans, cf. Poliakov, op. cit., pp. 183–91. Only German resistance to it caused Hitler to suspend the programme, but not before 70,000 mental patients had been so 'treated' (by August 1941).

113. cf. *Hitler's Table Talk*, pp. 424 *et seq.*, 588 *et seq.*, in Nolte, op. cit., p. 521.

114. On the final solution, cf. Poliakov, op. cit., and R. Hilberg, *The Destruction of the European Jews*, Quadrangle, Chicago 1961.

115. cf. the analysis in Nolte, op. cit., pp. 513 *et seq.*

116. The phrase is from Hitler's last testament, cited in Poliakov, op. cit., p. 285.
117. For the definition of 'caste' cf. E. Leach, 'Caste, Class and Slavery', in A. de Reuck and J. Knight (eds), *Caste and Race*, Ciba, London 1967. Also O. C. Cox, *Caste, Class and Race*, Doubleday, New York 1948.
118. On caste in India, cf. L. Dumont, *Homo Hierarchicus*, Weidenfeld & Nicolson, London 1970, and G. D. Berreman, 'Caste in India and the United States', *American Journal of Sociology* 66, 1960, 120–27. On 'caste situations' and 'pariah peoples', cf. the essays on the Burakumin by Wagatsuma and on medieval and modern European anti-Semitism by Cohn and Poliakov, in de Reuck and Knight, op. cit., pp. 118–65, 223–65.
119. On Hitler's 'anti-Semitism of reason', cf. Nolte, op. cit., p. 401.
120. cf. S. Baron, *Modern Nationalism and Religion*, Meridian Books, New York 1960, for the nationalist formulations of the founding fathers.
121. *Hitlers Tischgespräche*, p. 227, cited by Nolte, op. cit., p. 516. Throughout, the contrast is between fully fledged nazism and traditional nationalism.
122. A. Schweitzer, 'Nazification of the Lower Middle Class and Peasants', in *The Third Reich*, op. cit., and Gerth, op. cit.
123. But in Schleswig-Holstein, the Conservatives lost the support of the small property-owners but not that of the upper strata; cf. R. Heberle, *From Democracy to Nazism*, Louisiana State University Press, Baton Rouge, 1945. For the voting figures of the 1928–1933 German elections, cf. Lipset, op. cit., p. 141; for the argument that nazism left many Conservative Nationalist areas intact, cf. ibid., pp. 142–6. On the other hand, the Nationalist (DNVP) vote declined by 50 per cent in the 1930 election, compared with the 1928 election; cf. Bracher, op. cit., p. 233. On early big business support cf. ibid., p. 126.
124. cf. H. M. Pachter, 'Nazi and Fascist Propaganda for Power', in *The Third Reich*, op. cit., and Bracher, op. cit., pp. 117–18, 189–95. Hitler himself was preoccupied by questions of tactics and mass propaganda, as the discussions in *Mein Kampf* demonstrate: for example, his stress on the simplified slogan for intellectually limited 'masses', and the need for 'fanaticism' or mass hysteria; cf. *Mein Kampf* (Munich 1925–8), Boston 1962, pp. 197–8, analysed in W. Maser: *Hitler's Mein Kampf*, Faber & Faber, London 1969. For an interesting view which sees Nazi symbolism and liturgy as rooted in earlier German *völkisch*–artistic spatial and rhythmic national experiments, cf. G. Mosse, 'Mass Politics and the Political Liturgy of Nationalism', in Kamenka (ed.), op. cit., pp. 39–54.
125. On Hitler's and Nazi ideas of pan-Europeanism, and of the national aspirations of non-German European peoples, cf. Bracher, op. cit., pp. 505–8, 511–12; on Hitler's testament, cf. ibid., pp. 574–5.
126. cf. P. E. Mayo, *The Roots of Identity: Three National Movements in Contemporary European Politics*, Allen Lane, London 1974. Here we may cite the Basque, Catalan, Galician, Breton, Corsican, Scots, Welsh and Ulster movements, in addition to stirrings among the Manx, Cornish and Jurassiens, and the long-standing Flemish–Walloon dispute. On this, see ch. 6 (below).
127. For the didactic and heroic moralism of the *philosophes*, particularly Diderot, cf. J. A. Leith, *The Idea of Art as Propaganda in France, 1750–99*, University of Toronto Press, Toronto 1965, chs. 2–4.
128. cf. Goebbels's statement (radio address of 1 April 1933): 'The year 1789 is hereby eradicated from history' (J. Goebbels, *Revolution der Deutschen*, Oldenburg 1933, p. 155); cited and discussed in Bracher, op. cit., pp. 22–3; cf. also Fest, op. cit., p. 66.

129. Himmler's speech to a small circle of faithful SS chiefs at Poznan on 4 October 1943 (*Nürnberger Dokumente*, PS-1919, vol. XXIX, pp. 122–3), is partly reproduced in Bracher, op. cit., pp. 522–3, and Poliakov, op. cit., p. 214. More generally, cf. H. Bucheim *et al.*, *Anatomy of the SS State*, Collins, London 1968.
130. L. R. Franck, 'The Economic and Social Diagnosis of National-Socialism', in *The Third Reich*, op. cit.
131. It was in the East that 'secessionist' ethnic nationalism was particularly acute as a result of pre-existing ethnic antagonisms inflamed by the new urban competition for limited facilities; cf. B. Azkin, *State and Nation*, Hutchinson, London 1964, pp. 55 *et seq*. The relative failure of nationalism, even after it had achieved independence, to contain or dissipate the effects of economic and social insecurity, greater democracy, minority conflicts and the resort to large-scale violence, attracted increasing segments of the population of eastern Europe to anti-Semitic, specifically racialist and paramilitary solutions. At the same time, the 'race' and the élite could appear much more plausibly as extensions or 'true' interpretations of nationalist goals and categories, in an uncorrupted, pristine form.
132. On the impact of the World War on the 'rhythm' and *élan* of fascism, cf. Mosse, 'The Genesis of Fascism', op. cit., p. 17. On the early connection of poison gas in the Great War and the extermination of the 'Hebrews' in Hitler's mind, cf. Hitler, *Mein Kampf*, p. 722, cited in Nolte, op. cit., p. 524.
133. In Germany, especially, where defeat and a crushing peace had undermined the faith of many in the authoritarian–hierarchical state, the more 'inward' and 'spiritual' concept of the race could now break through into more general respectability. In this, too, the Great War proved a solvent of revolutionary dimensions; even if it did not destroy the idea of the *Obrigkeitsstaat*, it enabled it to be harnessed to, and incorporated by, the dynamic concept of racial warfare. Ludendorff's and Rohm's ideas of the 'armed state' were enveloped by Hitler's and Himmler's 'race state', cf. Nolte, op. cit., pp. 412–22.
134. T. Parsons, 'Democracy and Social Structure in Pre-Nazi Germany', and 'Some Sociological Aspects of the Fascist Movements' (both 1942) in Parsons, *Essays in Sociological Theory*, rev. ed., Free Press, Glencoe, Ill. 1964.
135. cf. M. Weber, 'Economy and Society' 3/9, in H. Gerth and C. W. Mills, *From Max Weber*, Routledge & Kegan Paul, London 1948.

CHAPTER 4

1. For other definitions, cf. K. Deutsch, *Nationalism and Social Communication*, MIT Press, New York 1966, ch. 1; and A. D. Smith, *Theories of Nationalism*, Duckworth, London 1971, ch. 7.
2. Further discussions of the concepts of the 'nation' and 'nationalism' are contained in G. Zernatto, 'Nation: The History of a Word', *Review of Politics* 6, 1944, 351–66, and recently in E. Kamenka, 'Political Nationalism – the Evolution of an Idea', in E. Kamenka (ed.), *Nationalism: The Nature and Evolution of an Idea*, Australian National University, Edward Arnold, London 1976, pp. 3–20.
3. The distinction between 'racism' and 'racialism', the former denoting racial theories or ideologies, the latter racial policies or actions, is taken from M. Banton, *Race Relations*, Tavistock Publications, London 1967, p. 8.

4. cf. P. van den Berghe, *Race and Racism*, John Wiley, New York 1967, pp. 10–11, for further comments on social and 'subjective' definitions.
5. Banton, op. cit., p. 18. Blumenbach's five races were the Caucasian (white), Mongolian (yellow), Ethiopian (black), American (red) and Malayan (brown), and Blumenbach maintained that they were formed as the result of inheritance of modifications induced by different environments.
6. Thus W. Boyd, 'The Contribution of Genetics to Anthropology', in A. Kroeber (ed.), *Anthropology Today*, University of Chicago Press, Chicago 1953, pp. 488–506, concentrated on the Rh blood group and ABO genes, which yielded a five-fold classification of European, African, Asiatic, American Indian and Australoid races; S. M. Garn, *Human Races*, Thomas, Springfield 1961, isolated nine 'geographical races'; and C. S. Coon, S. M. Garn and J. B. Birdsell, *Races*, Thomas, Springfield 1950, proposed a finer subdivision into thirty races which change over time and which result from combining different physical traits.
7. On 'methodological nationalism', cf. H. Martins, 'Time and Theory in Sociology', in J. Rex (ed.), *Approaches to Sociology, An Introduction to Major Trends in British Sociology*, Routledge & Kegan Paul, London 1974.
8. T. Dobzhansky, *Mankind Evolving*, Bantam Books, Toronto and New York 1962, p. 283.
9. van den Berghe, op. cit., pp. 9–10.
10. A. D. Smith, 'Ethnocentrism, Nationalism and Social Change', *International Journal of Comparative Sociology* 13, 1972, 1–20.
11. For such inscriptions, cf. J. B. Pritchard (ed.), *The Ancient Near East*, Princeton University Press, Princeton 1958, and C. H. Gordon, *The Ancient Near East*, 3rd rev. ed., Norton & Co., New York 1965.
12. cf. M. L. Gordon, 'The Nationality of Slaves under the Early Roman Empire', *Journal of Roman Studies*, 14, 1924, 93–111, reprinted in M. I. Finley (ed.), *Slavery in Classical Antiquity*, Heffer & Sons, Cambridge 1960.
13. Tacitus, *Germania*; and cf. E. A. Thompson, 'Slavery in Early Germany', *Hermathena* 89, 1957, 17–29, reprinted in Finley, op. cit.
14. Horace, *Odes* I (27) and III (3,4); cf. A. N. Sherwin-White, *Racial Prejudice in Imperial Rome*, Blackwell, Oxford 1952.
15. R. Schlaifer, 'Greek Theories of Slavery from Homer to Aristotle', *Harvard Studies in Classical Philology* 47, 1936, 165–204, in Finley, op. cit. On the Arabs, cf. P. Mason, *Patterns of Dominance*, Oxford University Press, London 1971, pp. 193–4, 206, 221; and J. Carmichael, *The Shaping of the Arabs*, Macmillan, London 1967, pp. 137, 236–8 (on the Zanj slave revolt of 869–83 A.D., mainly of Negroes brought by the African slave trade).
16. L. Poliakov, 'Racism in Europe', in A. de Reuck and J. Knight (eds): *Caste and Race*, Ciba Foundation, London 1967, 223–34, dates the birth of a 'racist mentality' to the period 1800–15, citing German books and pamphlets by Grattenauer (1803), Jahn (1810), Arndt and Fichte, mainly anti-Semitic tracts, as were Napoleon's statements about the '*sang vicie*' of '*la race juive*'. However, more theoretical racial Darwinist works appear after 1850, and Banton dates the high period of racist theory to the early 1850s (the works of Knox, Gobineau, Nott and Gliddon, and of Disraeli; later Hunt and Beddoe), cf. Banton, op. cit., pp. 28–35.

The origins of nationalism may be variously dated between the Corsican rising of Paoli in the 1750s and the first Partition of Poland in 1772, both of which evoked proto-nationalist advice from Rousseau, and the French Revolution, with accompanying movements in Holland, Switzerland and the United States.

17. cf. A. P. Whitaker and D. C. Jordan, *Nationalism in Contemporary Latin America*, Free Press, New York 1966, ch. 9.
18. van den Berghe, op. cit., p. 48; and J. Pitt-Rivers, 'Race, Color, and Class in Central America and the Andes', in C. S. Heller (ed.), *Structured Social Inequality*, Macmillan, London 1970, pp. 380–87.
19. van den Berghe, op. cit., p. 54.
20. Whitaker and Jordan, op. cit., p. 108.
21. On Sanchez and the Indian Renaissance, cf. K. Masur, *Nationalism in Latin America*, Macmillan, New York 1966, pp. 97–100.
22. On this *sertanismo*, cf. Whitaker and Jordan, op. cit., pp. 78–9; and Masur, op. cit., p. 124.
23. On Jaguaribe, cf. Whitaker and Jordan, op. cit., pp. 83–5.
24. van den Berghe, op. cit., pp. 69–75.
25. H. Martins, 'Ideology and Development: 'Developmental Nationalism' in Brazil', *Sociological Review Monograph* No. 11, 1967, 153–72. On race relations in Brazil, cf. C. Wagley (ed.), *Race and Class in Rural Brazil*, Unesco, Paris 1952, and A. W. Lind (ed.), *Race Relations in World Perspective*, University of Hawaii Press, Honolulu 1955, p. 461.
26. W. J. Argyle, 'European Nationalism and African Tribalism', in P. H. Gulliver (ed.): *Tradition and Transition in East Africa*, Pall Mall Press, London 1969; but cf. the differences with European ethnic nationalisms described by B. Neuberger: 'State and Nation in African Thought', *Journal of African Studies* 4/2, 1977, 198–205.
27. On this, cf. V. Olorunsola (ed.), *The Politics of Cultural Sub-nationalism in Africa*, Anchor Books, New York 1972; also B. Neuberger, 'The Western Nation-state in African Perceptions of Nation-building', *Asian and African Studies* 11/2, 1976, 241–61.
28. cf. C. Anderson, F. von der Mehden and C. Young, *Issues of Political Development*, Prentice-Hall, Englewood Cliffs, 1967, ch. 2.
29. G. von Grunebaum, 'Problems of Muslim Nationalism', in R. N. Frye (ed.), *Islam and the West*, Mouton, The Hague 1957. Also E. I. J. Rosenthal, *Islam in the Modern National State*, Cambridge Univeristy Press, Cambridge 1965, pp. 117–23.
30. For some of these ethnic conflicts, cf. 'Nationalism and Separatism', *Journal of Contemporary History* 6/1, 1971. On the Burakumin, cf. H. Wagatsuma, 'The Pariah Caste in Japan: History and Present Self-image', in de Reuck and Knight (eds), op. cit., pp. 118–40.
31. B. Akzin, *State and Nation*, Hutchinson University Library, London 1964, pp. 53 *et seq.*, and E. Gellner, 'Scale and Nation', *Philosophy of the Social Sciences* 3, 1973, 1–17.
32. van den Berghe, op. cit., pp. 12–13; Mason, op. cit., pp. 12–20.
33. B. Lewis, *The Emergence of Modern Turkey*, Oxford University Press, London 1968, pp. 345–8.
34. Z. N. Zeine, *Arab–Turkish Relations and the Emergence of Arab Nationalism*, Khayats, Beirut 1958, pp. 77–80.
35. Lewis, op. cit., pp. 352–4, 357–61.
36. Under the influence of al-Afghani and Abduh, and following the Arabic renaissance in Lebanon under the leadership of Butrus al-Bustani, writers like al-Yaziji, al-Kawakibi and Negib Azoury began to proclaim a secular Arab nationalism at the turn of the century. But a full pan-Arabism had to wait until the 1930s, when its chief exponents were Lebanese, Syrian and Iraqi nationalists like Edmond Rabbath, al-Alayili, Sami Shawkat and Sati al-Husri: cf. H. B. Sharabi, *Arab Intellectuals and the West: The Formative*

Years, 1875–1914, Johns Hopkins Press, Baltimore and London 1970, and S. Haim, *Arab Nationalism, An Anthology,* University of California Press, Berkeley and Los Angeles 1962, especially pp. 35 *et seq.*

37. On Axis influence in Iraq, cf. L. Hirscowicz, *The Third Reich and the Arab East,* Routledge & Kegan Paul, London 1966, pp. 77–8. The racial element is clearly found in the works of Rabbath and al-Alayili, cf. S. Haim: op. cit., pp. 37-8, 40-2, 68, 103-119, 124-6.

38. C. E. Dawn, 'From Ottomanism to Arabism: The Origin of an Ideology', *Review of Politics* 23, 1961, 379–400; and A. D. Smith, 'Nationalism and Religion: The Role of Religious Reform in the Genesis of Arab and Jewish Nationalism', *Archives de Sciences Sociales des Religions* 35, 1973, 23–43.

39. P. O. Esedebe, 'Origins and meaning of PanAfricanism', *Présence Africaine* 73, 1970, 109–27.

40. B. Neuberger, 'The African Concept of Balkanisation', *Journal of Modern African Studies,* 13, 1976, 523–29.

41. C. Legum, *PanAfricanism, A Short Political Guide,* Pall Mall Press, London and Dunmow 1962, pp. 33–4.

42. On pan-Slavism in general, cf. H. Kohn, *Pan-Slavism: Its History and Ideology,* 2nd rev. ed., Vintage Books, Random House, New York 1960. On some tensions of Russian nationalism, cf. H. Rogger, 'Nationalism and the State: A Russian Dilemma', *Comparative Studies in Society and History* 4, 1962, 253–64.

43. E. C. Thaden, *Conservative Nationalism in 19th Century Russia,* University of Washington Press, Seattle 1964.

44. Banton, op. cit., pp. 40–1, 45; Poliakov, op. cit., pp. 231–2; also H. Tint, *The Decline of French Patriotism, 1870–1940,* Weidenfeld & Nicolson, London 1964.

45. G. L. Mosse, *The Crisis of German Ideology: Intellectual Origins of the Third Reich,* Grosset and Dunlap, New York 1964, chs 2–4, 12.

46. H. Seton-Watson, 'Unsatisfied Nationalisms', *Journal of Contemporary History* 6/1, 1971, 3–14. On the German example, cf. C., L. and R. Tilly, *The Rebellious Century, 1830–1930,* J. M. Dent, London 1975, ch. 4. For the disunity in the Bismarckian Reich, cf. M. S. Anderson, *The Ascendancy of Europe, 1815–1914,* Longman, London 1972, pp. 124–7.

47. cf. L. Greenberg, *The Jews in Russia,* vol. II, Schocken Books, New York 1976 (1951), pp. 82–3, 87–8, for their activities.

48. H. Kohn, *The Mind of Germany,* Macmillan, London 1965, p. 87.

49. ibid., pp. 58–68. Also H. S. Reiss (ed.), *The Political Thought of the German Romantics, 1793–1815,* Blackwell, Oxford 1955; and J. Weiss, *Conservatism in Europe, 1770–1945,* Thames & Hudson, London 1977, pp. 41–5.

50. For this sense of the conservative state, cf. L. Krieger, *The German Idea of Freedom,* Beacon Press, Boston 1957; and K. D. Bracher, *The German Dictatorship,* Penguin, Harmondsworth 1973, pp. 31 *et seq.*

51. On the 'political anti-Semitism' of Marr, Dühring and von Glogau, and the rural populism of Langbehn, Fritsch and Willibald Hentschel, cf. P. Pulzer, *The Rise of Political AntiSemitism in Germany and Austria,* John Wiley, New York 1964, chs 6–7, and Mosse, op. cit., pp. 112–19; also Weiss, op. cit., ch. 7.

52. For an account, cf. H. Sachar: *The Course of Modern Jewish History,* Delta Books, Dell Publishing Co., New York, 1958, pp. 61–5.

53. cf. R. F. Byrnes: *AntiSemitism in Modern France,* Rutgers, New York 1950; and E. Nolte: *Three Faces of Fascism,* Mentor, New York 1969, pt. II.

54. G. Lichtheim: *Imperialism,* Penguin Books, Harmondsworth 1971, ch. 6, esp. pp. 88 *et seq.* On Germany, cf. K. D. Bracher: op. cit., pp. 34–5, 45, 50–1.

55. M. Banton: op. cit., pp. 32–3; E. Nolte: op. cit., pp. 354–7.
56. On Japan, cf. D. C. Holtom: *Modern Japan and Shinto Nationalism*, University of Chicago Press, Chicago 1943; for an interpretation of the Japanese variant of fascism, cf. Barrington Moore, Jr.: *Social Origins of Dictatorship and Democracy*, Allen Lane, The Penguin Press, London 1967, ch. 5, esp. pp. 291 *et seq.*
57. For Boer nationalism, cf. F. A. van Jaarsfeld: *The Awakening of Afrikaner Nationalism, 1868–91*, Human & Rosseau, Cape Town 1961, and P. van den Berghe: *South Africa: A Study in Conflict*, Wesleyan University Press, Middletown, Conn. 1965.
58. G. Barraclough, *An Introduction to Contemporary History*, Penguin, Harmondsworth 1967.
59. N. Cohn: 'The Myth of the Demonic Conspiracy of Jews in Medieval and Modern Europe', in de Reuck and Knight, op. cit., pp. 240–54.
60. cf. R. Segal, *The Race War*, Cape, London 1966; J. Rex: *Race Relations in Sociological Theory*, Weidenfeld & Nicolson, London 1970, p. 161. On black and white categories, cf. de Reuck and Knight, op. cit., pp. 255 *et seq.*
61. T. Draper, *The Rediscovery of Black Nationalism*, Secker & Warburg, London 1971, ch. 8.
62. A. Horton, 'Refutation of the Alleged Inferiority of the Negro Race', (1866), in D. Nicol (ed.), *Africanus Horton, The Dawn of Nationalism in Modern Africa*, Longman, London 1969, pp. 24–30.
63. A. Horton, *West African Countries and Peoples* (1868), in H. S. Wilson (ed.), *Origins of West African Nationalism*, Macmillan, London 1969, pp. 167–8.
64. Horton: op. cit., and his *Letters on the Political Condition of the Gold Coast*, both in Wilson, op. cit., pp. 168–70, 198–9: 'If Europe, therefore, has been raised to her present pitch of civilisation by progressive advancement, Africa too, with a guarantee of civilisation from the north, will rise into equal importance. The nucleus has been planted; it is just beginning to show signs of life and future vigour; . . . '
65. E. Blyden, *Our Origins, Dangers and Duties*, annual address before Mayor and Common Council of Monrovia, National Independence Day, 26 July 1865, cited in Wilson, op. cit., pp. 103–4.
66. R. July, *The Origins of Modern African Thought*, Faber & Faber, London 1968, pp. 222–3.
67. E. W. Blyden, 'Ethiopia Stretching Out Her Hands to God' (1880) in *Christianity, Islam and the Negro Race* (1887), pp. 13–29, in Wilson, op. cit., p. 246.
68. E. W. Blyden, 'Study and Race', *Sierra Leone Times*, 3 June 1893, in Wilson, op. cit., p. 250.
69. Thus in 1880 he wrote: 'The sentiment of race and nationality has attained wonderful development. . . . The efforts of men like Garibaldi and Cavour in Italy, of Kossuth in Hungary, of Bismarck in Germany, of the Ashantees and Zulus in Africa, have proved the indestructible vitality and tenacity of racism'. ('Ethiopia Stretching . . . ', op. cit., p. 245). Similarly, Horton can write of Sierra Leone in 1868: 'But the inhabitants of the colony have been gradually blending into one race, and a national spirit is being developed.' (*West African Countries and Peoples*, in Wilson, op. cit., p. 172).
70. July, op. cit., pp. 215–17; also H. R. Lynch, *Edward Wilmott Blyden: Pan-Negro Patriot, 1832–1912*, Oxford University Press, New York 1967.
71. E. W. Blyden, 'The Prospects of the African', p. 7, in July, op. cit., p. 219.
72. Wilson, op. cit., Introduction, pp. 40–1.
73. I. Geiss, *The Pan-African Movement*, Methuen, London 1974, pp. 116–18; July, op. cit., ch. 21.

74. G. Shepperson, 'Notes on Negro American Influence on African Nationalism', *Journal of African History* 1, 1960, 299–312.
75. Alexander Crummell, 'The Social Principle Among a People . . .' (1875), in J. H. Bracey, Jr, A. Meier, and E. Rudwick (eds), *Black Nationalism in America*, Bobbs-Merrill, Indianapolis and New York 1970, p. 130. Crummell actually sought the development of Negro race pride and self-help, to the point where Whites would concede race equality, and hence the 'ultimate extinction of caste, and all race distinctions' (ibid., p. 133).
76. Bishop Henry M. Turner, 'God is A Negro' (*Voice of Missions*, 1 February 1898), in Bracey, Meier and Rudwick, op. cit., pp. 154–5.
77. Cited in Legum, *Pan-Africanism*, op. cit., p. 20.
78. W. E. B. Du Bois, Editorial in *The Crisis* 20, October 1920; in Bracey, Meier, and Rudwick, op. cit., pp. 276–8.
79. W. E. B. Du Bois, 'Criteria of Negro Art', *The Crisis* 32, October 1926, in ibid., pp. 280–1.
80. Langston Hughes, cited in Legum, op. cit., p. 17.
81. Langston Hughes, *The Langston Hughes Reader*, Braziller, New York 1958, cited in Legum, op. cit., pp. 18–19.
82. In Olumbe Bassir (ed.), *An Anthology of West African Verse*, Ibadan 1957, in Legum, op. cit., p. 19.
83. On Césaire, cf. C. Wauthier, *The Literature and Thought of Modern Africa*, Pall Mall Press, London 1966, pp. 104–5, 111–2, 170–2; and Legum, op. cit., pp. 92–5.
84. In *Black Orpheus* 1958, in Legum, op. cit., p. 19.
85. On the Harlem renaissance, cf. H. Cruse, *The Crisis of the Negro Intellectual*, William Morrow, New York 1967.
86. Geiss, op. cit., pp. 320–1.
87. Legum, op. cit., pp. 34–7, 95–6, citing Senghor's statement of 1961 – 'I am not really a Pan-Africanist, I am a humanist' – and Césaire's:
. . . preserve me, heart, from all hatred
do not turn me into a man of hate whom I shall hate
for in order to emerge into this unique race,
you know my world-wide love
know it is not hatred against other races
that turns me into the cultivator of this one race . . . .
88. Cited in ibid., pp. 96–7, and Appendix 19, pp. 212–13 for the Resolution of the First Conference of Negro Writers and Artists, Paris 1956.
89. Négritude, *Black Orpheus* 1958, in ibid., p. 94; and Wauthier, op. cit., pp. 106, 278.
90. Geiss, op. cit., p. 319.
91. ibid., p. 319. Psychological interpretations are challenged by T. Hodgkin: 'The Relevance of "Western" Ideas in the Derivation of African Nationalism', in J. R. Pennock (ed.), *Self-government in Modernising Societies*, Prentice-Hall, Englewood Cliffs 1964.
92. A. A. Mazrui, *Towards a Pax Africana*, Weidenfeld & Nicolson, London 1966, ch. 3.
93. On these élites, cf. P. C. Lloyd (ed.), *New Elites in Tropical Africa*, Oxford University Press, London 1966.
94. cf. I. Wallerstein, *Africa, the Politics of Unity: An Analysis of a Contemporary Social Movement*, Pall Mall Press, London 1967.
95. On Nkrumah, cf. Geiss, op. cit., pp. 368–81, and the summing up on pp. 427–32.
96. E. Kedourie, *Nationalism*, Hutchinson, London 1960, ch. 4, and E. Gellner, *Thought and Change*, Weidenfeld & Nicolson, London 1964, ch. 7.

97. On vernacular renascences, cf. J. Fishman (ed.), *Language Problems in Developing Countries*, John Wiley, New York 1968.
98. The Egyptian and Ethiopian experience, despite their symbolism, seem to lie especially outside this experience; cf. Geiss, op. cit., p. 430.
99. cf. A. Hertzberg, *The Zionist Idea*, Meridian Books, New York 1960, Introduction.
100. Emotionally pan-Africanism must always react ambivalently to its continental political aims which naturally give equal status to the North African countries.
101. Racial bitterness becomes most evident in Garveyism; cf. E. D. Cronon, *Black Moses*, University of Wisconsin Press, Madison, Wisconsin 1955.

CHAPTER 5

1. As did the German Social Democrats who voted war credits for the Kaiser's war in 1914.
2. K. Marx, *Capital*, Modern Library, New York 1936, pp. 708–9.
3. This phrase comes from a speech, 'The Study of History', made by Banerjea to an audience of parents in the late 1870s, in which he argued that the study of India's 'past glories' is the key to moral, and hence social and political, regeneration, cf. R. C. Palit (ed.), *Speeches of Babu Surendra Nath Banerjea, 1876–80*, Calcutta 1880, pp. 1–18, cited in E. Kedourie (ed.), *Nationalism in Asia and Africa*, Weidenfeld & Nicolson, London 1970, pp. 225–44.
4. For mid nineteenth-century Japan, the external 'enemy' and catalyst was America in the form of its naval incursions into Japanese waters and it set a new standard of comparison for the dissatisfied samurai. Similarly, the continuous wars with England (Seven Years War, American War of Independence) brought home the contrast between 'English liberties' and the hedonistic tyranny of the court in Rococo France. Similar 'renewal' nationalisms bred by analogous feelings of decay and decline occurred in early twentieth-century Turkey and Persia.
5. K. Marx and F. Engels: *The German Ideology*, International Publishers, New York 1947, pp. 9, 21.
6. Cited in C. Legum, *PanAfricanism; A Short Political Guide*, Pall Mall Press, London and Dunmow 1962, p. 15.
7. L. Pinsker, *Autoemancipation*, Berlin 1882 (ZOA 1956), p. 19.
8. K. Marx, *Economic and Philosophic Manuscripts* (1844), in L. D. Easton and K. Guddat (eds), *Writings of the Young Marx on Philosophy and Society*, Anchor Books, Garden City, NY 1967, pp. 289–90.
9. K. Marx, *Critique of Hegel's Philosophy of the State* (1843), in Easton and Guddat, op. cit., p. 155.
10. K. Marx, *Excerpt-Notes of 1844*, in Easton and Guddat, op. cit., p. 266.
11. K. Marx, *Economic and Philosophic Manuscripts* (1844), in Easton and Guddat, op. cit., p. 297.
12. On this need to preserve one's links with the past, cf. S. M. Dubnow, *Nationalism and History*, ed. K. S. Pinson, Jewish Publication Society of America, Philadelphia 1958.
13. G. Mazzini, *Life and Writings of Joseph Mazzini*, Smith, Elder, London 1890, vol. I. pp. 226–90; cited in H. Kohn: *Nationalism, Its Meaning and History*, Van Nostrand, Princeton 1955, p. 118.
14. Mazzini, op. cit., ibid., p. 119.
15. D. Hyde, *Revival of Irish Literature and other Addresses*, Fischer Unwin, London

1894, pp. 117–31, cited in Kohn, op. cit., pp. 148–9.
16. cf. P. Calvert, 'On Attaining Sovereignty', in A. D. Smith (ed.), *Nationalist Movements*, Macmillan, London 1976, especially pp. 142–5.
17. K. Marx, *Capital*, vol. I, ch. 32, Lawrence and Wishart, London 1970.
18. K. Marx, *Werke* vol. IV, pp. 338–9; cited in S. Avineri, *The Social and Political Thought of Karl Marx*, Cambridge University Press, Cambridge 1968, p. 191.
19. K. Marx, *Economic and Philosophic Manuscripts* (1844), in Easton and Guddat, op. cit., p. 314.
20. K. Marx and F. Engels: *The German Ideology* (1846), in Easton and Guddat, op. cit., pp. 424–5.
21. K. Marx, *Economic and Philosophic Manuscripts* (1844), in Easton and Guddat, op. cit., p. 304.
22. K. Marx, *Critique of the Gotha Programme* (1875), in L. S. Feuer (ed.), *Marx & Engels: Basic Writings on Politics & Philosophy*, Anchor Books, Garden City, NY 1959, p. 119.
23. A. Müller, *The Elements of Politics* (1809), cited in E. Kedourie, *Nationalism*, Hutchinson, London 1960, p. 39.
24. J-J. Rousseau, *Projet Corse* (1765), cited by A. M. Cohler, *Rousseau and Nationalism*, Basic Books, New York 1970, p. 199, n. 23. Rousseau holds up the industrious, harmonious Swiss as a model for the Corsicans to follow in returning to their original estate, now that they have shaken off the Genoese tyranny.
25. J-J. Rousseau, *Considerations on the Government of Poland* (1772), in F. M. Watkins (ed.), *Rousseau, Political Writings*, Nelson, Edinburgh and London 1953, p. 165. Islanders are particularly likely to have a distinctive national character, 'being less mixed', says Rousseau, apropos of the Corsicans; ibid., p. 293.
26. E. Burke, *Reflections on the Revolution in France* (1790), cited in S. Baron, *Modern Nationalism and Religion*, Meridian Books, New York 1960, p. 30.
27. G. Mazzini, *Italia del Popolo*, 18 June 1848, article reprinted in G. Mazzini: *Scritti editi ed inediti Edizione nazionale*, 89 vols. Imola 1906–40, 38, 82; cited in Baron, op. cit., p. 49.
28. Territorial self-sufficiency and the agrarian ideal again find their classic expression in Rousseau's eulogies of the Swiss and the Corsicans. Thus: 'Agriculture is the only means of maintaining the external independence of a state', and 'Cultivation of the land cultivates the spirit; all agricultural peoples multiply. ...'; and of the Poles: 'Cultivate your fields well, and have no other care ... pay little attention to foreign countries, give little heed to commerce; but multiply as far as possible your domestic production and consumption of foodstuffs'; cited in Watkins, op. cit., pp. 283, 285, 226, 231.
    For Marx, of course, the 'idiocy of rural life' is another reason for favouring urban industrialism with all its attendant ills, but only so as to win through to socialism's abolition of the division of labour.
29. cf. W. MacGaffey and C. R. Barnett: *Cuba, Its People, Its Society, Its Culture*, HRAF Press, New Haven 1962, p. 20.
30. J. Carmichael, 'The Nationalist–Communist Symbiosis in the Middle East', *Problems of Communism*, 8/3, 1959, 35–41.
31. cf. R. Lowenthal, 'The Points of the Compass', in J. H. Kautsky (ed.), *Political Change in Underdeveloped Countries*, John Wiley, New York 1962, pp. 335–47, and J. H. Kautsky's *Introduction*, chs 3–4.
32. G. Amin, 'The Egyptian Economy and the Revolution', in P. J. Vatikiotis (ed.), *Egypt since the Revolution*, George Allen & Unwin, London 1968, pp. 40–9, and C. Issawi, *Egypt in Revolution: An Economic Analysis*, RIIA, Oxford 1963.
33. L. Binder, *The Ideological Revolution in the Middle East*, John Wiley, New

York 1964; and H. B. Sharabi, *Nationalism and Revolution in the Arab World*, Van Nostrand, Princeton 1966.

34. On Sékou Touré's views, cf. P. Worsley, *The Third World*, Weidenfeld & Nicolson, London 1964, pp. 127, 162, 179–80.

35. Notably to China, whose agricultural communes appear more relevant than Soviet factories. The Israeli *moshav*, too, is favoured; cf. P. Worsley, 'The Concept of Populism', in E. Gellner and G. Ionescu (eds), *Populism: Its Meanings and National Characteristics*, Weidenfeld & Nicolson, London 1970, pp. 212–50.

36. S. P. Huntington, *Political Order in Changing Societies*, Yale University Press, New Haven and London 1968, pp. 334 *et seq.*

37. F. Engels, *Friedrich Engels' Briefwechsel mit Karl Kautsky*, ed. B. Kautsky, Vienna 1955, pp. 5–53; cited in H. B. Davis, *Nationalism and Socialism*, Monthly Review Press, New York 1967, p. 17.

38. R. Lowenthal, 'Communism versus Nationalism', *Problems of Communism* 11, 1962, 37–44, on such communist 'polycentrism' since 1948.

39. C. Leiden and K. M. Schmitt, *The Politics of Violence*, Prentice-Hall, Englewood Cliffs 1968, ch. 10; and T. Draper, *Castroism: Theory and Practise*, Praeger, New York 1965.

40. D. A. Wilson, 'Nation-Building and Revolutionary War', in K. Deutsch and W. Foltz (eds), *Nation-building*, Atherton, New York 1963.

41. On Burma, cf. E. Sarkisyanz, *Buddhist Backgrounds of the Burmese Revolution*, Nijhoff, The Hague 1964. More generally, on cultural responses to westernisation and their politicisation, cf. the essays in D. E. Smith (ed.), *Religion and Political Modernisation*, Yale University Press, New Haven and London 1974, especially those by von der Mehden, Smith, Bechert and Lewy.

42. cf. Draper, op. cit., pp. 132–3.

43. Leiden and Schmitt, op. cit., pp. 188–9, 195–6.

44. C. Johnson, 'Building a Communist Nation in China', in R. A. Scalapino (ed.), *The Communist Revolution in Asia*, Prentice-Hall, Englewood Cliffs 1969, pp. 52–84.

45. R. V. Burks, *The Dynamics of Communism in Eastern Europe*, Princeton University Press, Princeton 1961, ch. 6, pp. 107 *et seq.*

46. ibid., pp. 118–30; I. J. Lederer, 'Nationalism and the Yugoslavs', in P. F. Sugar and I. J. Lederer (eds), *Nationalism in Eastern Europe*, University of Washington Press, Seattle and London 1969, especially pp. 433–8.

47. Johnson, op. cit., p. 52, quoting *The People's Daily* (Peking), 11 February 1963.

48. The strategies of Ho Chi Minh's Lao Dong party are analysed by J. C. Donnell and M. Gurtov, 'North Vietnam', in Scalapino, op. cit., pp. 151–84.

49. cf. R. Lowenthal, 'The Points of the Compass', in Kautsky, op. cit., pp. 335–47.

50. R. A. Scalapino, 'Communism in Asia', in Scalapino, op. cit., pp. 1–51, especially 7–8.

51. Some Asian examples are given by Scalapino, op. cit., pp. 10–18, 25–41. cf. also the essay by Donnell and Gurtov, op. cit.

52. K. Marx and F. Engels, *The Communist Manifesto*, in Feuer, op. cit., p. 26.

53. K. Marx and F. Engels, *The German Ideology*, International Publishers, New York 1963, p. 69.

54. Marx and Engels, *The Communist Manifesto*, in Feuer, op. cit., p. 11. This is in line with the movement from 'national seclusion and self-sufficiency' to 'universal interdependence of nations'.

55. Marx and Engels, *The German Ideology*, op. cit., p. 99.
56. K. Marx, 'Prospects in England and France', *New York Tribune*, 27 April 1855 (*Werke*, vol. XI, 182), cited in Davis, op. cit., p. 74.
57. The worker is just as likely to turn xenophobic in a national crisis as any other group, but in more quiescent times he tends to concentrate on improving his economic position in class or individualistic or family terms; cf. the responses of Egyptian workers to Lerner's surveys, in D. Lerner, *The Passing of Traditional Society*, Free Press, New York 1958.
58. The passage in question reads:

> Only under the rule of Christianity, which externalises all human relationships – national, natural, moral and theoretical – could bourgeois society detach itself entirely from the sphere of the state, destroy all those bonds which link men as a species, replace them with egotism and the demands of self-interest, and dissolve the human world into a world of atomized and mutually hostile individuals. '*Zur Judenfrage*,' *Deutsch-Französische Jahrbücher*, 1843–44 (*Werke* I, 376), cited in Easton and Guddat, op. cit., p. 247.

Davis, op. cit., pp. 6–7, points to a communist weakness in not embracing the 'nation' as the organising political unit of solidarity after the state had withered away.

59. F. Engels, *Po und Rhein* (1859), (*Werke* XIII, 267), cited by Davis, op. cit., pp. 60–1; and n. 37 *supra*.
60. Marx and Engels, *The Communist Manifesto*, in Feuer, op. cit., p. 19. At the same time, 'modern industrial labour' has stripped the proletarian of 'every trace of national character' (ibid. p. 18).
61. ibid., p. 26.
62. Though Engels's own susceptibility to German nationalism and to Hegel's theory of 'historyless peoples' made him more sensitive to the problem of nationalities in eastern Europe; cf. Davis, op. cit., pp. 18–23, 44–51.
63. K. Marx, Preface to *A Contribution to the Critique of Political Economy*, (1859), in Feuer, op. cit., pp. 43–4.
64. 'A nation is a historically evolved, stable community of language, territory, economic life, and psychological make-up manifested in a community of culture'; J. Stalin, *Marxism and the National Question* (1913), in J. Stalin, *Marxism and the National and Colonial Question*, Lawrence & Wishart, London 1936, p. 8. cf. also S. Shaheen: *The Communist Theory of Self-determination*, van Hoeve, The Hague 1956.
65. As with the German nationalist, Max Weber; cf. his 'Structures of Power: The Nation', in H. Gerth and C. W. Mills (eds), *From Max Weber: Essays in sociology*, Routledge & Kegan Paul, London 1947.
66. On these heroes of the French Revolution, cf. R. Herbert, *David, Voltaire, Brutus and the French Revolution*, Allen Lane, London 1972; and 'Neo-classicism and the French Revolution', in The Arts Council of Great Britain: *The Age of Neo-Classicism*, Shenval Press, London & Harlow 1972, lxxii–lxxv.
67. Stalin, op. cit., pp. 13–20.
68. cf. J. H. Kautsky, *Communism and the Politics of Development*, John Wiley, New York 1968; as Kautsky earlier pointed out in his Introduction to *Political Change in Underdeveloped Countries*, op. cit., pp. 74 *et seq.*, the neo-Maoist strategy adopted by communists after 1947 included the native capitalists, whom Marxists had always treated as the enemy, the exploiters *par excellence*. Now they too were to be united in the bloc of four classes (proletariat, peasantry, petty bourgeoisie and native capitalists) against 'imperialism'.

69. On the increasingly external orientation of national élites, cf. J. P. Nettl and R. Robertson, *International Systems and the Modernisation of Societies*, Faber, London 1968, Part II.
70. cf. E. Kedourie, *Nationalism in Asia and Africa*, op. cit., Introduction; and for communism's relations with tradition, the interesting symposium on the subject, S. N. Eisenstadt and Y. Azmon (eds), *Socialism and Tradition*, Humanities Press, Atlantic Highlands, NJ 1975.

CHAPTER 6

1. For an illuminating classification of political ideologies and their social and psychological roots, cf. H. Walsby, *The Domain of Ideologies, A Study of the Origin, Development and Structure of Ideologies*, William MacLellan, London 1947.
2. cf. the work of Ortega y Gasset, Karl Mannheim, Emil Lederer and Hannah Arendt; and W. Kornhauser, *The Politics of Mass Society*, Routledge & Kegan Paul, London 1959. For a critique of the 'mass society' approach, cf. J. Gusfield, 'Mass Society and Extremist Politics', *American Sociological Review* 27, 1962, 19–30.
3. A trend amply documented in G. van Benthem van den Berghe, 'Contemporary Nationalism in the Western World', *Daedalus* 95, 1966, 828–61.
4. For example, Denis de Rougemont's *The Meaning of Europe*, Sidgwick & Jackson, London 1965, and the survey by C. J. Friedrich, *Europe: An Emergent Nation?*, Harper & Row, New York 1969.
5. H. Seton-Watson, *Nationalism, Old and New*, Sydney University Press, Sydney 1965, and E. Gellner, *Thought and Change*, Weidenfeld & Nicolson, London 1964, ch. 7, especially p. 174.
6. On fascism and nationalism, cf. E. Nolte, *Three Faces of Fascism*, (trans. L. Vennewitz), Mentor, New York and Toronto 1969; and H. Seton-Watson, 'Fascism, Right and Left', *Journal of Contemporary History* 1/1, 1966, 183–97.
7. For typologies of modern nationalisms, cf. A. D. Smith, 'The Formation of Nationalist Movements', in Smith (ed.), *Nationalist Movements*, Macmillan, London 1976, pp. 1–30; and L. Snyder, *The New Nationalism*, Cornell University Press, Ithaca, NY 1968.
8. The large number of possible ethnic subunits in Europe is explored by J. Geipel, *The Europeans: The People – Today and Yesterday – Their Origins and Interrelations*, Pegasus, New York 1970; and in G. Heraud, *L'Europe des Ethnies*, Presses d'Europe, Paris 1963. cf. also the excellent discussion by J. Krejci; 'Ethnic Problems in Europe', in S. Giner and M. S. Archer (eds), *Contemporary Europe: Social Structures and Cultural Patterns*, Routledge & Kegan Paul, London 1978.
9. The larger ethnic movements have tended to evolve from a more inward-looking, traditional and defensive ethnocentrism to a much more secular, interventionist political nationalism, as in Quebec and Scotland. On Quebec, cf. R. Cook (ed.), *Canada and the French-Canadian Question*, Macmillan, Toronto 1967; and D. Smiley, *The Canadian Political Nationality*, Methuen, Toronto 1967.
10. Plaid Cymru Research Group, *An Economic Plan for Wales*, Cardiff 1970, p. 286; cited in M. Hechter, *Internal Colonialism: The Celtic Fringe in British National Development, 1536–1966*, Routledge & Kegan Paul, London 1975, an important study of Scots, Welsh and Irish nationalisms.
11. D. Simpson, 'Independence: The Economic Issues', in N. MacCormick (ed.),

The Scottish Debate, Essays on Scottish Nationalism, Oxford University Press, London 1970, pp. 128–9; and also I. S. M. MacCormick, 'The Case for Independence', in ibid., pp. 96–9.

12. On Corsica, cf. P. Savigear, 'Corsicans and the French Connection', *New Society*, 10 February 1977, pp. 273–4.

13. S. Payne, 'Catalan and Basque Nationalism', *Journal of Contemporary History* 6/1, 1971, 15–51.

14. J. Osmond, 'Centralism or Democracy', in *The Centralist Enemy* 1974, p. 13.

15. Hechter, op. cit., p. 310.

16. Payne, op. cit., and P. Mayo, *The Roots of Identity: Three National Movements in Contemporary European Politics*, Allen Lane, London 1974.

17. W. Petersen, 'On the Subnations of Western Europe', in N. Glazer and Daniel P. Moynihan (eds), *Ethnicity, Theory and Experience*, Harvard University Press, Cambridge, Mass. 1975, pp. 177–208.

18. This was part of the reaction to Adam Smith's rationalism and 'natural law' first enunciated by Adam Müller in his *Elemente der Staatskunst*, vol. I, of 1809. Müller's and List's ideas are briefly outlined by Arcadius Kahan, 'Nineteenth-Century European Experience with Policies of Economic Nationalism', in H. G. Johnson (ed.), *Economic Nationalism in Old and New States*, George Allen & Unwin, London 1968, pp. 17–30.

19. On Corsica in Rousseau's time, cf. P. Thrasher, *Pasquale Paoli*, Constable, London 1970, especially pp. 23 *et seq.* On Rousseau's nationalism, there are studies by A. Cobban, *Rousseau and the Modern State*, 2nd ed., Allen & Unwin, London 1964, and by Anne M. Cohler, *Rousseau and Nationalism*, Basic Books, New York 1970.

20. For discussions of nationalism's social composition, cf. V. G. Kiernan, 'Nationalist Movements and Social Classes', in A. D. Smith (ed.), *Nationalist Movements*, Macmillan, London 1976, pp. 110–33; and A. D. Smith, *Theories of Nationalism*, Duckworth, London 1971, pp. 123–33.

21. Mayo, op. cit., on Basques, Bretons and Welsh and their cultural revivals. On the languages of the smaller *ethnie*, cf. S. Potter, *Language in the Modern World*, Penguin, Harmondsworth 1968, pp. 104–8. On the early nationalists, cf. A. Kemilainen, *Nationalism, Problems concerning the Word, Concept and Classification*, Kustantajat Publishers, Yvaskyla 1964.

22. On Quebec nationalism today, and in the past, cf. T. Warburton, 'Nationalism and Language in Switzerland and Canada', in A. D. Smith (ed.), *Nationalist Movements*, op. cit., pp. 88–109; and G. Spry, 'Canada: Notes on Two Ideas of Nation in Confrontation', in *Journal of Contemporary History* 6/1, 1971, 173–96. For Scots and Welsh nationalisms, cf. the essays by H. M. Begg and J. A. Stewart, and by K. O. Morgan, in the same volume (pp. 135–52, 153–72).

23. Going back in Scotland, for example to John MacCormick's National Party of Scotland, founded in 1928 – cf. H. J. Hanham, *Scottish Nationalism*, Faber & Faber 1969, pp. 151–62, and ch. 8, 'The Scottish National Party'. But the first beginnings of Scots nationalism were traceable to the earlier nineteenth century; ibid. p. 73, and much the same development can be found in Catalonia, Wales and the Basque country, even though formal political organisations did not appear till later.

24. Mayo, op. cit., *passim*; and Warburton, op. cit. on the flexibility of Swiss (and to a lesser extent Canadian) political arrangements.

25. A distinction ably drawn in a lively essay by T. Nairn: 'Scotland and Wales: Notes on Nationalist Pre-history', in *Planet* 34, November 1976, 1–11.

26. Nairn, op. cit., makes use of the 'historic–nonhistoric' continuum, ultimately derived from Hegel and Engels, to explain some of the differences between

Welsh and Scots nationalism, but agrees that it cannot account for the general resurgence of western nationalism (p. 9). The term 'subnation', used by Petersen, op. cit., presupposes rather more than the specific 'ethnic group', which points up the sense of common origins and history, as vital for the nationalist movements.

27. On the geopolitical shift, cf. G. Barraclough, *An Introduction to Contemporary History*, Penguin, Harmondsworth 1967.

28. cf. Hanham, op. cit., and Savigear, op. cit., p. 273.

29. K. Kautsky, in *Neue Zeit*, 1886, pp. 522–5; cited in H. B. Davis, *Nationalism and Socialism*, Monthly Review Press, New York and London 1967, p. 142.

30. For a similar emphasis on the breakup of imperialism, which can equally be applied to the West itself, cf. D. Bell, 'Ethnicity and Social Change', in Glazer and Moynihan, op. cit., pp. 141–74, especially 169–71.

31. cf. the emphasis upon democracy by the Scottish nationalists in *S.N.P. and You: Aims and Policy of the Scottish National Party*, 3rd ed., SNP, Edinburgh 1968. (e.g. 'they illustrate the democratic non-sectarian nature of the National Party .... The National Party stands for a nation; all sections, all people in it; welded in a common purpose; devoted, dedicated to the social and economic improvement of all.')

32. The notion of a 'civil theology' is derived by Bell, op. cit., p. 144; from E. Voegelin, *The New Science of Politics*, Chicago University Press, Chicago 1952, pp. 81–3.

CHAPTER 7

1. E. Hobsbawm, 'Some reflections on "The Break-up of Britain"', *New Left Review* 105, 1977, 3–23. The term 'neo-nationalism' is used by T. Nairn, *The Break-up of Britain*, New Left Books, London 1977, p. 90.

2. R. Debray, 'Marxism and the National Question', *New Left Review* 105, 1977, 29–41.

3. G. Zernatto, 'Nation: the History of a Word', *Review of Politics* 6, 1944, 351–66.

4. By 1789 these mainly pre-industrial conditions – commerce, secularism, bureaucracy, the territorial state – provided the basis for a political nationalism; cf. H. Kohn, *Prelude to Nation-States: the French and German Experience, 1789–1815*, Van Nostrand, Princeton 1967.

5. For a classic statement, cf. W. Kornhauser, *The Politics of Mass Society*, Routledge & Kegan Paul, London 1959.

6. cf. A. W. Gouldner, 'Red Tape as a Social Problem', in R. K. Merton *et al.* (eds), *Reader in Bureaucracy*, Free Press, New York 1952.

7. The meanings of 'treason' are well analysed in M. Grodzins, *The Loyal and the Disloyal: Social Boundaries of Patriotism and Treason*, Meridian Books, Cleveland and New York 1956.

8. Arrangements analysed by T. Warburton, 'Nationalism and Language in Switzerland and Canada', in A. D. Smith (ed.), *Nationalist Movements*, Macmillan, London 1976.

9. cf. G. Almond and L. Pye (eds), *Comparative Political Culture*, Princeton University Press, Princeton 1965.

10. The growth of a national sentiment *pari passu*, and often in congruence with the State, in England and France, is described by J. Strayer, 'The Historical Experience of Nation-building in Europe', in K. Deutsch and W. Foltz (eds),

Nation-Building, Atherton, New York 1963.
11. R. I. Rotberg, 'African Nationalism: Concept or Confusion?', *Journal of Modern African Studies* 4, 1967, 33–46.
12. A diffusionist idea expounded, for example, by H. Trevor-Roper: *Jewish and other Nationalisms*, Weidenfeld & Nicolson, London 1961.
13. On this technological revolution, cf. G. Barraclough, *An Introduction to Contemporary History*, Penguin, Harmondsworth 1967, ch. 2.
14. For these definitions, cf. A. D. Smith, *The Concept of Social Change*, Routledge & Kegan Paul, London and Boston 1973, ch. 4.
15. cf. R. Hess, 'Ethiopia', in G. Carter (ed.), *National Unity and Regionalism in Eight African States*, Cornell University Press, Ithaca, NY 1966.
16. On the Marcusian and New Left idealist and irrationalist varieties of neo-Marxism, cf. N. McInnes, *The Western Marxists*, Alcove Press, London 1972, chs 5–7. He well illustrates the cultural élitism and chiliasm of some of their aspirations, e.g. Fanon's 'The revolution in depth, the real one ... changes man and renews society ... creates and orders a new humanity', or Dutschke's affirmation that the true revolutionary is an internationalist who 'must carry on total opposition for the salvation of the human race and for its emancipation'; ibid., p. 159.
17. My position modifies the usual approach which identifies the needs of the intelligentsia with the drive for modernisation, as in J. H. Kautsky (ed.), *Political Change in Underdeveloped Countries*, John Wiley, New York 1962, Introduction.
18. Ironically conveyed by Hobsbawm, op. cit., p. 13.

CHAPTER 8

1. On élite *linguae francae*, medieval and modern, cf. E. Haugen, 'Dialect, Language, Nation', *American Anthropologist* 68, 1966, 922–35. On the Marxist predictions, cf. ch. 5 above.
2. H. Seton-Watson, 'Unsatisfied Nationalisms', *Journal of Contemporary History* 6/1, 1971, 3–14.
3. E. Gellner, *Thought and Change*, Weidenfeld & Nicolson, London 1964, ch. 7.
4. E. Gellner, 'Scale and Nation', *Philosophy of the Social Sciences* 3, 1973, 1–17, especially p. 14.
5. B. Akzin, *State and Nation*, Hutchinson, London 1964, ch. 5.
6. cf. the analysis of anti-Semitism by S. Andreski, *Elements of Comparative Sociology*, Weidenfeld & Nicolson, London 1964, ch. 21.
7. Seton-Watson, op. cit., and *Nationalism, Old and New*, Sydney University Press, Sydney 1965.
8. cf. D. Apter, *Some Conceptual Approaches to the Study of Modernisation*, Prentice-Hall, Englewood Cliffs 1968.
9. Gellner, *Thought and Change*, op. cit., p. 174.
10. T. Warburton, 'Nationalism and Language in Switzerland and Canada', in A. D. Smith (ed.), *Nationalist Movements*, Macmillan, London 1976.
11. Gellner, 'Scale and Nation', op. cit., p. 15; see also ch. 3 above.
12. cf. M. Weber, *The Protestant Ethic and the Spirit of Capitalism*, George Allen & Unwin, London 1930, pp. 181–2.
13. cf. R. G. Hovannisian, *Armenia, the Road to Independence*, University of California Press, Berkeley 1963; and C. J. Edmonds, 'Kurdish Nationalism', *Journal of Contemporary History* 6/1, 1971, 87–107.

14. On terrorism generally, cf. P. Wilkinson, *Political Terrorism*, Macmillan, London 1974.
15. J. P. Nettl and R. Robertson, *International Systems and the Modernisation of Societies*, Faber, London 1968. The phrase, 'a system of locks' is Gellner's in *Thought and Change*, op. cit., p. 175.
16. Nettl and Robertson, op. cit., Pt I.
17. R. L. Merritt and S. Rokkan (eds), *Comparing Nations*, Yale University Press, New Haven 1966.
18. An interpretation also favoured by some Marxians such as A. G. Frank, *Latin America: Underdevelopment or Revolution?* Monthly Review Press, New York 1969.
19. H. Martins, 'Time and Theory In Sociology', in J. Rex (ed.), *Approaches to Sociology, An Introduction to Major Trends in British Sociology*, Routledge & Kegan Paul, London 1974.
20. Some 'nation-states', while much larger than villages or districts, are pretty small, for example Iceland, while others, such as China or India, resemble empires. This somewhat detracts from Gellner's object of analysis, the scale of nations.
21. cf. P. Mercier, 'On the Meaning of "Tribalism" in Black Africa', in P. L. van den Berghe (ed.), *Africa: Social Problems of Change and Conflict*, Chandler, San Francisco 1965.
22. cf. J. Galtung, *The European Community: a Superpower in the Making*, George Allen & Unwin, London 1973.
23. D. de Rougemont, *The Meaning of Europe*, Sidgwick & Jackson, London 1965.
24. For the notion of 'concentric circles', cf. J. S. Coleman, *Nigeria: Background to Nationalism*, University of California Press, Berkeley and Los Angeles 1958.

Bibliography

AKZIN, B., *State and Nation*, Hutchinson, London 1964.

ALMOND, G. and PYE, L. (eds), *Comparative Political Culture*, Princeton University Press, Princeton 1965.

AMIN, G., 'The Egyptian Economy and the Revolution', in P. J. Vatikiotis (ed.) *Egypt since the Revolution*, George Allen & Unwin Ltd., London 1968.

ANCHOR, R., *The Enlightenment Tradition*, Harper & Row, New York, Evanston and London 1967.

ANDERSON, C. W., VON DER MEHDEN, F. and YOUNG, C., *Issues of Political Development*, Prentice-Hall, Englewood Cliffs 1967.

ANDERSON, M. S., *The Ascendancy of Europe, 1815–1914*, Longman, London 1972.

ANDRESKI, S., *Elements of Comparative Sociology*, Weidenfeld & Nicolson, London 1964.

ANTAL, F., *Classicism and Romanticism, with other studies in Art History*, Routledge & Kegan Paul, London 1966.

APPEL, K., 'Nationalism and sovereignty: a psychiatric view', *Journal of Abnormal and Social Psychology* 40, 1945, 355–63.

APTER, D., *Some conceptual approaches to the study of modernisation*, Prentice-Hall, Englewood Cliffs 1968.

ARENDT, H., *The Origins of Totalitarianism*, Harcourt, Brace, New York 1951.

ARGYLE, W. J., 'European nationalism and African tribalism', in P. H. Gulliver (ed.), *Tradition and Transition in East Africa*, Pall Mall Press, London 1969.

ARGYLE, W. J., 'Size and scale as factors in the development of nationalist movements', in A. D. Smith (ed.), *Nationalist Movements*, Macmillan, London 1976.

AVINERI, S., *The social and political thought of Karl Marx*, Cambridge University Press, Cambridge 1968.

BALANDIER, G., *Sociologie actuelle de l'Afrique Noire*, Presses Universitaires de France, Paris 1955.

BALANDIER, G., 'Messianismes et nationalismes en Afrique Noire', *Cahiers Internationaux de Sociologie* 14, 1953, 41–65.

BANTON, M., *Race relations*, Tavistock Publications Ltd., London 1967.

BARBU, Z., 'Nationalism as a source of aggression', in *Conflict*, Ciba Foundation, London 1966.

BARNARD, F., *Herder's social and political thought: From enlightenment to nationalism*, Clarendon Press, Oxford 1965.

BARNARD, F., 'Culture and political development: Herder's suggestive insights', *American Political Science Review* 62, 1969, 379–97.

BARON, S., *Modern nationalism and religion*, Meridian Books, New York 1960.

BARRACLOUGH, G., *An Introduction to Contemporary History*, Penguin, Harmondsworth 1967.
BARRINGTON MOORE, Jr., *The social origins of Dictatorship and Democracy*, Allen Lane, Penguin, London 1967.
BARZUN, J., *The French Race: Theories of its origins and their social and political implications prior to the Revolution*, Columbia University Press, New York 1932.
BASTIDE, R., 'Messianisme et developpement economique et sociale', *Cahiers Internationaux de Sociologie* 31, 1961, 3–14.
BEALES, D., *The Risorgimento and the unification of Italy*, Allen & Unwin, London 1971.
BEGG, H. M. and STEWART, J. A., 'The nationalist movement in Scotland', in *Journal of Contemporary History* 6/1, 1971, 135–52.
BELL, D., 'Ethnicity and social change', in N. Glazer and D. P. Moynihan (eds), *Ethnicity, theory and experience*, Harvard University Press, Cambridge, Mass., and London, 1975.
BELLAH, R. (ed.), *Religion and Progress in Modern Asia*, Free Press, Glencoe 1965.
BENDIX, R., *Nation-Building and Citizenship*, John Wiley, New York 1964.
BENDIX, R., 'Social stratification and political power', in R. Bendix and S. M. Lipset (eds), *Class, Status and Power*, Free Press, Glencoe 1956.
BENNIGSEN, A. & LEMERCIER-QUELQUEJAY, C., *Les mouvements nationaux chez les musulmans de la Russie*, Mouton, Paris 1960.
BENTHEM VAN DEN BERGE, G. VAN, 'Contemporary nationalism in the Western world', *Daedalus* 95, 1966, 828–61.
BERLIN, I., 'Herder and the Enlightenment', in E. A. Wasserman (ed.), *Aspects of the eighteenth century*, Johns Hopkins University Press, Baltimore, 1965.
BERREMAN, G. D., 'Caste in India and the United States', *American Journal of Sociology* 66, 1960, 120–27.
BINDER, L., *The Ideological Revolution in the Middle East*, John Wiley, New York 1964.
BLAU, J. L., *Modern Varieties of Judaism*, Columbia University Press, New York 1966.
BOYD, W., 'The contribution of genetics to anthropology', in A. Kroeber (ed.), *Anthropology Today*, University of Chicago Press, Chicago 1953.
BRACEY, J. H., MEIER, A. & RUDWICK, E. (eds), *Black nationalism in America*, Bobbs-Merrill, Indianapolis and New York, 1970.
BRACHER, K. D., *The German Dictatorship; the origins, structure and effects of National Socialism*, Penguin, Harmondsworth 1973.
BRANDON, S. G. F., *Jesus and the Zealots*, Manchester University Press, Manchester 1967.
BRECHERT, H., 'Buddhism and Mass Politics in Burma and Ceylon', in D. E. Smith (ed.), *Religion and Political Modernisation*, Yale University Press, New Haven and London 1974.
BROWN, L. C., 'The Islamic Reformist movement in North Africa', *Journal of Modern African Studies* 2, 1964, 55–63.
BRUFORD, W., *Germany in the Eighteenth Century*, Cambridge University Press, Cambridge 1965.
BUCHEIM, H. et al., *Anatomy of the SS State*, Collins, London 1968.
BURKS, R. V., *The Dynamics of Communism in Eastern Europe*, Princeton University Press, Princeton 1961.
BURRIDGE, K., *New Heaven, New Earth*, Basil Blackwell, Oxford 1969.
BUTLER, R. D., *The Roots of National Socialism*, Faber & Faber, London 1941.
BYRNES, R. F., *Anti-Semitism in modern France*, Rutgers University Press, New York 1950.

CALVERT, P., 'On attaining sovereignty', in A. D. Smith (ed.), *Nationalist Movements*, Macmillan, London 1976.
CAMPBELL, J. K. and SHERRARD, P., *Modern Greece*, Ernest Benn Ltd., London 1968.
CARMICHAEL, J., *The Shaping of the Arabs*, Macmillan, London 1967.
CARMICHAEL, J., 'The Nationalist Communist Symbiosis in the Middle East', *Problems of Communism* VIII/3, 1959, 35–41.
CARRÈRE D'ENCAUSSE, H., *Réforme et Révolution chez les Musulmans de l'Empire Russe, Bukhara 1867–1924*, Armand Colin, Paris 1966.
COBBAN, A., *Rousseau and the modern state*, 2nd ed., Allen & Unwin, London 1964.
COBBAN, A., *Aspects of the French Revolution*, Paladin, London 1968.
COHLER, A., *Rousseau and Nationalism*, Basic Books, New York 1970.
COHN, N., *The Pursuit of the Millennium*, Secker & Warburg, London 1957.
COHN, N., 'Medieval millennarism: its bearings on the comparative study of millennarian movements', in S. Thrupp (ed.), *Millennial Dreams in Action*, Nijhoff, The Hague 1962.
COHN, N., 'The myth of the demonic conspiracy of Jews in medieval and modern Europe', in A. de Reuck and J. Knight (eds), *Caste and Race*, Ciba Foundation, London 1967.
COLEMAN, J. S., *Nigeria, Background to Nationalism*, University of California Press, Berkeley and Los Angeles 1967.
COLEMAN, J. S., 'Nationalism in tropical Africa', *American Political Science Review* 18, 1954, 404–26.
COOK, R. (ed.), *Canada and the French-Canadian Question*, Macmillan, Toronto 1967.
COON, C. S., GARN, S. M. and BIRDSELL, J. B., *Races*, Thomas, Springfield 1950.
COX, O. C., *Caste, Class and Race*, Doubleday, New York 1948.
CRANE, R. I., 'Problems of divergent developments within Indian nationalism, 1895–1905', in R. K. Sakai (ed.), *Studies on Asia*, University of Nebraska Press, Lincoln 1961.
CRONON, E. D., *Black Moses*, University of Wisconsin Press, Madison 1955.
CROWDER, M., *West Africa under colonial rule*, Hutchinson, London 1968.
CRUSE, H., *The Crisis of the Negro Intellectual*, William Morrow, New York 1967.
CURTIN, P., *The Image of Africa*, University of Wisconsin Press, Madison, Wisconsin 1964.

DAVIES, I., *African Trade Unions*, Penguin, Harmondsworth 1966.
DAVIS, H. B., *Nationalism and Socialism: Marxist and labour theories of nationalism*, Monthly Review Press, London 1967.
DAWN, C. E., 'From Ottomanism to Arabism: the origins of an ideology', *Review of Politics*, 23, 1961, 379–400.
DE REUCK, A. and KNIGHT, J. (eds), *Caste and Race*, Ciba Foundation, London 1967.
DE ROUGEMONT, D., *The Meaning of Europe*, Sidgwick & Jackson, London 1965.
DEBRAY, R., 'Marxism and the National Question', *New Left Review* 105, 1977, 29–41.
DESAI, A. R., *The social background of Indian Nationalism*, Bombay Publishing Company, Bombay 1954.
DEUTSCH, K. W., *Nationalism and social communication*, MIT Press, New York 1966.
DEUTSCH, K. W. and FOLTZ, W. (eds), *Nation-Building*, Atherton, New York 1963.
DOBZHANSKY, T., *Mankind Evolving*, Bantam Books, Toronto and New York 1962.
DONNELL, J. C. and GURTOV, M., 'North Vietnam', in R. A. Scalapino (ed.), *The Communist Revolution in Asia*, Prentice-Hall, Englewood Cliffs 1969.

DOOB, L., *Patriotism and Nationalism: Their psychological foundations*, Yale University Press, New Haven 1964.
DRAPER, T., *Castroism: Theory and Practise*, Praeger, New York 1965.
DRAPER, T., *The Rediscovery of Black Nationalism*, Secker and Warburg, London 1971.
DROZ, J., *Europe between Revolutions, 1815–48*, Collins, London and Glasgow 1967.
DUBNOW, S. M., *Nationalism and History*, ed. K. S. Pinson, Jewish Publication Society of America, Philadelphia 1958.
DUMONT, L., *Homo Hierarchicus*, Weidenfeld & Nicolson, London 1970.

EDMONDS, C. J., 'Kurdish nationalism', *Journal of Contemporary History* 6/1, 1971, 87–107.
EISENSTADT, S. N., (ed.), *Readings in Social Evolution and Development*, Pergamon Press, Oxford and London 1970.
EISENSTADT, S. N. and AZMON, Y. (eds), *Socialism and Tradition*, Humanities Press, Atlantic Highlands, New Jersey 1975.
ESEDEBE, P. O., 'Origins and meaning of panAfricanism', *Présence Africaine*, 73, 1970, 109–27.

FEST, J. C., *The Face of the Third Reich*, (tr. M. Bullock), Weidenfeld & Nicolson, London 1970.
FINLEY, M. I. (ed.), *Slavery in Classical Antiquity*, Heffer & Sons, Cambridge 1960.
FISCHER-GALATI, S., 'Rumanian nationalism', in P. F. Sugar and I. J. Lederer (eds), *Nationalism in Eastern Europe*, University of Washington Press, Seattle and London 1969.
FISHMAN, J. (ed.), *Language Problems in Developing Countries*, John Wiley, New York 1968.
FLORISOONE, M., 'The Romantic and Neo-Classical conflict', in The Arts Council, *The Romantic Movement*, London 1959, 21–26.
FRANCK, L. R., 'The Economic and social diagnosis of National Socialism', in *The Third Reich*, Praeger, New York 1955.
FRANK, A. G., *Latin America: Underdevelopment or Revolution?*, Monthly Review Press, New York 1969.
FRAZEE, C. A., *The Orthodox Church and independent Greece, 1821–52*, Cambridge University Press, Cambridge 1969.
FREUD, S., *Moses and Monotheism*, (tr. K. Jones), Hogarth Press, London 1939.
FRIEDLANDER, W., *David to Delacroix*, Schocken Books, New York 1968.
FRIEDRICH, C. J., *Europe: An Emergent Nation?*, Harper & Row, New York 1969.
FRYE, R. N. (ed.), *Islam and the West*, Mouton, The Hague 1957.

GALTUNG, J., *The European Community: a Superpower in the making*, George Allen & Unwin, London 1973.
GARN, S. M., *Human Races*, Thomas, Springfield 1961.
GAY, P. *The Enlightenment: an Interpretation*, 2 vols., Wildwood House, London 1973.
GEIPEL, J., *The Europeans: The People – Today and Yesterday – Their Origins and Interrelations*, Pegasus, New York 1970.
GEISS, I., *The Pan-African Movement*, Methuen & Co., London 1974.
GELLNER, E., *Thought and Change*, Weidenfeld & Nicolson, London 1964.
GELLNER, E., 'Scale and Nation', *Philosophy of the Social Sciences* 3, 1973, 1–17.
GELLNER, E. and IONESCU, G. (eds), *Populism, its meanings and national characteristics*, Weidenfeld & Nicolson, London 1970.
GERTH, H., 'The Nazi Party: its leadership and composition', *American Journal of Sociology* XLV, 1940, 517–41.

GIBB, H. A. R., *Modern Trends in Islam*, Chicago University Press, Chicago 1947.

GLAZER, N. and MOYNIHAN, D. P. (eds), *Ethnicity; theory and experience*, Harvard University Press, Cambridge, Mass. 1975.

GORDON, C. H., *The Ancient Near East*, third edn. revised, Norton & Co., New York 1965.

GORDON, M. L., 'The nationality of slaves under the early Roman Empire', *Journal of Roman Studies* 14, 1924, 93–111, reprinted in M. I. Finley (ed.), *Slavery in Classical Antiquity*, Heffer & Sons, Cambridge 1960.

GOULDNER, A. W., 'Red Tape as a social problem', in R. K. Merton et al. (eds), *Reader in Bureaucracy*, Free Press, New York 1952.

GREENBERG, L., *The Jews in Russia*, 2 vols., Schocken Books, New York 1976 (1951).

GRODZINS, M., *The Loyal and the Disloyal: social boundaries of patriotism and treason*, Meridian Books, Cleveland and New York 1956.

GRUNEBAUM, G. E. VON: 'Problems of Muslim nationalism', in R. N. Frye (ed.), *Islam and the West*, Mouton, The Hague 1957.

GUSFIELD, J., 'Mass society and extremist politics', *American Sociological Review* XXVII, 1962, 19–30.

GUSFIELD, J., 'Tradition and modernity: misplaced polarities in the study of social change', *American Journal of Sociology* 72, 1967, 351–62.

HAIM, S. (ed.), *Arab Nationalism, An Anthology*, University of California Press, Berkeley and Los Angeles 1962.

HALECKI, O., *A History of Poland*, rev. edn., J. M. Dent, London 1955.

HALES, E. E., *Mazzini and the secret societies: The making of a myth*, Kennedy, New York 1956.

HALPERN, M., *The Politics of social change in the Middle East and North Africa*, Princeton University Press, Princeton 1963.

HANDELSMAN, M., 'Le rôle de la nationalité dans l'histoire de l'antiquité', *Bulletin of the International Committee of Historical Science*, 2, 1929, 305–20.

HANHAM, H. J., *Scottish Nationalism*, Faber & Faber, London 1969.

HARRIS, C. P., *Nationalism and Revolution in Egypt: the role of the Muslim Brotherhood*, Mouton, The Hague 1964.

HARRIS, R. W., *Romanticism and the social order, 1780–1830*, Blandford Press, London 1969.

HAUGEN, E., 'Dialect, language, nation', *American Anthropologist* 68, 1966, 922–35.

HAYES, C. J. H., *The historical evolution of modern nationalism*, Smith, New York 1931.

HAYES, P. M., 'Quisling's political ideas', *Journal of Contemporary History* 1/1, 1966, 145–57.

HEBERLE, R., *From Democracy to Nazism*, Louisiana State University Press, Baton Rouge 1945.

HECHTER, M., *Internal Colonialism: The Celtic Fringe in British National Development, 1536–1966*, Routledge & Kegan Paul, London 1975.

HEER, F., *Europe, Mother of Revolutions*, Weidenfeld & Nicolson, London 1971.

HEIMSATH, C., *Indian nationalism and Hindu social reform*, Princeton University Press, Princeton 1964.

HELLER, C. S. (ed.), *Structured Social Inequality*, Macmillan, London 1970.

HERAUD, G., *L'Europe des Ethnies*, Presses d'Europe, Paris 1963.

HERBERT, R., *David, Voltaire, Brutus and the French Revolution*, Allen Lane, London 1972.

HERBERT, R. 'Neo-classicism and the French Revolution', in The Arts Council of Great Britain: *The Age of Neo-Classicism*, Shenval Press, London and Harlow 1972, lxxii–lxxv.

HERTZ, F., *Nationalism in history and politics*, Routledge & Kegan Paul, London 1944.

HERTZBERG, A., *The French Enlightenment and the Jews*, Schocken Books, New York 1968.

HERTZBERG, A. (ed.), *The Zionist Idea, A Reader*, Meridian Books, New York 1960.

HESS, R., 'Ethiopia', in G. Carter (ed.), *National Unity and Regionalism in eight African states*, Cornell University Press, Ithaca 1966.

HILBERG, R., *The Destruction of the European Jews*, Quadrangle, Chicago 1961.

HIRSCOWICZ, L., *The Third Reich and the Arab East*, Routledge & Kegan Paul, London 1966.

HOBSBAWM, E., *Primitive Rebels*, Manchester University Press, Manchester 1959.

HOBSBAWM, E., 'Some reflections on "The Break-up of Britain"', *New Left Review* 105, 1977, 3–23.

HODGKIN, T., *Nationalism in colonial Africa*, Muller, London 1956.

HODGKIN, T., 'A note on the language of African nationalism', *St. Antony's Papers*, 10, 1961, 22–40.

HODGKIN, T., 'The relevance of 'Western' ideas in the derivation of African nationalism', in J. R. Pennock (ed.), *Self-government in modernising societies*, Prentice-Hall, Englewood Cliffs 1964.

HOFFMAN, S., *Le Mouvement Poujade*, Armand Colin, Paris 1956.

HOLTOM, D. C., *Modern Japan and Shinto Nationalism*, University of Chicago Press, Chicago 1943.

HONOUR, H., *Neo-Classicism*, Penguin, Harmondsworth 1968.

HOVANNISIAN, R. G., *Armenia, the Road to Independence*, University of California Press, Berkeley 1963.

HUMPHREYS, R. A. and LYNCH, J. (eds), *The origins of the Latin American revolutions, 1808–26*, A. Knopf, New York 1965.

HUNTINGTON, S. P., *Political Order in Changing Societies*, Yale University Press, New Haven and London 1968.

HYSLOP, B., *French nationalism in 1789 according to the general cahiers*, Columbia University Press, New York 1934.

IRWIN, D., *English Neo-Classical Art*, Faber & Faber, London 1966.

ISSAWI, C., *Egypt in Revolution; an Economic Analysis*, R.I.I.A., Oxford 1963.

JARVIE, I. C., *The Revolution in Anthropology*, Routledge & Kegan Paul, London 1964.

JEDLICKA, L. 'The Austrian Heimwehr', *Journal of Contemporary History* 1/1, 1966, 127–44.

JOHNSON, C., 'Building a communist nation in China', in R. A. Scalapino (ed.), *The Communist Revolution in Asia*, Prentice-Hall, Englewood Cliffs 1969.

JOHNSON, H. G., 'A theoretical model of economic nationalism in new and developing states', *Political Science Quarterly*, 80, 1965, 169–85.

JOHNSON, H. G., (ed.), *Economic Nationalism in Old and New States*, Allen and Unwin, London 1968.

JOHNSON, J., 'The new Latin American nationalism', *The Yale Review*, 54, 1965, 187–204.

JULY, R., *The origins of modern African thought*, Faber & Faber, London 1968.

KAHAN, A., 'Nineteenth-century European experience with policies of economic nationalism', in H. G. Johnson (ed.), *Economic Nationalism in Old and New States*, George Allen & Unwin Ltd., London 1968.

KAMENKA, E. (ed.), *Nationalism; the Nature and Evolution of an Idea*, Australian National Press, Canberra 1973 and Edward Arnold, London 1976.
KAPLOW, J. (ed.), *New Perspectives on the French Revolution*, John Wiley, New York 1965.
KATZ, J., 'Jews and Judaism in the 19th century', *Journal of World History* 4, 1958, 881–900.
KAUTSKY, J. H. (ed.), *Political Change in Underdeveloped Countries*, John Wiley, New York 1962, Introduction: 'An essay in the Politics of Development'.
KAUTSKY, J. H., *Communism and the Politics of Development*, John Wiley, New York 1968.
KEDOURIE, E., *Nationalism*, Hutchinson, London 1960.
KEDOURIE, E., *Afghani and Abduh*, Cass, London and New York 1966.
KEDOURIE, E. (ed.), *Nationalism in Asia and Africa*, Weidenfeld & Nicolson, London 1971.
KEDWARD, R. (ed.), *The Dreyfus Affair*, Longman, London 1965.
KEMILAINEN, A., *Nationalism, Problems concerning the Word, Concept and Classification*, Kustantajat Publishers, Yvaskyla 1964.
KIERNAN, V., 'Nationalist movements and social classes', in A. D. Smith (ed.), *Nationalist Movements*, Macmillan, London 1976.
KILSON, M., 'Nationalism and social classes in British West Africa', *Journal of Politics*, 20, 1958, 268–87.
KIMBLE, D., *A political history of Ghana: the rise of Gold Coast nationalism, 1850–1928*, Clarendon Press, Oxford 1963.
KOHN, H., *The Idea of Nationalism*, (1944), Collier Books, Macmillan, London 1967.
KOHN, H., *Nationalism: its meaning and history*, Van Nostrand, Princeton 1955.
KOHN, H., *Nationalism and Liberty: the Swiss Example*, Macmillan, London 1956.
KOHN, H., *Pan-Slavism: Its history and ideology*, 2nd ed. revised, Vintage Books, Random House, New York 1960.
KOHN, H., *Prophets and Peoples*, Macmillan, New York 1961.
KOHN, H., *Prelude to Nation-States: the French and German experience, 1789–1815*, Van Nostrand, Princeton 1967.
KOHN, H., *The Mind of Germany: the education of a nation*, Scribners, New York 1960; Macmillan, London 1965.
KOHN, H., 'The origins of English nationalism', *Journal of the History of Ideas* I, 1940, 69–94.
KOLARZ, W., *Peoples of the Soviet Far East*, Philip, London 1954.
KORNHAUSER, W., *The Politics of Mass Society*, Routledge & Kegan Paul, London 1959.
KRIEGER, L., *The German Idea of Freedom*, Beacon Press, Boston 1957.

LACLOTTE, M., 'J-L. David, Reform and Revolution', in The Arts Council: *The Age of Neo-Classicism*, Shenval Press, London 1972, pp. lxvi-lxxi.
LADNER, G., *The Idea of Reform*, Harvard University Press, Cambridge, Mass. 1959.
LANTERNARI, V., *The Religions of the Oppressed*, Mentor Books, New York 1965.
LARTICHAUX, J-Y., 'Linguistic Politics during the French Revolution', *Diogenes*, 97, 1977, 65–84.
LEACH, E., 'Caste, class and slavery', in A. de Reuck and J. Knight (eds), *Caste and Race*, Ciba Foundation, London 1967.
LE BON, G., *The Crowd*, Unwin, London 1896.
LEDERER, I., 'Nationalism and the Yugoslavs', in P. F. Sugar and I. J. Lederer (eds), *Nationalism in Eastern Europe*, University of Washington Press, Seattle and London 1969.

LEGUM, C., *PanAfricanism, a short political guide*, Pall Mall Press, London and Dunmow 1962.
LEIDEN, C. and SCHMITT, K. M., *The Politics of Violence*, Prentice-Hall, Englewood Cliffs 1968.
LEITH, J. A., *The Idea of Art as Propaganda in France, 1750–99*, University of Toronto Press, Toronto 1965.
LERNER, D., *The Passing of Traditional Society*, Free Press, New York 1958.
LEVENSON, J. R., *Liang Ch'i Ch'ao and the mind of modern China*, 2nd edn revised, University of California Press, Berkeley and Los Angeles 1959.
LEWIS, B., *The Emergence of Modern Turkey*, Oxford University Press, London 1968.
LICHTHEIM, G., *Imperialism*, Penguin Books, Harmondsworth 1971.
LIND, A. W. (ed.), *Race Relations in World Perspective*, University of Hawaii Press, Honolulu 1955.
LIPSET, S. M., *Political Man*, William Heinemann Ltd., London 1960.
LIVELEY, J. (ed.), *The Enlightenment*, Longman, London 1966.
LLOYD, P. C., *Africa in social change*, Penguin, Harmondsworth 1967.
LLOYD, P. C. (ed.), *New elites in tropical Africa*, Oxford University Press, London 1966.
LOWENTHAL, R., 'Communism versus nationalism', *Problems of Communism* 11, 1962, 37–44.
LOWENTHAL, R., 'The points of the compass', in J. H. Kautsky (ed.), *Political Change in Underdeveloped Countries*, John Wiley, New York 1962.
LYNCH, H. R., *Edward Wilmot Blyden, Pan-Negro Patriot, 1832–1912*, Oxford University Press, London, Oxford, New York 1967.

MACCOBY, H., *Revolution in Judaea*, Ocean Books, London 1974.
MACCORMICK, I. S. M., 'The case for Independence', in N. MacCormick (ed.), *The Scottish debate, Essays on Scottish Nationalism*, Oxford University Press, London 1970.
MACCORMICK, N. (ed.), *The Scottish debate, Essays on Scottish Nationalism*, Oxford University Press, London 1970.
McCRAE, D. G., *Ideology and Society*, Heinemann, New York 1961.
McCULLEY, B. T., *English Education and the origins of Indian nationalism*, Smith, Gloucester, Mass. 1966.
McDOUGALL, W., *The Group Mind*, Methuen, Cambridge 1920.
MacGAFFEY, W. and BARNETT, C. R., *Cuba, Its People, Its Society, Its Culture*, HRAF Press, New Haven 1962.
McINNES, N., *The Western Marxists*, Alcove Press, London 1972.
MANNHEIM, K., *Ideology and Utopia*, Routledge & Kegan Paul, London 1936.
MARCUS, J. (ed.), *The Jew in the Medieval World*, Harper & Row, New York 1965.
MARMORSTEIN, E., 'Religious opposition to nationalism in the Middle East', *International Affairs* 28, 1952, 344-59.
MARTIN, D., *Pacifism*, Routledge & Kegan Paul, London 1965.
MARTINS, H., 'Ideology and Development: 'Developmental nationalism' in Brazil," *Sociological Review Monograph* No. 11, 1967, 153–72.
MARTINS, H., 'Time and Theory in Sociology', in J. Rex (ed.), *Approaches to Sociology, An Introduction to major trends in British sociology*, Routledge & Kegan Paul, London 1974.
MARUYAMA, M., *Thought and behaviour in modern Japanese politics*, ed. Ivan Morris, Oxford University Press, London 1960.
MARX, K., *Capital*, Modern Library, New York 1936, Lawrence & Wishart Books 1970.

MARX, K., *Writings of the Young Marx on Philosophy and Society*, ed. L. D. Easton and K. H. Guddat, Anchor Books, Garden City, New York 1967.

MARX, K. and ENGELS, F., *The German Ideology*, International Publishers, New York 1947 (1963).

MARX, K. and ENGELS, F., *Basic Writings on Politics and Philosophy*, ed. L. S. Feuer, Anchor Books, Garden City, New York 1959.

MASER, W., *Hitler's Mein Kampf*, Faber & Faber, London 1969.

MASON, P., *Patterns of Dominance*, Oxford University Press, London 1971.

MASUR, K., *Nationalism in Latin America*, Macmillan, London 1966.

MAYO, P., *The Roots of Identity: Three National Movements in Contemporary European Politics*, Allen Lane, London 1974.

MAZRUI, A. A., *Towards a Pax Africana*, Weidenfeld & Nicolson, London 1966.

MERCIER, P., 'On the meaning of 'tribalism' in Black Africa', in P. L. van den Berghe (ed.), *Africa: Social problems of change and conflict*, Chandler Publishing Co., San Francisco 1965.

MERRITT, R. L. and ROKKAN, S. (eds), *Comparing Nations*, Yale University Press, New Haven 1966.

MEYER, M. A., *The origins of the modern Jew: Jewish identity and European culture in Germany, 1749–1824*, Wayne State University Press, Detroit 1967.

MINOGUE, K., *Nationalism*, Batsford, London 1967.

MISRA, B. B., *The Indian middle classes: their growth in modern times*, Oxford University Press, London 1961.

MORGAN, K. O., 'Welsh Nationalism: the historical background', *Journal of Contemporary History*, 6/1, 1971, 153–172.

MOSSE, G., *The Crisis of German Ideology: Intellectual origins of the Third Reich*, Grosset and Dunlap, New York 1964.

MOSSE, G., 'The mystical origins of National Socialism', *Journal of the History of Ideas*, 22, 1961, 81–96.

MOSSE, G., 'The genesis of Fascism', *Journal of Contemporary History*, 1/1, 1966, 14–26.

— MOSSE, G., 'Mass Politics and the Political Liturgy of Nationalism', in E. Kamenka (ed.), *Nationalism; the Nature and Evolution of an Idea*, Australian National Press, Canberra 1973.

MUSSOLINI, B., *The Political and Social Doctrine of Fascism*, Hogarth Press, London 1936.

NAIRN, T., *The Break-up of Britain; Crisis and Neo-Nationalism*, New Left Books, London 1977.

NAIRN, T., 'Scotland and Wales: Notes on Nationalist Prehistory', *Planet*, 34, 1976, 1–11.

NETTL, J. and ROBERTSON, R., *International Systems and the modernisation of societies*, Faber, London 1968.

NEUBERGER, B., 'The African concept of Balkanisation', *Journal of Modern African Studies*, XIII, 1976, 523–29.

NEUBERGER, B., 'The Western nation-state in African perceptions of nation-building', *Asian and African Studies* 11/2, 1976, 241–61.

NEUBERGER, B., 'State and Nation in African Thought', *Journal of African Studies* 4/2, 1977, 198–205.

NEUMANN, F., *Behemoth, the Structure and Practise of National Socialism, 1933–44*, Oxford University Press, New York 1944.

NICOL, D. (ed.), *Africanus Horton, The Dawn of Nationalism in modern Africa*, Longman, London 1969.

NOLTE, E., *Three Faces of Fascism*, (tr. L. Vennewitz), Mentor Books, New York and Toronto 1969.

NYE, R. B., *The Cultural Life of the New Nation, 1776–1830*, Hamish Hamilton, London 1960.

OLORUNSOLA, V. (ed.), *The Politics of Cultural Subnationalism in Africa*, Anchor Books, New York 1972.

OLSEN, M., 'Rapid growth as a destabilising force', *Journal of Economic History* 23, 1963, 519–52.

PACHTER, H. M., 'Nazi and fascist propaganda for power', in *The Third Reich*, Praeger, New York 1955.

PARSONS, T., 'Sources and patterns of aggression', in P. Mullahy (ed.), *A Study of Interpersonal Relations: New Contributions to Psychiatry*, Hermitage Press, New York 1949.

PARSONS, T., 'Democracy and social structure in pre-Nazi Germany', and 'Some sociological aspects of the Fascist movements', in T. Parsons, *Essays in Sociological Theory*, rev. edn, Free Press, Glencoe Ill. 1964.

PAYNE, S., 'Catalan and Basque Nationalism', *Journal of Contemporary History* 6/1, 1971, 15–51.

PEPELASSIS, A., 'The image of the past and economic backwardness', *Human Organisation* 17, 1958, 19–27.

PETERSEN, W., 'On the Subnations of Western Europe', in N. Glazer and D. P. Moynihan (eds), *Ethnicity, Theory and Experience*, Harvard University Press, Cambridge, Mass. 1975.

PETROVICH, M. B., *The Emergence of Russian Pan-Slavism, 1856-70*, Columbia University Press, New York 1956.

PIERCE, R., *Russian Central Asia, 1867–1917; A study in colonial rule*, University of California Press, Berkeley 1960.

PITT-RIVERS, J., 'Race, Color and Class in Central America and the Andes', in C. S. Heller (ed.), *Structured Social Inequality*, Macmillan, London 1970.

PLAMENATZ, J., 'Two Types of Nationalism', in E. Kamenka (ed.), *Nationalism: The Nature and Evolution of an Idea*, Australian National Press, Canberra 1973.

POCOCK, D., 'Notes on the interaction of English and Indian thought in the 19th century', *Journal of World History*, 4, 1958, 833–48.

POLIAKOV, L., *Harvest of Hate*, Syracuse University Press, New York 1954.

POLIAKOV, L., 'Racism in Europe', in A. de Reuck and J. Knight (eds), *Caste and Race*, Ciba Foundation, London 1967.

POPPER, K., *The Open Society and Its Enemies*, 2 Vols, 4th edn, Routledge and Kegan Paul, London 1962.

POTTER, S., *Language in the Modern World*, Penguin, Harmondsworth 1968.

PRITCHARD, J. B. (ed.), *The Ancient Near East*, Princeton University Press, Princeton 1958.

PRUSZYNSKI, K., *Adam Mickiewicz, 1798–1855*, Polish Cultural Institute, London 1955.

PULZER, P., *The Rise of Political AntiSemitism in Germany and Austria*, John Wiley, New York 1964.

REID, A., 'Nineteenth century pan-Islam in Indonesia and Malaysia', *Journal of Asian Studies*, 26, 1967, 267–83.

REISS, H. S. (ed.), *The Political Thought of the German Romantics, 1793–1815*, Blackwell, Oxford 1955.

REX, J., *Race Relations in Sociological Theory*, Weidenfeld & Nicolson, London 1970.

RITTER, G., 'The historical foundations of the rise of National Socialism', in *The Third Reich*, Praeger, New York 1955.

Robson-Scott, W. D., *The Literary Background of the Gothic Revival in Germany*, Clarendon Press, Oxford 1965.

Roff, W., *The origins of Malay nationalism*, Yale University Press, New Haven 1967.

Rogger, H., 'Nationalism and the State: a Russian Dilemma', *Comparative Studies in Society and History* 4, 1962, 253–64.

Rogger, H. and Weber, E. (eds), *The European Right: A Historical Profile*, University of California Press, Berkeley, Calif. 1965.

Rogowski, R., 'The Gauleiter and the social origins of Fascism', *Comparative Studies in Society and History* 19, 1977, 399–430.

Rosberg, C. G. and Nottingham, J., *The Myth of Mau Mau: Nationalism in Kenya*, Praeger, New York 1966.

Rosenblum, R., *Transformations in late 18th century Art*, Princeton University Press, Princeton 1967.

Rosenthal, E. I. J., *Islam in the modern national State*, Cambridge University Press, Cambridge 1965.

Rotberg, R., 'African nationalism: concept or confusion?', *Journal of Modern African Studies* 4, 1967, 33–46.

Rotberg, R. and Mazrui, A. A. (eds), *Protest and Power in Black Africa*, Oxford University Press, New York 1970.

Sachar, H., *The Course of Modern Jewish History*, Delta Books, Dell Publishing Company, New York 1958.

Safran, N., *Egypt in Search of Political Community*, Harvard University Press, Cambridge, Mass. 1961.

Sarkisyanz, E., *Buddhist Backgrounds of the Burmese Revolution*, Nijhoff, The Hague 1965.

Savigear, P., 'Corsicans and the French Connection', *New Society*, 10 February 1977, 273–4.

Scalapino, R. A. (ed.), *The Communist Revolution in Asia*, Prentice-Hall, Englewood Cliffs 1969.

Schlaifer, R., 'Greek theories of slavery from Homer to Aristotle', *Harvard Studies in Classical Philology* 47, 1936, 165–204, reprinted in M. I. Finley (ed.), *Slavery in Classical Antiquity*, Heffer & Sons, Cambridge 1960.

Schweitzer, A., 'Nazification of the lower middle classes and peasants', in *The Third Reich*, Praeger, New York 1955.

Segal, R., *The Race War*, Cape, London 1966.

Seton-Watson, H., *Nationalism, Old and New*, Sydney University Press, Sydney 1965.

Seton-Watson, H., 'Fascism, Right and Left', *Journal of Contemporary History* 1/1, 1966, 183–97.

Seton-Watson, H., 'Unsatisfied nationalisms', *Journal of Contemporary History* 6/1, 1971, 3–14.

Shafer, B. C., 'Bourgeois nationalism in the Pamphlets on the eve of the French Revolution', *Journal of Modern History* 10, 1938, 31–50.

Shaheen, S., *The Communist theory of Self-determination*, van Hoeve, The Hague 1956.

Shapiro, L., *Rationalism and Nationalism in Russian 19th century political thought*, Yale University Press, New Haven and London 1967.

Sharabi, H., *Nationalism and Revolution in the Arab World*, Van Nostrand, Princeton 1966.

Sharabi, H., *Arab Intellectuals and the West: The formative years, 1875–1914*, Johns Hopkins Press, Baltimore and London 1970.

SHEPPERSON, G., 'Ethiopianism and African nationalism', *Phylon* 14, 1953, 9–18.
SHEPPERSON, G., 'Notes on Negro American Influence on African Nationalism', *Journal of African History* I, 1960, 299–312.
SHEPPERSON, G. and PRICE, T., *Independent African: John Chilembwe and the origins, setting and significance of the Nyasaland Native Rising of 1915*, Edinburgh University Press, Edinburgh 1958.
SHERWIN-WHITE, A. N., *Racial Prejudice in Imperial Rome*, Blackwell, Oxford 1952.
SHILS, E., 'Intellectuals in the political development of new states', *World Politics*, 12, 1960, 329–68.
SHILS, E., *Political Development in the New States*, Humanities Press, New York 1964.
SIMPSON, D., 'Independence: the Economic Issues', in N. MacCormick (ed.), *The Scottish Debate, Essays on Scottish Nationalism*, Oxford University Press, London 1970.
SINGH, K., *Prophet of Indian Nationalism*, Allen & Unwin, London 1963.
SMELSER, N. J., *A Theory of Collective Behaviour*, Routledge & Kegan Paul, London 1962.
SMILEY, D., *The Canadian Political Nationality*, Methuen, Toronto 1967.
SMITH, A. D., *Theories of Nationalism*, Duckworth, London 1971, Harper & Row, New York 1972.
SMITH, A. D., *The Concept of Social Change*, Routledge & Kegan Paul, London and Boston 1973.
SMITH, A. D., *Social Change*, Longman, London and New York 1976.
SMITH, A. D. (ed.), *Nationalist Movements*, Macmillan, London 1976, St. Martin's Press 1977.
SMITH, A. D., 'Nationalism, A Trend Report and Bibliography', *Current Sociology* 21/3, 1973, Mouton, The Hague.
SMITH, A. D., 'Ethnocentrism, Nationalism and Social Change', *International Journal of Comparative Sociology*, 13, 1972, 1–20.
SMITH, A. D., '"Ideas" and "structure" in the formation of independence ideals' *Philosophy of the Social Sciences* 3, 1973, 19–39.
SMITH, A. D., 'Nationalism and Religion: the role of religious reform in the genesis of Arab and Jewish nationalism', *Archives de Sciences Sociales des Religions*, 35, 1973, 23–43.
SMITH, A. D., 'The diffusion of nationalism: some historical and sociological perspectives', *British Journal of Sociology* XXIX/2, 1978, 234–48.
— SMITH, D. E., *Religion and Politics in Burma*, Princeton University Press, Princeton 1965.
— SMITH, D. E. (ed.), *Religion and Political Modernisation*, Yale University Press, New Haven and London 1974.
SNYDER, L., *The Meaning of Nationalism*, Rutgers University Press, New Brunswick 1954.
SNYDER, L., *The New Nationalism*, Cornell University Press, Ithaca 1968.
SNYDER, L. (ed.), *The Dynamics of Nationalism: A Reader*, Van Nostrand, New York 1964.
SOUCY, J., 'The nature of Fascism in France', *Journal of Contemporary History* 1/1, 1966, 27–55.
SPRY, G., 'Canada: Notes on Two Ideas of Nation in Confrontation', *Journal of Contemporary History* 6/1, 1971, 173–96.
STALIN, J., *Marxism and the National and Colonial Question*, Lawrence and Wishart, London 1936.
STAVRIANOS, L., *The Balkans Since 1453*, Holt, New York 1961.
STAVRIANOS, L., 'Antecedents of the Balkan revolutions of the 19th century', *Journal of Modern History*, 29, 1957, 333–48.

STOIANOVITCH, T., 'The pattern of Serbian intellectual evolution', *Comparative Studies in Society and History* I, 1958, 242–72.

STONE, L., 'The English Revolution', in R. Forster and J. P. Greene (eds), *Preconditions of Revolution in Early Modern Europe*, Johns Hopkins University Press, Baltimore and London 1972.

STRAYER, J., 'The historical experience of nation-building in Europe', in K. Deutsch and W. Foltz (eds), *Nation-Building*, Atherton, New York 1963.

SUGAR, P. and LEDERER, I. (eds), *Nationalism in Eastern Europe*, Far Eastern and Russian Institute, University of Washington, Seattle 1969.

SYMMONS-SYMONOLEWICZ, K., *Nationalist Movements: a comparative view*, Maplewood Press, Meadville, Pa., 1970.

SYMMONS-SYMONOLEWICZ, K., 'Nationalist Movements: an attempt at a comparative typology', *Comparative Studies in Society and History* 7, 1965, 221–30.

SZPORLUK, R., 'Nationalities and the Russian Problem in the USSR: an historical outline', *Journal of International Affairs* 27, 1973, 22–40.

TALMON, J., *Political Messianism, the Romantic Phase*, London 1960.

TALMON, J., *Israel among the Nations*, Weidenfeld & Nicolson, London 1970.

TALMON, Y., 'The pursuit of the millennium – the relation between religious and social change', *European Journal of Sociology* 3, 1962, 125–48.

THADEN, E. C., *Conservative Nationalism in 19th century Russia*, University of Washington Press, Seattle 1964.

The Third Reich, a study published under the auspices of the International Council for Philosophy and Humanistic Studies, with the assistance of Unesco, Praeger, New York 1955.

THOMAS, H., 'The Hero in the Empty Room: Jose Antonio and Spanish Fascism', *Journal of Contemporary History* 1/1, 1966, 174–82.

THOMPSON, E. A., 'Slavery in Early Germany', *Hermathena* 89, 1957, 19–29, reprinted in M. I. Finley (ed): *Slavery in Classical Antiquity*, Heffer & Sons, Cambridge 1960.

THRASHER, P., *Pasquale Paoli*, Constable, London 1970.

TIBAWI, A. L., 'The American Missionaries in Beirut and Butrus al-Bustani', *St. Antony's Papers* 16, 1963, 137–82.

TILLY, C. L. and R., *The Rebellious Century, 1830–1930*, J. M. Dent & Sons Ltd., London 1975.

TINKER, H., 'Politics in Burma', in S. Rose (ed.), *Politics in Southern Asia*, Macmillan, London 1963.

TINT, H. *The decline of French Patriotism, 1870–1940*, Weidenfeld & Nicolson, London 1964.

TIPTON, C. L. (ed.), *Nationalism in the Middle Ages*, Holt, Rinehart and Winston, New York 1972.

TREVOR-ROPER, H., *Jewish and other nationalisms*, Weidenfeld & Nicolson, London 1961.

VAN DEN BERGHE, P. L., *South Africa: a study in conflict*, Wesleyan University Press, Middletown, Conn. 1965.

VAN DEN BERGHE, P. L. (ed.), *Africa: Social Problems of Change and Conflict*, Chandler Publishing Company, San Francisco 1965.

VAN DEN BERGHE, P. L., *Race and Racism*, John Wiley, New York 1967.

VAN JAARSFELD, F. A., *The Awakening of Afrikaner Nationalism, 1868–91*, Human and Rosseau, Cape Town 1961.

VERMEIL, E., 'The origin, nature and development of German nationalist ideology in the 19th and 20th centuries', in *The Third Reich*, Praeger, New York 1955.

VOEGELIN, E., *The New Science of Politics*, Chicago University Press, Chicago 1952.

WAGATSUMA, H., 'The pariah caste in Japan: history and present self-image', in A. de Reuck and J. Knight (eds), *Caste and Race*, Ciba Foundation, London 1967.

WAGLEY, C. (ed.), *Race and Class in Rural Brazil*, Unesco, Paris 1952.

WALCH, P., 'Charles Rollin and early NeoClassicism', *Art Bulletin* XLIX, 1967, 123–27.

WALLACE, A., 'Revitalisation Movements', *American Anthropologist* LVIII/2, 1956, 264–81.

WALLERSTEIN, I., *Africa, the politics of unity; an analysis of a contemporary social movement*, Pall Mall Press, London 1967.

WALLERSTEIN, I., 'Elites in French-speaking West Africa', *Journal of Modern African Studies* 3, 1965, 1–33.

WALSBY, H., *The Domain of Ideologies, A Study of the Origin, Development and Structure of Ideologies*, William MacLellan, London 1947.

WARBURTON, T. R., 'Nationalism and language in Switzerland and Canada', in A. D. Smith (ed.), *Nationalist Movements*, Macmillan, London 1976.

WATKINS, F. M. (ed.), *Rousseau, Political Writings*, Nelson, Edinburgh and London 1953.

WAUTHIER, C., *The Literature and Thought of Modern Africa*, Pall Mall Press, London 1966.

WEBER, E., 'Romania', in H. Rogger and E. Weber (eds), *The European Right: A Historical Profile*, University of California Press, Berkeley, Calif. 1965.

WEBER, E., 'The Men of the Archangel', *Journal of Contemporary History*, 1/1, 1966, 101–26.

WEBER, M., *The Protestant Ethic and the Spirit of Capitalism*, George Allen & Unwin, London 1930.

WEBER, M., *From Max Weber, Essays in Sociology*, ed. H. Gerth and C. W. Mills, Routledge & Kegan Paul, London 1948.

WEISS, J., *Conservatism in Europe, 1770–1945*, Thames & Hudson, London 1977.

WERBLOWSKY, R. J., 'Messianism in Jewish History', in H. H. Ben-Sasson and S. Ettinger (eds), *Jewish Society through the Ages*, Valentine, Mitchell, London 1971.

WERTHEIM, W. F., 'Religious reform movements in South and Southeast Asia', *Archives de Sociologie des Religions* 12, 1961, 53–62.

WHITAKER, A. P., *Nationalism in Latin America, past and present*, University of Florida Press, Gainesville, Fla., 1962.

WHITAKER, A. P. and JORDAN, D. C., *Nationalism in Contemporary Latin America*, Free Press, New York 1966.

WILKINSON, P., *Political Terrorism*, Macmillan, London 1974.

WILSON, B., *Sects and Society*, Oxford University Press, Oxford 1971.

WILSON, B., 'Millennialism in Comparative Perspective', *Comparative Studies in Society and History* 6, 1964, 93–114.

WILSON, D. A., 'Nation-building and revolutionary war', in K. W. Deutsch and W. Foltz (eds), *Nation-Building*, Atherton, New York 1963.

WILSON, H. S. (ed.), *Origins of West African Nationalism*, Macmillan & Co., London 1969.

WORSLEY, P., *The Third World*, Weidenfeld & Nicolson, London 1964.

WORSLEY, P., *The Trumpet Shall Sound*, 2nd edn, MacGibbon & Kee, London 1968.

WORSLEY, P., 'The concept of Populism', in E. Gellner and G. Ionescu (eds), *Populism, its meanings and national characteristics*, Weidenfeld & Nicolson, London 1970.

WRIGHT, M. C., *The last stand of Chinese Conservatism*, Stanford University Press, Stanford 1957.

ZEINE, Z. N., *Arab–Turkish Relations and the Emergence of Arab Nationalism*, Khayats, Beirut 1958.

ZENOVSKY, S., *Pan-Turkism and Islam in Russia*, Harvard University Press, Cambridge, Mass. 1960.

ZENKOVSKY, S., 'A century of Tatar revival', *Slavic Review* 12, 1953, 303–18.

ZERNATTO, G., 'Nation: the history of a word', *Review of Politics* VI, 1944, 351–66.

ZNANIECKI, F., *Modern nationalities*, University of Illinois Press, Urbana, Illinois 1952.

Index